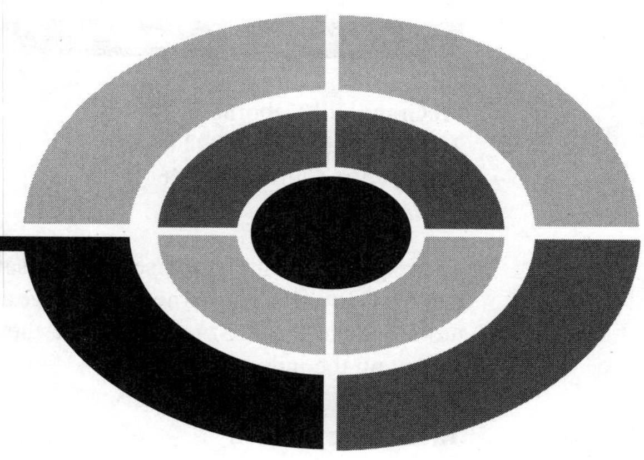

JAVA DEMYSTIFIED

JIM KEOGH

McGraw-Hill/Osborne

New York Chicago San Francisco Lisbon London
Madrid Mexico City Milan New Delhi San Juan
Seoul Singapore Sydney Toronto

The McGraw-Hill Companies

McGraw-Hill/Osborne
2100 Powell Street, 10th Floor
Emeryville, California 94608
U.S.A.

To arrange bulk purchase discounts for sales promotions, premiums, or fund-raisers, please contact **McGraw-Hill**/Osborne at the above address. For information on translations or book distributors outside the U.S.A., please see the International Contact Information page immediately following the index of this book.

Java Demystified

1234567890 FGR FGR 01987654

ISBN 0-07-225454-8

Publisher
Brandon A. Nordin

Vice President & Associate Publisher
Scott Rogers

Editorial Director
Wendy Rinaldi

Project Manager
Janet Walden

Project Editor
Carolyn Welch

Acquisitions Coordinator
Athena Honore

Technical Editor
Derek Lindner

Copy Editor
Bart Reed

Proofreader
Susie Elkind

Indexer
Claire Splan

Composition
Apollo Publishing Services, Tara A. Davis

Illustrators
Kathleen Edwards, Melinda Lytle

Cover Series Design
Margaret Webster-Shapiro

Cover Illustration
Lance Lekander

This book was composed with Corel VENTURA™ Publisher.

This book is dedicated to Anne, Sandy, Joanne, Amber-Leigh Christine, and Graaf, without whose help and support this book couldn't be written.

ABOUT THE AUTHOR

Jim Keogh is a member of the faculty of Columbia University where he teaches courses on Java Application Development, and is also a member of the Java Community Process Program. He developed the first e-commerce track at Columbia and became its first chairperson. Jim spent more than a decade developing advanced systems for major Wall Street firms and is also the author of several best-selling computer books.

CONTENTS AT A GLANCE

CONTENTS

INTRODUCTION

This book is for everyone who wants to learn the basics of the Java programming language without taking a formal course. This book also serves as a supplemental classroom text. For best results, you should start at the beginning of the book and go straight through.

If you are confident about your basic knowledge of programming, skip the first chapter but take the quiz at the end of the chapter to see if you are actually ready to jump into Java.

If you get 90 percent of the answers correct, you're ready. If you get 75 to 89 percent correct, skim through Chapters 1 and 2. If you get less than 75 percent of the answers correct, then find a quiet place and begin reading Chapter 1. Doing so will get you in shape to tackle the rest of the chapters on Java.

In order to learn Java, you must have some computer skills. If we were to tell you otherwise, we'd be cheating you. Don't be intimidated. None of the computer knowledge you need goes beyond basic use of the operating system and how to enter text into an editor.

This book includes a practice quiz at the end of every chapter. These quizzes contain questions that are similar to the kinds of questions used in a Java course. You can and should refer to the chapters when taking the quizzes. When you think you're ready, take a quiz, write down your answers, and then give your list of answers to a friend. Have your friend tell you your score, but not which questions you answered incorrectly. You'll find the answers in the back of the book. Stay with one chapter until you pass the quiz.

There is also a final exam at the end of this book. The questions are practical and are drawn from all chapters in the book. Take the exam when you have finished all the chapters and have completed all the quizzes. A satisfactory score is at least 75 percent correct answers. Have a friend tell you your score without letting you know which questions you missed on the exam.

We recommend that you spend an hour or two each day with the book. You should expect to complete one chapter each week. Take it at a steady pace. Take time to absorb the material. Don't rush. You'll complete the course in a few months, and then you can use this book as a comprehensive permanent reference.

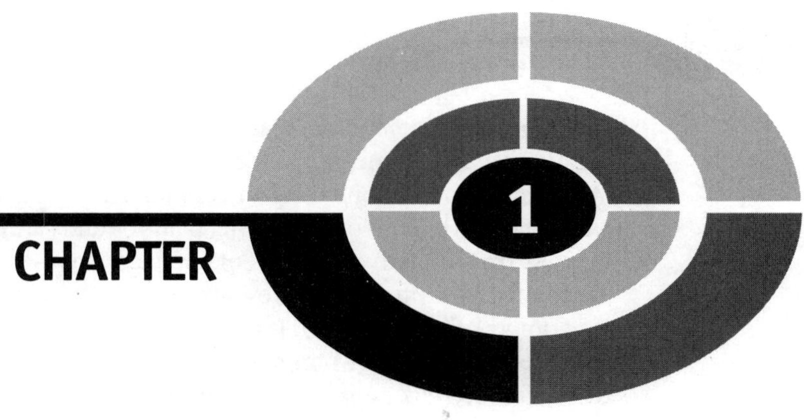

Inside Java

Computer programming might seem mystifying and something that should be left to university scientists, but it isn't. With a little time and effort you can easily master computer programming and take control over your computer in a way you never thought you could. If you can read this book and take a few notes, you have all the skills needed to write a computer program. A computer program is a set of instructions for the computer to follow. Those instructions are written in a programming language that is very similar to English. There are many computer languages. One of the more popular is Java. By now you probably have heard all the hoopla about Java and how Java is revolutionizing the world of computer programming. You'll be in the forefront of this revolution by learning how to put your computer through its paces by writing your own Java program. Let's begin at the beginning with the basics and then work up to everything you need to know to write a Java program.

Computer Programs

You probably use a personal computer; however, a personal computer is only one kind of computer. Other kinds of computers include personal digital assistants

(PDAs), powerful computers that run corporations, and tiny computers in automobiles, aircraft, and home appliances.

All computers have one thing in common: They perform computations and make logical decisions billions of times faster than you and I are capable of doing. Technically, computers perform only two kinds of computations—addition and subtraction.

Ready for your first quiz? How would you know whether two numbers are the same number? Subtract them. If the difference is zero, the numbers are the same. If the difference is a positive number, the first number is larger than the second number. If the difference is a negative number, the first number is smaller than the second number. This is the way a computer makes a logical decision.

A computer programmer instructs a computer how to perform a computation and how to make a logical decision by writing a computer program. A computer program contains all the steps that must be followed in a specific order to perform a computation and to reach a logical decision.

Data

Many computer instructions require the computer to manipulate information that is provided by the programmer, by a person who uses the computer, or by another computer. This information is called *data*.

You provide a program with data each time you enter your ID and password into your computer. The program receives your ID and password and then validates them before giving you access to your computer. Here's another quiz. What computation is used to validate your ID and password? Subtraction! The program subtracts the ID and password that you enter into your computer from the valid ID and password. If the difference is zero, they match and access is granted.

A programmer can enter data directly into an instruction if the programmer provides the data. For example, here is an instruction telling the computer to add two numbers (the programmer placed these numbers into the instruction):

```
10 + 15
```

Surprised to see how simple a computer instruction can be? If so, you're in for a treat because many of the instructions you write using the Java programming language are simple to understand and simple to write.

Many times the programmer doesn't have data for an instruction at the time when the program is written, such as a user's ID and password. The person who uses the program must then enter this data when the program runs.

However, the instruction still must be aware of the data when the program is written, so the programmer uses a placeholder for data in the instruction. You can think of a placeholder as a temporary label for the data. Programmers call these labels *variables*, which you'll learn more about later in this book. The following example is the same instruction used to add two numbers, except the letters `A` and `B` are placeholders for the numbers:

```
A + B
```

The computer replaces these letters with numbers when the person who uses the program enters numbers into the program or when the numbers are provided to the program by another computer program.

Programming Languages

A computer programming language such as Java makes it easy for a programmer to write instructions for a computer because those instructions are written using English-like words. However, a computer doesn't understand those English-like words. Instead, a computer understands instructions written in machine language. Machine language instructions consist of a series of zeros and ones that are understood by the computer's central processing unit (CPU), which is the part of the computer where all the processing occurs.

Although programmers tend to refer to machine language as a single language, there are actually different versions of machine language. Think of these versions as dialects. A CPU understands only one dialect of a machine language. This means that a program written in one dialect can be run only on computers that have a CPU that understands that dialect. This makes the program *computer dependent*, sometimes referred to as *machine dependent*. That is, a machine language program written for one kind of computer cannot run on a different kind of computer.

You don't need to be a rocket scientist to see problems writing programs using machine language. First, who in their right mind wants to write a program using only a series of zeros and ones? We think in words, not numbers. Also, who would want to spend all this time writing a program when it can run on only one kind of computer?

The introduction of assembly language addressed at least one of these problems. Assembly language is another programming language that consists of English abbreviations called *assembly language instructions*, each of which represents an elementary operation of the computer.

A programmer first decided what operation needed to be performed and then used the assembly language instruction to tell the computer to perform the operation. The computer still only understands zeros and ones, so a program called an *assembler* is used to translate assembly language instructions into machine language.

Here is an example of an assembly language program. You can probably figure out what operation the computer is being told to perform. The computer is being told to sum 10 and 15.

```
ADD 10, 15
```

You must admit that assembly language had a big advantage over machine language—the programmer could use English-like words to write instructions for the computer. However, there were critical disadvantages, too.

The programmers had to learn many assembly language abbreviations that weren't intuitive, such as POP and PUSH. Also, many instructions were necessary to carry out fundamental operations. And the biggest headache was portability. Each kind of computer understood its own dialect of assembly language, making it practically impossible to write an assembly language program that could run on different kinds of computers without having to rewrite the program.

Assembly language evolved into high-level programming languages that are intuitive because they use English-like words, statements (sentences), and punctuation to instruct the computer to do something. C, C++, and Java are popular high-level programming languages used today.

In addition, a single instruction can be written to perform a related set of operations. No longer must a programmer write one instruction for each operation. Also, programs written in a high-level programming language can be run on different computers without the programmers having to rewrite them.

Here's how a high-level programming language works: A programmer uses keywords of a programming language to form statements that tell a computer to do something. Keywords are similar to English words that you use to form sentences to tell someone to do something.

You've probably surmised that the computer doesn't understand a program written in a high-level computer language because computers only understand machine language. Therefore, the high-level computer language program must be translated into machine language.

This translation process involves two steps. First, the program is translated into an intermediate stage called an *object file*. Second, the object file is converted into the machine language program that can be run on the computer.

Translating the program into an object file is called *compiling* and is performed by a translator program called a *compiler*. The process of converting an object file into a machine language program is called *linking* and is performed by a program called a *linker*.

You might be wondering why the program isn't compiled directly to machine language. The reason is because a typical program has two or more object files that must be joined together to form the machine language program. Programmers call joining object files *linking*.

Compiling and linking are important features of a high-level programming language because these two processes enable a program to run on different kinds of computers without the programmer having to rewrite the program.

This is made possible because there is a different compiler and linker for each kind of computer that is capable of translating a specific high-level programming language into machine language for a specific kind of computer. For example, a program written in C++ can be compiled and linked so that it runs on different kinds of computers without having to be rewritten.

Here is the high-level programming language version of the assembly language example shown previously in this section:

```
10 + 15
```

In the Beginning

In the 1950s, FORTRAN (FORmula TRANslator) and COBOL (COmmon Business Oriented Languages) were two popular high-level computer languages, and they're still in use today.

FORTRAN, developed by IBM, is a high-level programming language designed to perform complex mathematical computations for scientific and engineering applications. COBOL, developed by the federal government, is designed to process and manipulate large amounts of data. Although both of these languages achieved their objectives very well, they were not flexible and lacked the capabilities required to build compilers and operating systems.

Therefore, engineers sought to develop a more versatile high-level programming language, and by the late 1960s a new programming language was developed by Martin Richards. It was called the *BCPL programming language* and was used to write compilers. Soon after the introduction of BCPL, Ken Thompson developed an enhanced version of BCPL and called it the *B programming language*. The B programming language was used to create the first versions of the Unix operating system at Bell Laboratories.

BCPL and the B programming languages had a major disadvantage in the way they used computer memory. Today, computer memory is relatively inexpensive. However, in the 1960s, computer memory was expensive, and both BCPL and B used computer memory inefficiently.

Think of computer memory as a bunch of boxes. Each box can store one bottle of soda (data). You must reserve a box before you can store a bottle of soda in a box. Therefore, it makes sense that you reserve ten boxes if you have to store ten bottles of soda and that you reserve five boxes if five bottles of soda are to be stored. BCPL and B required that the same number of boxes be reserved regardless of the number of soda bottles being stored. So, let's say that each time you wanted to store one soda bottle, you had to reserve ten boxes. This meant that nine boxes went unused and were therefore wasted.

In 1972, Dennis Ritchie created the C programming language at Bell Laboratories. It overcame the failings of BCPL and B. The C programming language incorporated many of the features found in BCPL and B, plus it introduced new features that, among other things, enabled a programmer to specify exactly the amount of memory needed to store data in computer memory.

Although the C programming language addressed the drawbacks of BCPL and B, some programmers felt that it lacked the capability to mimic the way we look at the real world. This is an important drawback because computer programs are designed to simulate the real word inside a computer. Therefore, the C programming language couldn't simulate the real world to meet the desire of programmers.

We look at the real world as objects. Those objects have attributes (data) and behaviors. Take a window, for example. The dimensions of the window are attributes. Also, the window can be opened and closed, which are functionalities associated with a window.

The C programming language is a procedural language that is focused on mimicking real-world behavior inside a computer. Unfortunately, the C programming language doesn't provide a way to combine behavior with attributes.

In 1980, Bjarne Stroustrup developed a new programming language at Bell Laboratories called C++. The most outstanding advancement of C++ was the capability to combine attributes and functionality into objects. And with this came the growth of object-oriented design and object-oriented programming (see *Object-Oriented Programming Demystified* for more on this subject).

You are probably wondering why Stroustrup used the ++ instead of coming up with a completely new name for the language. The ++ is the incremental operator in C (and in Java), which you'll learn about later in this book. For now, it is important to know that the incremental operator adds 1 to the current value. C++ is said to increment the C programming language by incorporating all the features found in C and then adding new features. Therefore, you can think of C++ as an extension of the C programming language.

How a Computer Language Becomes a Standard

Did you ever wonder how a computer language is developed? It takes a lot of perseverance and luck. Let's backtrack a bit and recall the components of a programming language. All programming languages consist of keywords and functionality.

A keyword is an English-like word. Functionality is the action performed by the computer when the keyword is used in a program. Think of functionality as the definition of the keyword.

The initial step in developing a programming language is to come up with a list of keywords and functionality. Ideally, the keywords and functionality of your programming language provide a much-needed improvement over an existing programming language; otherwise, no one except you will use your new language.

Next, get the word out among the members of the technical community and stir up an interest in the new programming language. If there is enough of a buzz and a real benefit, leaders in technology and industry will push to standardize the new programming language.

Standardization is the formal process where the technical community, through a standards organization, agrees to a set of keywords and corresponding functionality. The well-known standards organizations are the American National Standards Institute (ANSI; www.ansi.org) and the International Standards Organization (ISO; www.iso.ch). The Java Community Process (www.jcp.org) establishes standards for the Java programming language.

Once standards are established, software tools manufacturers develop compilers, linkers, and other software tools that recognize programs written in the new programming language and converts those programs to machine language programs so they can run on different kinds of computers. The new programming language is also taught in institutions, written about in books, and used by programmers to write programs.

And Then Java

C++ and the other high-level programming languages all had one drawback: Programs written in those languages had to be recompiled in order to run on different kinds of computers. Business organizations wanted a programming language that enables them to develop a program that can run on all computers without having to recompile the program.

In a round about way, Sun Microsystems met this demand with the introduction of the Java programming language. In 1991, Sun Microsystems launched the Green project to develop a programming language suited for writing programs for consumer electronic devices such as televisions and computers used in automobiles. They expected this to become a hot new market.

James Gosling, one of the chief engineers on the Green project, created the Oak programming language to meet this objective. It was named for the tree outside his office. However, there was a problem. A programming language called Oak already existed. Gosling and other Green project engineers sat around a coffeehouse trying to come up with a new name of their language—thus, Java was born.

The need for programs to run consumer electronic devices never materialized, but in 1993 the World Wide Web exploded. What once was a communications network for academia and governments became a new means for commerce and the general public to communicate with each other.

The web page became a key way to communicate. Each web page was written manually using the Hypertext Markup Language (HTML) to display text and graphics on remote computers. These are known as *static* web pages because the content remains static each time the web page is viewed.

However, web page developers wanted a robust way to build dynamic web pages that could be customized for each person who visits the website. They wanted web pages generated by a computer program that could also interact automatically with databases and computer systems used throughout an organization.

Gosling's Java programming language was perfect for creating dynamic web pages with interactive content that enables the web page to be customized for each visitor to the website. In addition, Java ran on practically any kind of computer without having to be recompiled.

Sun Microsystems formally introduced Java in 1995, and it became the programming language of choice for large-scale enterprise applications built around the World Wide Web four years later.

Today, the Java programming language has grown to include several versions called *editions*. The most commonly used edition is the Java 2 Standard Edition (J2SE), which is the one we'll be exploring in this book. There is also the Java 2 Enterprise Edition (J2EE), which is used to build applications for corporations. Java 2 Micro Edition (J2ME) is yet another common edition of Java; it's designed for building applications for mobile devices such as cell phones and personal digital assistants. You can learn more about J2EE by picking up a copy of *J2EE: The Complete Reference*. And you can learn more about J2ME by reading *J2ME: The Complete Reference*.

An Inside Look at Java

Let's get down to some basics about Java. A *program* is a series of instructions written in a programming language that tell a computer to perform specific tasks. This is like directions you write telling a friend how to drive to your house. Each instruction must be precisely written so that the computer understands what you want it to do.

No doubt you've heard the term *computer application*. A computer application is typically a group of related programs that collectively tell a computer how to mimic the real world. For example, your local supermarket has a transaction-processing application that is used to record, process, and report on purchases. The most visible part of the transaction-processing application is the scanner at the checkout counter. The transaction-processing application used by your supermarket consists of many programs.

A Java program consists of one or more Java classes that are written using the Java programming language. A class is like a cookie cutter that is used to define a real-world object inside your computer. Much like a cookie cutter defines what a cookie looks like, a class defines what an object looks like. And like a cookie cutter, a class is used to make a real object in your program. You'll see how this is done in Chapter 7.

These classes contain instructions that tell a computer what to do as well as the data necessary for the computer to carry out the task. Classes are written into a Java source code file using an editor. A Java source code file is similar to a word processing document. However, instead of containing text, the Java source code file has instructions written in the Java programming language. An editor is a barebones word processor that doesn't have all the fancy formatting capabilities you typically find in a word processor.

You write Java source code, which becomes a Java program. The source code must be saved to a disk in a file that has the file extension `.java`.

Java works differently than C++ and other high-level programming languages. High-level programming languages must be compiled into object code that is linked by a linker to form the machine language program that runs on a computer.

Java source code is not compiled into object code. Instead, Java source code is compiled into bytecode and saved in a file that has the file extension `.class`. The Java compiler is a component of the Java 2 Software Development Kit (J2SDK) that is available for downloading, free of charge, from the java.sun.com website.

NOTE: *The Java compiler is also a component of commercially available Java Integrated Development Environments (IDEs) such as Borland's JBuilder. Besides the Java compiler, an IDE includes an editor, debugger, and other timesaving software tools.*

The bytecode that is generated by the Java compiler is interpreted by the Java Virtual Machine (JVM), which translated bytecode into machine language that runs on the computer. Today, a Java Virtual Machine is available for most kinds of computers and can be downloaded free of charge from the java.sun.com website.

The Java Virtual Machine is key to the success of Java because the bytecode produced by the Java compiler is readable by every Java Virtual Machine, regardless of the kind of computer that is running the Java Virtual Machine. The goal of the industry has been finally achieved. A program can be compiled once and run on practically any computer without having to be recompiled or modified in any way.

Java Program from Scratch

Before getting into the details of Java, let's jump into the waters and write, compile, and run the traditional HelloWorld program, which is the first program every programmer writes. It contains all the basic elements of a Java program and will help to build your confidence as you learn all the ins and outs of Java throughout this book.

Begin by downloading the Java 2 Software Development Kit from java.sun.com. It will take a few minutes before the entire file is copied onto your computer. Once the download is completed, click the J2SDK icon and install the development kit. Make sure that you add the `/bin` subdirectory to your path so you can compile your Java program in any directory on your computer.

After the J2SDK is installed on your computer, you are ready to write your first Java program. You'll need to write Java instructions into an editor. Most computers come with an editor. If you are using a Windows computer, open Notepad. If you are using a Unix/Linux-based computer, open vi. Enter Figure 1-1 into your editor. This is the HelloWorld Java program.

Save the file as `HelloWorld.java`. Make sure that the filename is spelled exactly the same way as shown here. Otherwise, you'll receive a compiler error. The class name and filename are case sensitive.

```
class HelloWorld {
  public static void main ( String args[] )
  {
     System.out.println("Hello world!");
  }
}
```

Figure 1-1 The HelloWorld program

If you are using Notepad, select Save As. You'll notice that the default file name is `*.txt`. Replace this with `HelloWorld.java`. To open this file in Notepad, you'll need to change File Type from Text Document (*.txt) to All Files (*.*) in order to see files that have extensions other than `*.txt`.

Compiling a Java Program

I'll explain the parts of the `HelloWorld.java` program in the next section. For now, let's compile and run the program. You run the compiler from the command line. If you are using a Windows computer, open a Command Prompt window. If you are using a Unix/Linux computer, you'll need to open a shell window.

Type following at the prompt and then press ENTER:

```
javac HelloWorld.java
```

A new command prompt appears on the screen if the Java program successfully compiled. If you display the directory, you'll see `HelloWorld.class`, which is the bytecode file of your program. On a Windows computer, you display the directory at the command prompt by typing `dir` then pressing ENTER. On a Unix/Linux computer, type `ls` and press ENTER.

If compiling was not successful, you might see a variety of things on the screen. Here are some of them, along with possible solutions:

- **'javac' is not recognized as an internal or external command, operable program or batch file** There are two likely causes of this type of error. First, you downloaded the J2SDK but didn't install it. If this is the case, you need to install the J2SDK. Second, you installed the J2SDK but didn't place the J2SDK's `bin` subdirectory on your computer's path. If this is the case, you need to place the `bin` subdirectory on your computer's path.
- **"...should be declared in a file named ..."** If you see this as part of the message displayed on the screen after you tried to compile the Java program, the likely cause is you didn't use the exact spelling shown in this chapter. Filenames must be typed just as they appear in this chapter, including upper- and lowercase letters. Double-check the spelling and the case.
- **javac: invalid flag:** If you see this message followed by a long list of words that begin with a hyphen, the compile likely can't find the Java program file. Display the current directory to be sure you see `HelloWorld.java` in the directory. If you don't see it there, then resave the Java program file to that directory. Another possibility is that you misspelled the name of the file when you tried to compile it.

Try again, making sure you spell the filename correctly. Another common problem is that you did not include the file extension with the filename when you compiled the file. You must include `.java` when compiling a file.

- **HelloWorld.java:6: ';' expected** Any time you see a message displayed that contains the word *expected*, suspect that a syntax error has occurred. A syntax error simply means that the compiler didn't understand something you wrote in your program file. The message is usually followed by the part of your program the compiler didn't understand. Here's how to fix the problem: The number next to the filename in the message tells you the line number of the program that is likely to have caused the problem. In this example, line 6 contains the problem instruction. Alongside the line number is the Java syntax the compiler expected to see in your program. In this example, the compiler expected to see a semicolon. Also, look carefully at the code displayed along with the message. You'll see a caret (^) pointing to the place in the code where the compiler discovered the problem. With all these clues at hand, your job is to display your Java program in your editor, make the necessary corrections, and then recompile your program.

Running a Java Program

Once you've successfully compiled your Java program, it's time to run it. Type the following line at the command prompt and press ENTER:

```
java HelloWorld
```

You should see "Hello world!" displayed on the screen in the Command Prompt window. If you don't see it, one of two common problems has occurred:

- **'java' is not recognized as an internal or external command, operable program or batch file** If you see this message, your computer cannot find the java class loader. Make sure that the Java Virtual Machine is installed on your computer. If it's not, download the Java Virtual Machine for you computer from java.sun.com.
- **Exception in thread "main" java.lang.NoClassDefFoundError:** You probably entered `HelloWorld.java` or `HelloWorld.class` instead of `HelloWorld` when trying to run your program. Don't include the file extension when running your Java program.

Taking Apart a Java Program

Now that you've compiled and run your first Java program, let's take a closer look at it to see how the HelloWorld program works. There are three parts to this program: the class definition, the method definition, and a statement.

Class Definition

The class definition in the HelloWorld program contains all the pieces of the program necessary to display "Hello world!" on the screen. The class definition, shown in Figure 1-2, consists of the following:

- The `class` keyword
- The class name
- The class body

The keyword `class` informs the compiler that you are defining a class. The keyword `class` must be followed by the name of the class. In this example, `HelloWorld` is the class name. The class name in the HelloWorld program must be the same as the program's filename. Both names must match exactly; otherwise, you'll receive a compiler error when you compile the program.

Notice that the name of this class is made up of two words: Hello and World. Java doesn't permit you to use spaces in a class name; however, it is a good idea to capitalize the first letter of each word used in the class name. This makes it easier for you and other programmers to read.

The class body is where attributes are declared and methods defined. The class body begins with a left brace ({), called an *open brace*, and ends with a right brace (}), called a *close brace*.

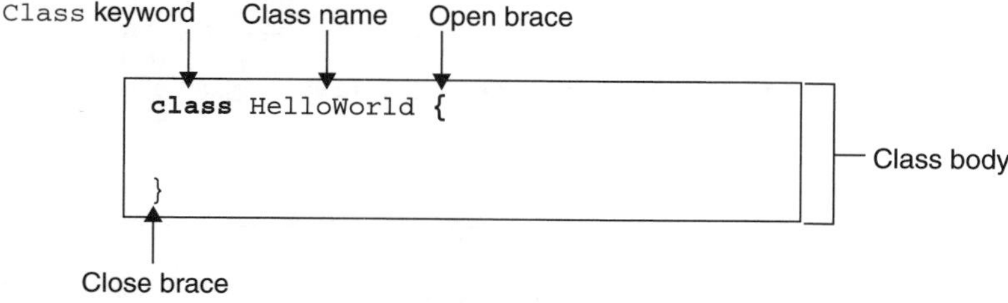

Figure 1-2 The class definition must have these components.

Method Definition

Previously in this chapter you learned that a class has two elements. These are attributes and behaviors, which are called *methods*. An attribute is data that is associated with the class, and a method is a functionality of the class. An attribute isn't a required part of a class, but every Java application must define one method—the `main()` method. The `main()` method, shown in Figure 1-3, is where the Java program begins.

A method definition consists of the following items:

- Method name
- Method argument
- Method body
- Method return value

The method name is used to identify the method and to call the method whenever you need the program to perform the functionality provided by the method. You'll learn all about methods in Chapter 5. For now, simply understand that the Java Virtual Machine calls the `main()` method when the program runs.

The method argument is the data identified between the parentheses to the right of the method name and is used by the method to provide the necessary functionality. The `main()` method in the HelloWorld program has one method argument: `String args[]`. You'll learn about this argument in Chapter 5. For now, we'll hold off discussing it because the HelloWorld program doesn't use it.

The method body is where you place statements that instruct the computer to perform specific functionality. A pair of braces similar to the class body defines the method body. Statements contained in a method body are executed sequentially. The program terminates when the last statement in the `main()` method executes.

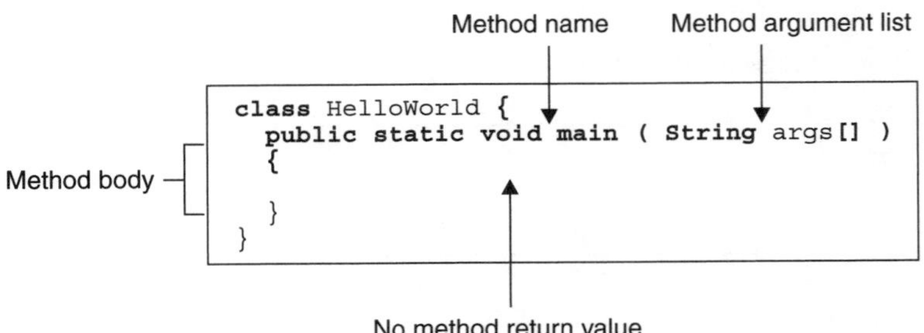

Figure 1-3 All Java applications must have a `main()` method because the `main()` method is the entry point to the application.

The method's return value is the data returned to the part of the program that requested the method to perform its functionality. Not all methods have a return value, which you'll learn about in Chapter 5. In this example, the `main()` method doesn't have a return value. Therefore, we must precede the name of the method with the keyword `void`, which indicates there isn't a return value.

You'll notice that two other keywords are used alongside the name of the `main()` method. These are `public` and `static`. The keyword `public` means that the method can be called from outside the class definition. The `main()` method is also public because it is called by the Java Virtual Machine. The keyword `static` is an advanced topic that is discussed in Chapter 5. For now, simply know that the `static` keyword must appear in the method definition.

Statement

As you learned earlier in this chapter, a *statement* is an instruction to the computer to do something. This example contains one statement that tells the computer to display the words "Hello world!" on the screen.

As shown in Figure 1-4, this statement calls one of Java's standard methods: `println()`. You'll learn about the `println()` method in Chapter 5. For now, it is important to understand that the functionality of the `println()` method is to display data on the screen. However, you must tell the `println()` method what data you want displayed. You do this by placing the data between the parentheses when calling the `println()` method. In this case, the words "Hello world!" are placed between the parentheses and appear on the screen.

Finally, every statement in a Java program must end in a semicolon (;). Otherwise, the compiler won't recognize the statement and is likely to display an error message when you try to compile the program.

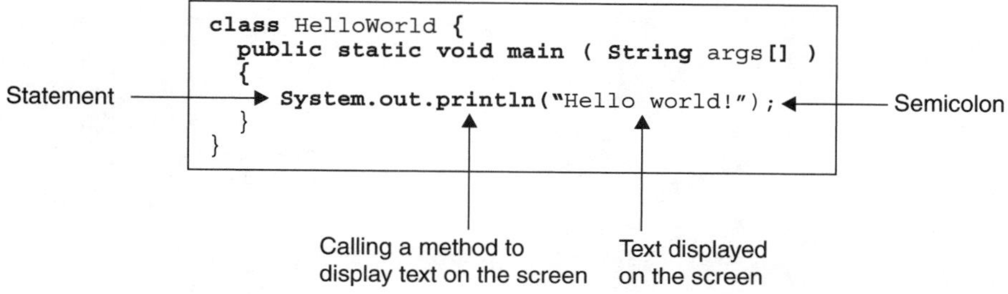

Figure 1-4 This statement tells Java to display "Hello world!" on the screen.

Quiz

1. What is a compiler?
2. What is a high-level programming language?
3. What is machine language?
4. What is a key difference between C and Java?
5. What is a key difference between C++ and Java?
6. What is bytecode?
7. What is the Java Virtual Machine?
8. What is the purpose of the `main()` method in a Java application?
9. Must all Java classes have at least one attribute declared?
10. What happens after the last statement in the `main()` method executes?

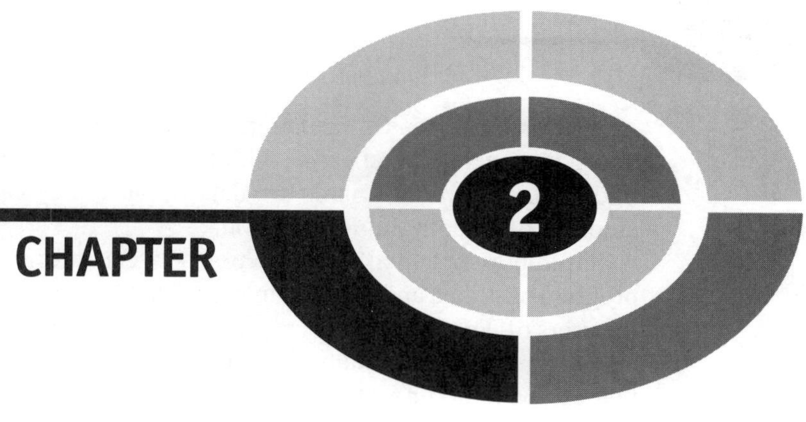

Data Types and Variables

Practically every Java program you write focuses on data and instructions. Data is information used by a computer to execute an instruction given to it by you, the programmer. Let's begin our trek toward mastering Java by taking a close look at data. You'll learn what data is, how to store data in memory, and how your Java programs can use data to achieve the goals of your program.

Data and Numbers

For many of us, the terms *information* and *data* are synonymous. However, information and data are distinctly different. Data is the smallest amount of meaningful information. No doubt this sounds like technical double talk, so let's look at an example to illustrate the difference between data and information.

A person's name is information and not data because a person's name can be reduced to a person's first name, middle name, and last name. A person's first name, middle name, and last name are data because they cannot be reduced to smaller amounts of meaningful information.

It is important to make a distinction between information and data because a Java program uses data and not information. That is, you don't instruct a computer to ask the users of your program to enter their name. Instead, the users are prompted to enter a first name, middle name, and last name. We view data as one or more characters that can be a mixture of alphabetical characters, numeric characters, and symbols such as punctuation. However, a computer sees data as a series of numbers represented as numbers of the binary numbering system. These are the much talked about zeros and ones.

Numbering system is one of those intimidating terms that conjure images of dreaded math courses. However, a number system is nothing more than a way of counting, something you probably learned in the third grade.

We use the decimal numbering system all the time to count. The decimal number system has ten digits, which are 0 through 9. When we reach 9, we carry over 1 to the left column and begin counting again from 0.

```
  9
+ 1
 10
```

However, many other numbering systems exist. All of them do exactly the same thing. They are used to count. The only difference among numbering systems is the number of digits. You'll encounter three numbering systems as you read computer books: the octal numbering system, the hexadecimal numbering system, and the binary numbering system.

The octal numbering system consists of eight digits, from 0 through 7. When you reach 7, you carry over 1 to the left column and begin counting again. This is illustrated in the follow example. The sum of this addition calculation looks wrong because we've learned that 7 + 1 = 8 and not 10. However, this is only true if we use the decimal numbering system. However, the octal numbering system is used in this example, so the following sum is correct:

```
  7
+ 1
 10
```

The hexadecimal numbering system has 16 digits. Hex, which is what programmers called the hexadecimal numbering system, is baffling at first glance because it is difficult to imagine digits beyond 9. Letters *A* through *F* are used for numbers 10 through 15.

Take a look at the following example. It probably resembles a strangely formatted algebra problem. It isn't algebra because letters *A* and *B* are not placeholders for real digits. These letters are real digits in the hex numbering system.

```
  A
+ 1
---
  B
```

Let's convert the previous problem from the hexadecimal number system to the decimal numbering system so you can have a better understanding of the calculation. Here's the same calculation in decimal:

```
 10
+ 1
---
 11
```

The binary numbering system is probably the most talked about numbering system aside from the decimal numbering system because the binary numbering system is used to represent data and instructions inside a computer.

The binary numbering system consists of two digits: 0 and 1. When counting, you carry over 1 to the left column when you reach digit 1 and then begin counting again. This is shown in the next example. No doubt the next example looks strange, but that's because we tend to assume that all calculations are performed using the decimal numbering system:

```
  1
+ 1
---
 10
```

The binary numbering system is the natural choice for representing numbers inside a computer because a computer is really a bunch of tiny switches. The binary digit 0 is used to represent a switch that is turned off, and the binary digit 1 represents a switch that is turned on. Programmers call each of these switches a *bit.* Those not familiar with computers usually think the term *bit* refers to a "little bit of information." That's incorrect. The term *bit* is an abbreviation for binary digit.

It is important to understand that any number you can write using the decimal numbering system can also be written in other numbering systems, regardless of the number of digits used by a numbering system.

Likewise, any calculation that can be performed using the decimal numbering system can be performed using any numbering system. This means you can perform complex calculus using the binary numbering system if you wish, although not many of us would do such a thing.

Playing with Numbering Systems

You can show off your new understanding of number systems by using the Calculator that comes with Windows to convert from one numbering system to another. Here's what you need to do:

1. Open the Windows Calculator. You'll find it under Programs | Accessories.
2. Select View from the menu bar and then Scientific from the drop-down menu. The image of the calculator expands to show, among other things, the four numbers systems spoken about in this section.
3. Select the Dec radio button, if it is not already selected, and enter the number 15.
4. Select the Hex radio button, and the letter *F* appears, which is the equivalent of the decimal value 15 in hexadecimal.
5. Select the Oct radio button, and the number 15 is converted to 17, which is how the number 15 is represented in the octal numbering system.
6. Select the Bin radio button and the number 15 is converted to 1111. This is the binary numbering system's representation of the decimal value 15.

Numbers and Characters

Computer memory is really a bunch of switches. When you want to place a decimal number in memory, the number is converted to the binary numbering system's representation of the number and then switches (computer memory) are turned on and off to represent the number.

Therefore, if we wanted to store the number 15 in memory, the number is first converted to its binary equivalent, which is 1111. Next, four switches (computer memory) are turned on. As you'll recall from the previous section, placing the switch in the "on" position represents a binary 1.

Fortunately, you don't have to turn on or turn off any switches. As you'll see later in this chapter, the Java compiler does this for you.

Computer memory is divided into groups of eight switches, called a *byte.* Each group is uniquely identified inside the computer by an address called a *memory address.* A byte is the minimum amount of switches (memory) used store a number. This means that the decimal number 15 is represented as 00001111 in memory. The first four zeros are called *leading zeros.* Therefore, 1111 and 00001111 are equivalent.

The largest decimal value that can be stored in a byte of memory is 255, which is the equivalent of 11111111 in binary. Numbers larger than 255 can be stored by using more than one byte of memory to store the number.

Now that you understand how numbers are stored in a computer, you're probably wondering how letters, punctuation, and other characters found on the keyboard are stored. The answer lies in a secret code. Well, it is really a not-so-secret code.

A consortium of hardware and software manufacturers in the late 1980s assigned a unique 16-digit (decimal numbering system) number to each character used in the languages throughout the world. They called it Unicode. Unicode has room to represent 1,114,112 individual characters, although about 95,221 characters are currently represented in Unicode, which includes nearly all characters used in the languages around the world. Each character requires two bytes of memory (16 switches) in order to store the character in memory.

Prior to the adoption of Unicode, programmers used the American Standard Code for Information Interchange (ASCII) code to represent characters. The ASCII code uses one byte of memory, but it is based on seven bits of the byte, so it has room to represent 128 characters. It soon became apparent that the ASCII code wasn't sufficient as computer usage spread around the global, because languages such as Russian, Arabic, Japanese, and Chinese have more than 128 characters. For example, Chinese ideographs have 21,000 characters. The adoption of Unicode addresses this concern. The first 128 characters and corresponding values in Unicode are the same as in ASCII. Fortunately, you don't have to be concerned about Unicode or ASCII because the Java compiler automatically converts characters to the binary equivalent of their Unicode value.

Let's say your program has prompted a user to enter his first name (in this case, Bob) and has saved it to memory. Each letter of the name is converted to its equivalent Unicode value, which is shown in Table 2-1 as a decimal number. The equivalent binary value of the Unicode value is used to determine switch (memory) settings.

Upper- and lowercase letters are assigned their own Unicode value. Numbers that are used as characters also have a Unicode value. These are typically numbers used for street addresses, ZIP codes, and other situations where the number is not used in a calculation.

It is important to understand that the Unicode value is a number just like any number. For example, the Unicode value 66 is the number 66. The computer treats the Unicode value 66 the same as if you entered the number 66 into the computer. There is no difference.

Character	Unicode (Decimal)	Binary
B	66	0000000001000010
o	111	0000000001101111
b	98	0000000001100010

Table 2-1 Unicode and Binary Values of Bob

You are probably wondering how a program knows that the number 66 really means the character B and not simply the number 66. It knows the difference because of the way the programmer writes the program. If the programmer uses the keyword `char` in the program, then the number is converted to its Unicode letter. If the programmer uses the keyword `int` (or one of a number of similar keywords, which you'll learn about later in this chapter), then the number is treated as a number.

Looking Up the Unicode Value

The Unicode value of a character can be determined in a number of ways. The most direct way is to let the computer tell you the Unicode value. You can do this by running the following Java program. Replace the letter *B* with the character you want to look up. Make sure you place the character within single quotations. The program displays the Unicode decimal value of the character. You'll learn the details of how this program works later in this chapter when you learn about data types and variables:

```
class Demo {
   public static void main( String args[]) {
      char x = 'B';
      double a = x;
      System.out.println("Unicode is " + a);
   }
}
```

Literals

Data is a number or character that is represented as a literal. Think of a literal as a number or character that you enter directly into your Java program. For example, the letter *B* used in the preceding program is a literal character.

Java has five kinds of literals:

- Integer
- Floating point
- Boolean
- Character
- String

Integer Literals

An *integer* is a whole number, which is a number that doesn't have a decimal value. An integer literal is a whole number entered directly into your Java program. The whole number can be entered as a decimal value, octal value, or a hexadecimal value, although most times you'll use a decimal value.

You enter an integer literal into your program the normal way you write a number. For example, here is how you would enter the decimal value 5 as an integer literal:

```
class Demo {
   public static void main( String args[]) {
      System.out.println("Decimal Integer Literal:  "
           + 5);
   }
}
```

Octal values are written in a slightly different format. An octal value must always be written with a leading zero. The leading zero is the signal to the Java compiler that the integer literal is written using the octal numbering system. Remember that 7 is the largest digit used as an octal value. Here's how would you write the decimal value 5 using octal:

```
class Demo {
   public static void main( String args[]) {
      System.out.println("Octal Integer Literal:  " + 05);
   }
}
```

An integer literal written in the hexadecimal numbering system also has a special format. Hexadecimal must be written with a leading zero followed by an *x,* which is then followed by the hexadecimal value. Remember that the largest digit in the hexadecimal numbering system is 15. Letters *A* through *F* represents values 11 through 15. Here's how to write an integer literal in hexadecimal:

```
class Demo {
   public static void main( String args[]) {
      System.out.println("Octal Integer Literal:  "
            + 0x5);
   }
}
```

Floating-point Literals

Floating point is the term programmers use to refer to a real number. A real number is composed of a whole number and a fraction that is represented as a decimal value. Real numbers are referred to as a *floating-point numbers* because of the way com puters notate a decimal value. Instead of placing a decimal in a real number, the computer notates the real number as a whole number and then notates the decimal position separately.

Let's say that 5.55 is a real number that needs to be stored by a program. Because this contains a decimal value, the number must be notated as a floating-point number. The number is stored as 555. Notice that the decimal is missing. However, the position of the decimal is notated separately. Behind the scenes, the computer might say something like, "Place the decimal between the first and second occurrences of the digit 5." Fortunately, you don't need to be concerned how a floating-point number is notated. All you need to do is to write the floating-point number into your program.

You can write a floating-point number in one of two ways. Either you can enter the number into your program the same way you enter a real number anywhere (that is, you can simply write 5.55), or you can write a real number using scientific notation. Scientific notation is typically used whenever you need to write a very large or very small number. Instead of writing a long series of digits that seem to go on forever, you can use an exponent. An exponent specifies a power of ten by which a value is multiplied.

You write an exponent in your program by preceding the exponent with the letter *E* or *e.* Either a plus sign or negative sign follows this symbol to indicate whether the number is very large (plus sign) or very small (negative sign). If you leave out the sign, the computer assumes that exponent is positive.

The following example illustrates how to write a real number in your program using scientific notation:

```
class Demo {
   public static void main( String args[]) {
      System.out.println("Scientific Notation.:  "
            + 5E+10);
      System.out.println("Scientific Notation.:  "
            + 5E-20);
      System.out.println("Scientific Notation.:  "
            + 5E30);
   }
}
```

Real numbers written in scientific notation typically have many digits following the decimal. However, all those digits may not be important to your program. Let's look at a simple example so that you understand this point. Let's say you have the real number 5.5543213421. Suppose this number represented the change someone is to receive after making a purchase. Only two of the ten digits following the decimal are important because the smallest denomination of U.S. currency is a penny. Therefore, the change is $5.55.

Programmers call the numbers following the decimal that are important to the program *significant numbers.* In the previous example, there are two significant numbers: 55. The other numbers (43213421) are insignificant and can be ignored by your program.

Some Java programs require that a number have a specific degree of accuracy. This is called *precision.* For example, the previous example requires two significant digits of precision because the customer expects to receive every penny of change that is due.

Floating-point literals are stored with a precision of approximately seven significant digits or approximately 15 significant digits. Seven-digit precision is called *single precision,* whereas 15-digit precision is called *double precision.* The word *approximately* is used because values may not correspond exactly to decimal digits because numbers are represented as binary values.

By default, floating-point values are stored using single precision. Therefore, 5.12345678910111213 14 is stored as 5.1234567. If your program requires more than seven significant digits, you need to store the value using double precision. Using the symbol *F* or *f* at the end of the value, as shown in this example, specifies double precision:

```
class Demo {
   public static void main( String args[]) {
      System.out.println("Scientific Notation.:   "
            + 5E+10F);
      System.out.println("Scientific Notation.:   "
            + 5E-20F);
      System.out.println("Scientific Notation.:   "
            + 5E30f);
   }
}
```

Boolean Literals

Whenever you see the term *Boolean,* you should think of true and false, yes and no, on and off, and 0 and 1, because a Boolean value can be one of two values. A Boolean value cannot be yes, no, and maybe. It must be one value or another value.

You write a Boolean literal by using the Boolean operators true and false. You'll learn more about these in the next chapter. In this example, two Boolean literals are assigned to variables. You'll learn about variables later in this chapter. For now, think of a variable as an empty box into which your program places a Boolean value. The box is actually computer memory that is identified by a label. We use `box1` and `box2` as labels for memory in the following example:

```
class Demo {
   public static void main( String args[]) {
      boolean box1 = true;
      boolean box2 = false;
}
}
```

Character Literals

A character is a letter, number, punctuation, or any other character defined in Unicode. It is easy to become confused between a number that is treated as a character and a number that is treated as a numeric value because they look very much alike. For example, the house number in the address 121 Gordon Street is treated as a character, as compared to the expression 5 + 10, which contains numeric values.

However, programs treat these differently. A numeric value can be directly used in a calculation, whereas a number character is a Unicode value that must be converted to a numeric value.

A character literal is a character defined by Unicode that you write into your program by placing the character between single quotations. Be careful. Placing a character literal in double quotations is a common error made when writing a character literal. As you'll learn in the next section, double quotations are used to write a string literal, which is materially different from a character literal.

Here's how to write a character literal in your program:

```
class Demo {
   public static void main( String args[]) {
      System.out.println("Character Literal:  " + 'A');
}
}
```

As good practice, don't write numeric values as character literals if they will be used in a calculation. Numeric values should be written as integer literals or as floating-point literals; otherwise, you'll need to convert the character literal version of the number of an integer literal or floating-point literal before it can be used in a calculation.

Escape Characters

Not all characters used in your program are printable characters. Some characters cannot be printed on the screen. These are called *nonprintable characters* and are used to give special direction to the computer and to programs. Nonprintable characters are the first 32 characters defined in the Unicode table. Table 2-2 shows the more commonly used nonprintable characters.

For example, you use a nonprintable character each time you want a new line to appear in a word processing document. You don't see the newline character because it isn't displayed on the screen. Instead, the word processor recognizes the newline character as a special command to move the cursor to the beginning of a new line.

You write a nonprintable character into your program by using the escape character followed by the symbol in the Unicode table that is used to represent the nonprintable character. The forward slash (\) is the escape character in Java. The combination of the escape character and the symbol used to represent the nonprintable character is called an *escape sequence.* The escape sequence is also referred to as a *control sequence* or *control character* because nonprintable characters are commonly used to control the behavior of programs and sometimes hardware.

The follow example illustrates how to write an escape sequence in a program. Here, the newline escape sequence (\n) is used to place the second portion of the text on its own line. Notice that the escape sequence consists of two characters. The first character is the forward slash, and the second character is the symbol found on the Unicode table. However, the escape sequence is enclosed within single quotation marks because both characters are treated as single characters and not as two characters.

```
 class Demo {
   public static void main( String args[]) {
      System.out.println("Line 1" + '\n' + "Line 2");
}
}
```

Escape Character	Description
\n	Newline character (also called a linefeed character)
\t	Tab character
\r	Carriage return character
\f	Formfeed character
\b	Backspace character

Table 2-2 Escape Characters

String Literals

A *string* is a series of related characters, such as the name Amber Leigh. You write a string literal in a program by enclosing the series of characters in double quotations on a single line. The most common use of a string literal in a program is to initialize a String object. You'll learn about String objects in Chapter 7. For now, think of a String object as something that is used to store a string literal in memory and lets you do things with the string literal such as counting the number of characters in it.

The following example shows how to write a string literal to initialize a String object:

```
class Demo {
   public static void main( String args[]) {
      String name = "Amber Leigh";
}
}
```

Data Types

When some people who are learning computer programming hear the term *memory,* they go into a state of panic because memory is something abstract. It is difficult to imagine what memory is because no one can really feel and touch it.

However, there isn't any need to panic when learning about memory. Think of memory as a bunch of empty boxes. Each box can hold eight binary digits (bits), collectively known as a *byte,* as you learned in Chapter 1. A number called a *memory address* uniquely identifies each "box."

Fortunately, you don't have to be concerned about memory addresses because Java handles memory addresses for your. However, you do have to be concerned about telling Java how many boxes you'll need to store data in memory.

Let's say your program needs to store an integer into memory. An integer takes up four boxes (four bytes). Therefore, you need to tell Java to reserve four boxes of memory for your program before your program can store the integer into memory.

No programmer wants to memorize the number of boxes (bytes) needed to store various kinds of data into memory. So, instead of telling Java to reserve a specific number of boxes, programmers simply use a keyword that tells Java the kind of data the program needs to store in memory. This keyword is called a *data type.* A data type tells Java how much memory to reserve and the kind of data that will be stored in that memory location. A data type also tells Java the kinds of operation that can be performed using the data stored at that memory location. Table 2-3 lists the data types used to tell Java the amount of boxes (bytes) of memory to reserve.

Data Type	Data Type Size in Bits	Range of Values	Group
byte	8	–128 to 127	Integer
short	16	–32,768 to 32,767	Integer
int	32	–2,147,483,648 to 2,147,483,647	Integer
long	64	–9,223,372,036,854,775,808 to 9,223,372,036,854,775,807	Integer
char	16 (Unicode)	65,000 (Unicode)	Character
float	32	3.4e-038 to 3.4e+038	Floating point
double	64	1.7e-308 to 1.7e+308	Floating point
boolean	1	0 or 1	Boolean

Table 2-3 Simple Java Data Types

Your job is to select the data type that provides your program with sufficient memory to store data. Table 2-3 shows the range of values that can be stored in each data type. Refer to this table whenever you are choosing a data type for your application in order to ensure you reserve enough memory to store the data.

Let's say your program needs to store –2,147,483,650 in memory. By consulting Table 2-3, you'll notice that this value is beyond the range of the int data type. This means if you had told Java to reserve an int data type and your program stored –2,147,483,650 into that memory location, some of the data would be lost because there is simply not enough room to store this number. The long data type is the preferred choice because this value fits within the range of the long data type.

Every data type falls into one of four of the following groups:

- **Integer** Stores whole numbers and signed numbers
- **Floating point** Stores real numbers (whole numbers and fractional values)
- **Character** Stores characters
- **Boolean** Stores a true or false value

Integer Data Types

The integer data type group contains four data types: byte, short, int, and long. These are used to store signed values. (A signed value is a number that is either positive or negative.) Unlike other programming languages, such as C++, Java doesn't permit the storage of unsigned values.

You might be curious about the importance of signed and unsigned numbers. The issue surrounds the largest value of a signed number that can be stored in memory.

As you can see in Table 2-3, the byte data type reserves one box (a byte) that holds eight bits. One of those bits is used to represent the sign. The other seven bits are used to hold the value of the number. The smallest value can be –128, and the largest value can be 127. However, by treating the value as an unsigned number, we can use all eight bits to represent the value. This means the smallest value is 0 and the largest is 256. A larger number can be stored in same memory size if the number is always positive.

byte

The byte data type is the smallest data type in the integer group. You tell Java to reserve enough memory to store a byte by using the keyword `byte`. You won't use the byte data type often in your program unless your program sends and receives information to and from a file or over a computer network. Programmers use the byte data type when working with binary data that isn't compatible with other data types, such as reading a graphics file that contains a picture.

short

The short data type is the least used of the data types in the integer data type group. This is because programmers have traditionally used the short data type for programs that took advantage of the efficiencies of a 16-bit computer. However, 16-bit computers have been replaced with 64-bit computers, making the short data type practically obsolete.

int

The int data type is the most frequently used data type in the integer data type group. It is used for control variables (Chapter 4) and array indexes (Chapter 5), and it's used for performing integer math.

You'll notice in Table 2-3 that an int data type tells Java to reserve 32 bits of memory. Depending on the nature of their program, some programmers feel 32 bits is too much memory for the value they intend to store in memory. Therefore, they use a byte or short data type instead of an int data type.

This is a false savings because the choice of data type tells Java the kind of data your program will store in memory. Your choice doesn't direct Java to use the data type you choose. The Java Virtual Machine has the ultimate say in deciding how much memory to reserve. However, you can be assured that the Java Virtual Machine will reserve sufficient memory to store the value placed there by your program.

long

The long data type is the best choice whenever your program needs to store very large whole numbers that are beyond the range of the int data type. Always consult Table 2-3 to determine whether an integer value used by your program is beyond the range of the int data type.

Floating-point Data Types

The floating-point data type group consists of data types used to store real numbers. A real number contains a whole number and a decimal value. There are two data types in the floating-point data type group: float and double.

float

A float data type is used to store single-precision values and is perfect for storing United States currency, where a fraction of a penny isn't critical to the program. However, you should always verify the result of any calculation that uses a data type in the floating-point data type group to ensure that the value isn't truncated. Truncation occurs when one or more digits to the left of the decimal are dropped because of insufficient room in memory to store those digits.

double

The double data type is used when you have very large or very small values that are beyond the range of a float. A double data type is used to store double-precision values.

Character Data Type

The character data type group contains the char data type, which is used to store a character in memory. Previously in this chapter, you learned that each character is assigned an integer in Unicode. It is this integer that is stored in memory.

Besides telling Java that the program needs to store a character in memory, the char data type tells Java how to interpret the integer that represents the character. As you saw at the beginning of this chapter, the letter *B* is assigned the integer 66 in Unicode. This means when your program stores the letter *B* in memory, Java stores the integer 66 in memory (66 is a number, just as if you stored the number 66 in memory). However, by using the char data type, you are telling Java that 66 must be interpreted as Unicode and not as a number. This means that the character *B* is used within the program and not the integer 66.

Boolean Data Type

The Boolean data type group consists of the boolean data type. The boolean data type tells Java to reserve memory sufficient to store a Boolean value. A Boolean value is either true or false.

You should use a boolean data type whenever your program needs to store one of two possible values that represents the state of a condition, such as on/off, true/false, yes/no, or 0/1. Java will then decide how to efficiently store this condition in memory.

Casting Data Types

Sometimes your program will call a method that performs a specific functionality and then returns a value to your program. However, the value returned by the method maybe of a data type different from the data type you used to tell Java to reserve memory for your program.

Let's say the prompt needs to read a character from the keyboard. In order to do this, you need to call the `System.in.read()` method. You'll learn how to do this in Chapter 11. For now, you need to know that this method returns the character entered into the keyboard as the integer that corresponds to the character's Unicode value.

Suppose that your program saves the return value from the `System.in.read()` method as a character instead of as an integer, as shown in the following example. The name choice is called a *variable.* You'll learn about variables in the next section. For now, think of a variable as a name that you assign to the box of memory that is used to store the character read from the keyboard. Also notice that the char data type is used to tell Java to reserve enough memory to store the character. You're also telling Java that you'll be using the name choice throughout your program to refer to that memory location (box of memory).

```
class Demo {
   public static void main( String args[]) {
      char choice = System.in.read();
   }
}
```

There is a problem, however. The `System.in.read()` method returns an integer (technically a byte data type). Memory is reserved to store a char data type. These are unlike data types. An error message is displayed when you try compiling this example.

You can temporarily change the data type returned by the `System.in.read()` method from an integer to a char data type by *casting* the value this method returns. Casting temporarily changes a value from one data type to another data type in order to carry out an operation. In the previous example, the operation is to store the character entered into the keyboard in memory.

You cast a value by placing the temporary data type within parentheses, as shown in the next example:

```
class Demo {
   public static void main( String args[])
               throws java.io.IOException {
      char choice = (char) System.in.read();
   }
}
```

Here's what happens when a value is cast:

1. The method `System.in.read()` returns an integer representing the character entered into the keyboard.
2. The return value (integer) is temporarily converted to (cast as) a char data type, making it the same data type as the `choice` variable.
3. The converted integer is assigned to the `choice` variable.

You probably noticed something a little different in the previous example. Alongside the `main()` method name is "`throws java.io.IOException`". This is telling Java that an `IOException` will be created by the method if something doesn't go right when a character is read from the keyboard. You'll learn about exceptions in Chapter 9.

Variables

Previously in this chapter, you learned that computer memory is divided into chucks of eight bits (one byte). Each byte is identified by a unique memory address similar to how each house in your town in identified by a unique address.

However, you might be more comfortable thinking of each chuck of memory as an empty box that is identified by a unique number. Using numbers to identify boxes (memory location) isn't the most intuitive way for you to keep track of them within your program. A more appropriate way is to assign a name to the boxes that is meaningful to you and that you tell Java to reserve for your program.

In the previous example, we use the word *choice* for the name of the box (memory location) that Java reserved to store the character entered at the keyboard. We refer to the word *choice* in the program whenever the program needs to access data stored in the corresponding box (memory location). Java is smart enough to translate the word *choice* into the actual address of the box (memory address).

The memory location that a program reserves is referred to as a *variable,* and the name you give to the variable is called an *identifier.* Therefore, *choice* is an identifier that refers to a memory location called a *variable.*

Java automatically relates the identifier to the variable's memory address. Each time you refer to the identifier in your program, Java looks up the memory address that corresponds to the identifier and accesses that memory address. This process is called *resolving*.

Declaring a Variable

Your program must tell Java to reserve memory before your program can store data in memory. The instruction to reserve memory is called *declaring a variable.* You declare a variable by using a declaration statement within your program. A declaration statement consists of three components:

- Data type
- Identifier
- Semicolon

The data type is one of the keywords described in Table 2-3, and it tells Java the kind of data your program will be storing in memory. Java then knows how much memory to reserve. The identifier is the name you will use within your program to refer to that memory location. The semicolon is Java punctuation that tells Java it has reached the end of the statement.

Here's how to declare a variable. In this example, Java is told to reserve enough memory to store an int and that you will use the identifier `grade` within the program to refer to that memory location:

```
class Demo {
   public static void main( String args[]) {
      int grade;
   }
}
```

The name you select as the identifier for the variable should be meaningful and represent the nature of data that is stored in the corresponding memory location. The previous example stores a grade in memory. Therefore, it makes sense to use the word *grade* as the identifier. In this way, we will always remember the nature of data.

There are some restrictions that apply to choosing an identifier, however:

- An identifier cannot begin with a number.
- An identifier cannot contain spaces.
- An identifier cannot be one of the following Java keywords:

abstract	do	instanceof	static	while
assert	double	int	strictfp	
boolean	else	interface	super	
break	extends	long	switch	
byte	final	native	synchronized	
case	finally	new	this	
catch	float	package	throw	
char	for	private	throws	
class	goto	protected	transient	
const	if	public	try	
continue	implements	return	void	
default	import	short	volatile	

The identifier name must be unique within the code block within which the variable is declared and the outer code blocks (see "Scope of a Variable" later in this chapter). This means you cannot declare two variables using the same identifier within the same code block; otherwise, there will be a compiler error. However, you can declare variables in different code blocks using the same identifier.

Java Naming Convention

Java programmers have developed a unique naming style, called the Java Naming Convention, that is used when naming identifiers. The Java Naming Convention isn't a steadfast rule that is enforced by the Java compiler. Instead, it is a style that is adhered to voluntarily by Java programmers. Therefore, you, too, should use the Java Naming Convention when naming identifiers in your program.

The Java Naming Convention calls for identifiers used for variables to begin with a lowercase letter and then for concatenated words used in the identifier to start with an uppercase letter. Suppose we changed the identifier used in the previous example from `grade` to `mygrade`. To conform to the Java Naming Convention, we must write the identifier as `myGrade` because the word *grade* is concatenated to the word *my* and therefore the concatenated word must begin with an uppercase letter.

Declaring Multiple Variables

Variables are typically declared at the beginning of a program, at the beginning of a method definition, or at the beginning of a class definition. In this way, you don't have to look all over your code for the definition of a variable.

Variables can be declared in separate statements or in one statement if variables are the same data type. Variables of different data types must be declared in different statements. You can declare variables of the same data type in the same statements by placing identifiers along side each other and separating them with commas.

Here is an example of how to declare multiple variables in a program. The first statement declares three variables in one statement. The other statements each declare a variable. We could have declared all these variables in one statement because they are the same data type, but we didn't in order to illustrate an alternative way of declaring a variable.

```
class Demo {
   public static void main( String args[]) {
      int projectGrade, finalGrade, midTermGrade;
      int quiz1;
      int quiz2;
      int quiz3;
   }
}
```

Initializing a Variable

Whenever you declare a variable, it is always best to store an initial value in the corresponding memory location. In this way, you won't experience an error if you try to use the value assigned to the variable before you actually assign a value to the variable. That would be like drinking a glass of water before you filled the glass with water.

The process of storing an initial value to a variable is called *initialization* and is typically performed in the statement that declares the variable by using the assignment operator (=). You'll learn about operators in Chapter 3. For now, you need to know that the assignment operator is an equal sign and that it copies the value on its right to the variable on its left.

Behind the scenes, Java stores a copy of the value that appears on the right of the assignment operator and stores the copy in the memory address that corresponds to the variable identifier in the statement.

A variable can be initialized using the following:

- A literal
- An expression
- Another variable

The following example illustrates how to initialize a variable using literal values:

```
class Demo {
   public static void main( String args[]) {
      int projectGrade = 0,
                  finalGrade = 0, midTermGrade = 0;
      int quiz1 = 0;
      int quiz2 = 0;
      int quiz3 = 0;
   }
}
```

As you'll learn in the next chapter, an expression is a mathematical statement that contains operators and operands. An operator is a symbol you use in arithmetic. An operand is the value used by the operator to perform the operation. For example, 5 + 10 is an expression. The addition sign is the operator, and each of the numbers is an operand.

You can use the result of an expression to initialize a variable. This is illustrated in the following example:

```
class Demo {
   public static void main( String args[]) {
      int totalFee = 50 + 100 + 50;
   }
}
```

You can also initialize a variable by using another variable that has already been initialized. This is illustrated in the next example, where four variables are declared. The first three variables declare individual fees, each of which is initialized. The last variable contains the total fee, which is initialized by using the previously declared variables.

Here's what Java is told to do: In the first declaration statement, Java is told to reserve memory sufficient to store an int, and that memory location will be called `fee1` throughout the program. Java is then told to copy the value 50 to that memory location. A similar process occurs for the next two variables.

The last statement tells Java to reserve memory for another int, which will be called `totalFee` in the program. Java is then told to add the values stored in `fee1`, `fee2`, and `fee3` and copy the sum to the memory location that is associated with the variable `totalFee`. It is important to understand that values stored in `fee1`, `fee2`, and `fee3` remain intact while Java executes the last statement.

```
class Demo {
   public static void main( String args[]) {
      int fee1 = 50;
      int fee2 = 100;
      int fee3 = 50;
      int totalFee = fee1 + fee2 + fee3;
   }
}
```

Scope of a Variable

A Java application is divided into sections of code call *code blocks*. The beginning of a code block is defined by an open brace ({) and ends with a closed brace (}). As you'll see in later chapters, code blocks are used to define methods, classes, and control structures, such as `if` statements and loops.

We'll explore each of these later in this book. For now, it is important to understand that a code block also defines the scope of a variable. Other statements within the same code block can access a variable that is declared within a code block. Statements outside the code block cannot access the variable, with a few exceptions that we'll talk about in the appropriate chapters.

A statement that can access a variable is said to be *within the scope of the variable.* Programmers sometimes say that a variable is *visible* to the statement. A statement that cannot access a variable is out of scope of the variable. Programmers say the variable is *hidden* from the statement.

As you'll see in the next example, a code block can be placed within another code block. This is referred to as *nesting.* Variables declared in the outer code block are within the scope of statements in the inner code block. However, variables declared in the inner code block are not within the scope of statements in the outer code block.

The next example contains three code blocks. The outermost code block is used to define the class. The next code block is used to define the `main()` method. The innermost code block is used to define the `if` statement. Statements within the `if` statement code block execute only if the value stored in the `grade` variable is zero.

The grade variable is declared in the main() method code block and is initialized to zero, causing statements within the if statement to execute because the value stored in the grade variable is zero. Notice that the value of the grade variable is displayed on the screen by the System.out.println() method. This is possible because the grade variable is declared in an outer code block.

Now take a look at the last statement in the program and you'll see the System.out.println() method try to display the value of variable x. When you compile this program, you'll receive an error message because variable x is not declared. This can become confusing because variable x is declared within the if statement code block. The problem is that the statement that is trying to display the value of variable x in the outer code block and therefore is out of scope of variable x. Simply said, the statement cannot access variable x because variable x cannot be seen from the outside code block.

You can avoid this problem by declaring variables in the outermost code block if the variables need to be accessed by statements contained in other code blocks.

```
class Demo {
   public static void main (String args[]) {
      int grade = 0;
      if (grade == 0)
      {
         int x = 0;
         System.out.println (grade);
      }
      System.out.println(x);
   }
}
```

The Life of a Variable

Java continues to reserve memory for a variable as long as the variable remains within scope. Once the variable goes out of scope, the program can no longer access that memory location. Values stored there are lost forever.

A variable goes out of scope when the program executes the last statement within the code block where the variable is declared. In the previous example, variable x is destroyed after the statement displays the value of the grade variable on the screen. The program then leaves the if statement code block and continues with the statement that follows the closed brace of the if statement code block.

Programmers define the life of a variable beginning when the variable is declared and ending when the variable goes out of scope.

Quiz

1. What is the purpose of a data type?
2. Can variables of different data types be declared in the same statement?
3. What is the purpose of casting?
4. How would you determine the proper data type for a variable?
5. What is a variable identifier?
6. What is the relationship between a variable identifier and a memory address?
7. What is the scope of a variable?
8. What is precision?
9. What value is stored in memory when you assign a character to a char variable?
10. Do the float and double data types have the same precision?

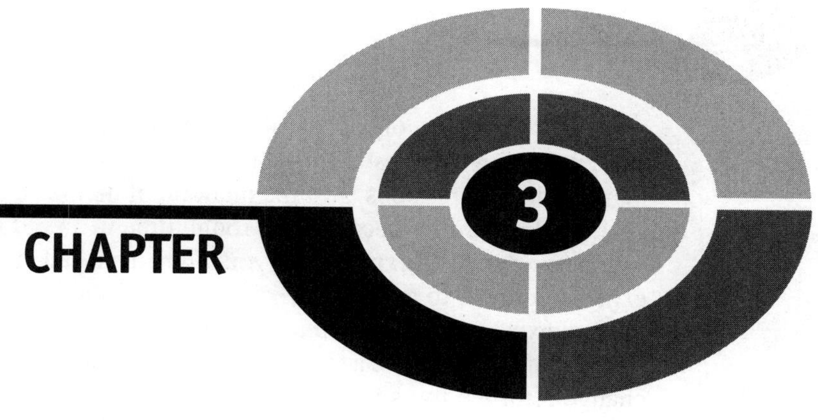

Expressions and Statements

If only you knew how to express yourself, you could have any computer eating out of your hands. Well, using a few choice words won't let you feed a computer, but it will give you the capability to put nearly any computer through its paces to automate a process or solve a problem. In the previous chapter, you learned how to store information in a computer's memory. In this chapter, you'll learn how to do something with that information by creating expressions and then using them to form statements that tell the computer to do something.

Expressions

You express your thoughts and ideas to friends and family by organizing nouns, verbs, and other types of words together into a sentence. If you construct the sentence properly, another person will understand what you are trying to say.

Nearly the same concept applies when you convey your thoughts and ideas to a computer. However, instead of nouns and verbs, you express yourself using mathematical-like expressions. Just the mention of math is enough to make some people shun reading further because of a rough time in an old math class.

Put aside any bad experiences you might have had in math class. Learning how to express yourself to a computer isn't at all difficult because you'll be using mathematical expressions that you use every day.

Most of us never give a second thought to calculating a sales price or counting the change returned to us after making a purchase. And yet to do these tasks we use mathematical expressions. That is, we use numbers, an equal sign, a plus sign, a minus sign, a multiplication sign, and a division sign in the correct order to perform such calculations. The order in which we place numbers and mathematical signs is a mathematical expression.

Programmers have their own terms for numbers and mathematical signs. Numbers in an expression are called *operands,* and mathematical signs are called *operators.* In the following expression, 5 and 10 are operands and the plus sign is an operator:

```
5 + 10
```

In Java, an expression has an operator and at least one operand, although many expressions have two operands. An operator is a symbol that tells Java to perform an operation using the operands. Although we think of an operand as a number, an operand can also be a variable or the result of another expression.

Here is an example of how two variables are used as operands in an expression. As you'll recall from the previous chapter, a *variable* is a name that corresponds to a memory address. Java replaces the variable with the value stored in the memory address before performing the operation specified in an expression. In this example, Java replaces A with the value stored in the corresponding memory address. Likewise, B is replaced with the value stored in its corresponding memory address. Java then adds both values.

```
A + B
```

The next example illustrates how the result of another expression is used as an operand. Two expressions are shown here. The first is addition, and the second expression subtracts 5 from the result of the first expression. Java performs the addition before the subtraction in this example.

```
5 + 10 - 5
```

Types of Expressions

There are two types of expressions: simple expressions and compound expressions. A simple expression is an expression that contains one operator. A compound expression is an expression that contains two or more operators.

Here is an example of a simple expression:

```
5 + 10
```

And here is an example of a compound expression:

```
5 + 10 - 5
```

Compound expressions can be baffling because it usually isn't clear which operation is performed first. Programmers refer to this as the *order of operation.* Does Java perform subtraction or addition first in the previous example?

It really doesn't matter because you'll arrive at the same answer whether you perform subtraction or addition first. However, that's not always going to be the case, and the order in which operations are performed can affect the result of the expression.

As an example, evaluate this compound expression:

```
10 * 5 + 2
```

Puzzling isn't it? The result of the compound expression could be 52 if multiplication is performed before addition. It could also be 70 if addition is performed before multiplication.

In order to determine how Java evaluates a compound expression, programmers consult the Java Precedence Table (see Table 3-1). The Java Precedence Table lists each operator in the order in which its operation is performed by Java. Operators having a higher precedence value are evaluated before operators that have a lower precedence value. You'll be introduced to all these operators later in this chapter.

Order of Operation	Type of Operator	Operator
1	Postfix operators	[] . *(params) expr++ expr--*
2	Unary operators	*++expr --expr +expr -expr* ~ !
3		creation or cast
4		new *(type)expr*
5	Multiplicative	* / %

Table 3-1 Java Precedence Table

Order of Operation	Type of Operator	Operator
6	Additive	+ -
7	Shift	<< >> >>>
8	Relational	< > <= >= instanceof
9	Equality	== !=
10	Bitwise AND	&
11	Bitwise exclusive	OR ^
12	Bitwise inclusive	OR |
13	Logical AND	&&
14	Logical OR	||
15	Conditional	? :
16	Assignment	= += -= *= /= %= &= ^= |= <<= >>= >>>=

Table 3-1 Java Precedence Table *(continued)*

Notice that addition and subtraction operators have the same precedence value. Therefore, Java performs operations left to right in the 5 + 10 – 5 compound expression. That is, addition followed by subtraction.

However, Java performs multiplication before addition in the 10 * 5 + 2 compound expression, thus making 52 the correct result. This is because multiplication has a higher precedence than addition.

NOTE: *Operators evaluate left to right if there are multiple operators at the same precedence level in an expression.*

Admittedly, order of operations confuses even a seasoned Java programmer. And let's face it: Some Java programmers don't want to take the time to look up an operator on the Java Precedence Table. So here's the shortcut they use: Instead of referring to the Java Precedence Table, programmers place parentheses around portions of a compound expression that they want evaluated before other portions. Notice that parentheses have the highest order of operation in the Java Precedence Table.

Let's say that we're unsure whether multiplication or addition is performed first in a compound expression. Rather than look up these operators in the Java Precedence Table, we could simply place parentheses around the portion of the expression

that we want evaluated first. In the following example, addition is performed before multiplication:

```
10 * (5 + 2)
```

A compound expression can contain multiple parentheses in two possible forms. Sets of parentheses can appear in multiple levels or the same level within the expression. Here's a compound expression that uses multiple levels of parentheses. Programmers call these *nested parentheses*. The highest-level parentheses are (20*4). The lower-level parentheses are (5 +2 + (20 * 4)).

```
10 * (5 + 2 + (20 * 4))
```

Java begins evaluating with the expression contained in the highest-level parentheses and then works its way down to the next-highest-level parentheses. Therefore, Java evaluates (20 * 4) first and then adds the product with 7 before multiplying the sum by 10.

Java evaluates parentheses from left to right if two sets of parentheses are on the same level as shown here. In this example, (5 +2) is evaluated before (20 * 4):

```
10 * (5 + 2) + (20 * 4)
```

Although using parentheses clarifies the order of operation for you and for Java, expect to run into the common problem of unbalanced parentheses, which occurs when there is an uneven number of an opening and closing parentheses in a compound expression. Even experienced Java programmers make this mistake, so don't be embarrassed if you join their ranks. Here's an example of unbalance parentheses. Note that there are more opening parentheses than closing parentheses.

```
10 * (5 + 2 + (20*4)
```

Here's a trick you can use to help reduce the likelihood of making this mistake. Count the number of opening parentheses and the number of closing parenthesis in a compound expression. Both counts should be the same. If they're not, there is an unbalanced parenthesis, and you need to match each pair to find the missing parenthesis. If you don't, your program won't compile.

Operators

Two general types of operators are available in Java: binary operators and unary operators. A binary operator requires two operands, such as the addition operator used in previous examples in this chapter. A unary operator requires one operand. For example, the incremental operator (++), which you'll learn about later in this chapter, is a unary operator because it increments the value of an operand. That is, it adds one to the value of the operand.

Operators are also organized into the following four groups:

- Arithmetic operators
- Relational operators
- Logical operators
- Bitwise operators

Arithmetic Operators

Arithmetic operators perform arithmetic operations. Table 3-2 contains a list of arithmetic operators. You are already familiar with many of these operators because they are the same operators you use everyday to perform arithmetic. However, you'll notice a few that are unusual, so we'll take a close look at those in this section.

Operation	**Operator**
Addition	+
Subtraction and unary minus	-
Multiplication	*
Division	/
Modulus	%
Addition assignment	+=
Subtraction assignment	-=
Multiplication assignment	*=
Division assignment	/=
Modulus assignment	%=
Increment	++
Decrement	--

Table 3-2 Arithmetic Operators

Modulus Operator

The modulus operator is probably the first operator that catches your eye as being strange. It looks as if it should return the percentage of an operand because the symbol for the modulus operator is a percentage symbol. However, the modulus operator has nothing to do with percentage. Instead, the modulus operator returns the remainder of the division of two operands. This sounds confusing, so let's go directly to an example and see how the modulus operator works. Run the following example and you'll see "modulus: 4" displayed on the screen (4 is the remainder of 14 / 5).

```
class Demo {
   public static void main (String args[]) {
      System.out.println ("modulus: " + 14%5);
   }
}
```

Assignment Operator

The assignment operator (=) is probably one of the most misleading of all the operators because the symbol for the assignment operator is commonly used to express equality. That is, two values are the same.

However, the assignment operator in Java tells Java to copy the value of the right operand and place it in the left operand. This is illustrated in the next example, where the assignment operator in the first statement within the `main()` method tells Java to copy the value 5 (right operand) to the variable a (left operand):

```
class Demo {
   public static void main (String args[]) {
      int a = 5;
      System.out.println ("assignment operator: " + a);
   }
}
```

There is a tendency to say "a equals 5," but that's not what is happening here. Instead, we should say "a is assigned the value 5." Later in this chapter, you'll learn about the relational equivalent operator (==), which is used to determine whether two operands are equal.

Combined Assignment Operator

You'll notice several strange-looking arithmetical operators in Table 3-2 that seem to use two operator symbols, such as +=. These operators combine two operations into one operation. Notice that the first operator symbol is an arithmetical operator. The second operator symbol is the assignment operator.

Here's how this works: First, Java performs the operation specified by the first operator using the operand on the left and right of the operator. The result is then assigned to the left operand.

The next example illustrates how each of these combined operators works. The first statement assigns the value 5 to variable a, which is then displayed on the screen. Next, the += operator is used. First, Java adds 5 to the value stored in variable a. Remember that the variable a represents the value 5. The sum of these values is 10. Next, Java assigns the sum to the left operand, which is variable a. The new value of variable a is 10.

See if you can determine what happens when the other statements are executed in this example and then run the example to check your answers:

```
class Demo {
   public static void main (String args[]) {
      int a = 5;
      System.out.println ("a = 5:  " + a);
      a += 5;
      System.out.println ("a += 5:  " + a);
      a -= 5;
      System.out.println ("a -= 5:  " + a);
      a *= 2;
      System.out.println ("a *= 2:  " + a);
      a /= 5;
      System.out.println ("a /= 5:  " + a);
      a %=5;
      System.out.println ("a %= 5:  " + a);
   }
}
```

Increment and Decrement Operators

The increment (++) and decrement (--) operators are two operators you might not have seen used outside of Java programming circles. Two aspects of these operators may seem unusual. First, each operator's symbol is a combination of two other operators. The increment operator uses two addition symbols, and the decrement operator uses two subtraction symbols. The other unusual feature is that both use one operand. That is, they are unary operators.

The increment operator adds 1 to the value of its operand and then assigns the sum to the operand. The decrement operator subtracts 1 from its operand and then assigns the difference to the operand. Both operators are illustrated in the next example.

First, the value 5 is assigned to the variable a, which is then displayed on the screen. The increment operator then increases the value of variable a by 1. Variable a is then displayed on the screen once again. The decrement operator then decreases the value of variable a by 1, and it is again displayed on the screen.

```
class Demo {
    public static void main (String args[]) {
        int a = 5;
        System.out.println ("Initial value: " + a);
        a++;
        System.out.println ("increment operator: " + a);
        a--;
        System.out.println ("decrement operator: " + a);
    }
}
```

The increment and decrement operators can be placed on either side of the operand. Their position tells Java when to add 1 to and subtract 1 from the operand. Placing the increment or decrement operator on the left of the operand tells Java to increment or decrement the operand before performing any additional operation on the operand. Placing the increment or decrement operator on the right of the operand tells Java to increment or decrement the operand after performing any additional operations on the operand.

This is a bit confusing, especially when you view the previous example, because only one operation is being performed with the operand. It doesn't make any difference where you place the increment or decrement operator because you always end up with the same result.

However, the increment and decrement operators are commonly used in compound expressions where the positions of these operators have a material effect on the result of the expression, as you'll see in the next example.

Notice the first expression that uses the increment operator (b = a++). What is the value of variable b? What is the value of variable a? Variable b is assigned the value of variable a before Java increments the value of variable a. Therefore, variable b is assigned the value 5 and variable a is then incremented by 1 to have a value 6.

However, the operation changes in the second expression that uses the increment operator (b = ++a). Remember that before this statement executes, variable b has the value 5 and variable a has the value 6. Because the increment operator appears to the left of variable a, Java increments the value of variable a before assigning its value to variable b. After this statement executes, variable a has the value 7 and variable b is assigned the value 7.

The position of the decrement operator has a similar effect as the increment operator. See if you can determine the value of variable a and variable b each time the decrement operator is used in the next example. Run the example to check your answers.

```
class Demo {
   public static void main (String args[]) {
      int a = 5, b = 0;
      System.out.println ("Initial value: a = " + a + " b =  "
              + b);
      b = a++;
      System.out.println (" b = a++ value: a = " + a + " b =  "
           + b);
      b = ++a;
      System.out.println ("b = ++a value: a = " + a + " b =  "
        + b);
      b = a--;
      System.out.println ("b = a-- value: a = " + a + " b =  "
       + b);
      b = --a;
      System.out.println ("b = --a value: a = " + a + " b =  "
           + b);

   }
}
```

Here are the rules for using the increment and decrement operators:

- Placing the incremental/decrement operator to the left of the variable causes the value of the variable to be incremented/decremented *before* the value is used in another operation.
- Placing the increment/decrement operator to the right of the variable causes the value of the variable to be incremented/decremented *after* the value is used in another operation.

Relational Operators

Many of your programs will compare two values to determine whether they are or are not the same or to determine the relationship between the two values. This happens each time you enter a password into a program. The program compares the password that you enter with the known password. It also happens when a program determines whether your final grade is equal to or greater than the passing grade for a course.

The operators that tell Java to determine this relationship are called *relational operators* because they determine the relationship between two operands. A relational

operator is used in a condition expression in order to test whether a particular kind of relationship exists between two operands, as called for by the program.

For example, a program may need to determine whether both operands are the same. Another program may need to know whether the left operand is greater than the right operand. And still another program might want to find out whether the operands are not the same. A relational operator enables you to test for any relationship between two operands.

All relational operators direct Java to return a Boolean value that indicates whether the relationship that is being tested is true or false. You'll recall from the previous chapter that a Boolean value is either true or false.

A conditional expression is used by Java to determine whether a portion of the program should or should not be executed. As you'll learn in Chapter 4, you can use a control statement to tell Java whether or not to execute one or multiple statements based on a condition.

One of the most commonly used control statements is the `if` statement, which tells Java to test a condition. (If the condition is true, then execute one or more statements. If the condition is not true, then don't execute those statements.) The expression that states the condition is called a *conditional expression,* and it uses one or more relational operators. Table 3-3 lists the relational operators. The following example illustrates how to use a relational operator in an `if` statement within your program.

Operation	Operator	Example
Equal to	==	`a == b`
Not equal to	!=	`a != b`
Greater than	>	`a > b`
Less than	<	`a < b`
Greater than or equal to	>=	`a >= b`
Less than or equal to	<=	`a <= b`

Table 3-3 Relational Operators

The following example gives you a peek at how the `if...else` constructor is used in a program. You'll be formally introduced to it in Chapter 4; however, let's see how a relational operator is used to have Java make a decision.

The `if...else` statement is fairly intuitive. It tells Java that if the conditional expression is true, then execute the statement within the body of the `if` statement. If it isn't true, then execute the statement in the body of the `else` statement. Only one statement will be executed depending on the evaluation of the conditional expression. The other statement will not be executed.

The conditional expression in this example uses the greater than or equal to (>=) relational operator. Java is told to compare the value of variable b to the value of variable a. If variable b is greater than or equal to variable a, then the conditional expression is true; otherwise, the conditional expression is false.

```
class demo {
   public static void main (String args[]) {
      int a = 5, b = 7;
      if ( b >= a)
      {
         System.out.println (
                  " b is greater than or equal to a");
      }
      else
      {
         System.out.println (
                  " b is not greater than or equal to a");
      }
   }
}
```

Logical Operators

As you saw in the previous section, an if statement is a conditional statement that tells Java to evaluate a relational expression. Based on whether or not the relational expression is true, Java either executes or skips statements within an if statement.

There are times when you'll need Java to evaluate two relational expressions to determine whether statements are to be executed or not. This happens when your program validates a user ID and password. In this case, both conditions must be true for Java to execute statements contained in the if statement.

There are other occasions when statements are executed if either relational expression is true. For example, a person might enter a valid user ID or a guest ID into your program. Either is acceptable.

In order to have Java evaluate two relational expressions, those expressions must be linked together using a logical operator. There are three logical operators, as shown in Table 3-4. These are AND (&&), OR (||), and the ternary (?:) operators.

Operation	Operator	Comment	Example
AND	&&	If the first relational expression is false, then the second relational expression is not evaluated.	`a == b && b == c`
OR	||	If the first relational expression is true, then the second relational expression is not evaluated.	`a == b || b == c`
AND	&	If the first relational expression is false, then the second relational expression is also evaluated.	
OR	|	If the first relational expression is true, then the second relational expression is also evaluated.	
Ternary if-then-else	?:	If the conditional expression is true, then use the first value (i.e., b), otherwise, use the second value (i.e., c).	`a == 50 ? b : c`

Table 3-4 Logical Operators

The AND Logical Operator (&&)

The AND logical operator is used to check to see if the results of two relational expressions are true. If both relational expressions are true, then the AND logical operator returns a Boolean true. If one or both relational expression is false, then the AND logical operator returns a Boolean false.

The following example illustrates how to use the AND logical operator in a program. This example determines whether a student passes or fails a course. The first statement within the `main()` method declares two integer variables that are used to store the grade for the final exam and the grade for the class project. Both of these are initialized with a grade.

Two relational expressions are used in an `if` statement to determine whether the word *pass* or *fail* should be displayed on the screen. These expressions are linked together using the AND logical operator. This might look a bit confusing, but it isn't. Here's what Java is being told to do: First, Java is told to evaluate the relational expression on the left of the AND logical operator. This relational expression asks the question, is the value of the `gradeFinalExam` variable greater than or equal to 70? The answer is true. The value of `gradeFinalExam` is 80.

Next, Java is told to evaluate the relational expression on the right of the AND logical operator. This relational expression asks the question, is the value of variable `gradeClassProject` greater than or equal to 70? The answer is true because the value of the `gradeClassProject` variable is 90.

Java is then asked to compare the results of both of these relational expressions. The AND logical operator asks the question, are both relational expressions true? If so, then Java is told to execute the statement within the `if` statement. If either relational expression is false, then Java is told to execute the statement within the `else` statement.

```
class Demo {
   public static void main (String args[]) {
      int gradeFinalExam = 80, gradeClassProject =90;
      if (gradeFinalExam >= 70 && gradeClassProject >= 70)
      {
         System.out.println ("Pass");
      }
      else
      {
         System.out.println ("Fail");
      }
   }
}
```

The OR Logical Operator (||)

The OR logical operator is also used to check the results of two relational expressions to see if they are true. However, only one of those relational expressions needs to be true for the OR logical operator to return a Boolean true. The OR logical operator returns a Boolean false only if both relational expressions are false.

Let's take a look at how this works in this next example. This example is a slight modification of the previous example. Notice that the grade for the final exam is initialized to 60. However, the student needs only to receive a passing grade for either the final exam or the class project in order to pass the course.

The OR logical operator is used to link together both relational expressions in the `if` statement. Java is told to perform basically the same evaluations of these relational expressions as performed in the previous example. However, the final step is for Java to determine whether either of the relational expressions is true. If so, then the OR logical operator returns a Boolean true, which is the case in this example.

```
class Demo {
   public static void main (String args[]) {
      int gradeFinalExam = 60, gradeClassProject =90;
      if (gradeFinalExam >= 70 || gradeClassProject >= 70)
      {
         System.out.println ("Pass");
      }
      else
      {
         System.out.println ("Fail");
      }
   }
}
```

Single AND Operator (&) and OR Operator (|)

Java has two versions of the AND logical operator and the OR logical operator. The first version uses a double ampersand (&&) and double vertical bar (||). The double ampersand tells Java to evaluate the first relational expression. If the first relational expression is false, then Java does not evaluate the second relational expression because both relational expressions must be true in order for the AND logical operator to return a Boolean true. If the first relational expression is false, then the AND logical operator must return a false.

Likewise, the double vertical bar (||) tells Java to evaluate the first relational expression. If the first relational expression is true, then Java does not evaluate the second relational expression because only one relational expression must be true in order for the OR logical operator to return a Boolean true. If the first relational expression is true, then the OR logical operator must return a true.

The single ampersand (&) and single vertical bar (|) versions of these logical operators tell Java to evaluate both relational expressions regardless of whether or not the first relational expression returns a true or false.

The Ternary Operator (?:)

The ternary logical operator is more similar to an `if...else` statement than it is to the AND logical operator and the OR logical operator. This is because the ternary logical operator is used to have Java make a decision.

The ternary logical operator is composed of three elements—a relational expression and two values. If the relational expression is true, then Java uses the first value. Otherwise, the second value is used.

The following example illustrates the ternary logical operator. It begins by declaring an integer variable called gradeClassProject and initializing it with the grade 90. The next statement declares a char variable called grade and uses the ternary logical operator to determine the initial grade.

To the left of the question mark is the relational expression that asks Java to determine if the value of the gradeClassProject is greater than or equal to 70. If this expression is true, then the value to the right of the question mark is used. If this expression is false, then the value to the right of the colon is used.

Although this example uses one relational expression, you can use two or more relational expressions if they are linked together using the AND logical operator or the OR logical operator.

```
class Demo {
   public static void main (String args[]) {
      int gradeClassProject = 90;
      char grade = gradeClassProject >= 70 ? 'P' : 'F';
      System.out.println( "Course grade: " + grade);
   }
}
```

Bitwise Operators

Previously in this book, you learned that information is stored inside a computer as numbers represented in the binary numbering system. Most of us know this as zeros and ones. You normally don't use the binary numbering system in your program. Instead, you use the decimal numbering system to represent numbers, and you use the characters on your keyboard to represent characters. Java takes and converts these values to binary for you when you compile and run your program.

However, more advanced Java programmers sometimes have a need to work with binary digits (bits). This is common for programmers who write network communications programs. These programmers use bitwise operators to change the value of a bit from zero to one, or vice versa.

I'll show you how to use bitwise operators in this section, but you may simply want to give it a glance or skip it altogether until you move into the advanced Java programmer ranks.

Working at the bit level can become confusing because we normally don't view data as a bit. If you decide to plunge into this section, then take your time. Analyze each bitwise operation by writing the bits on paper and then change its value just as the bitwise operator tells Java to change the bit value inside your computer. After you have a understanding of how a bitwise operator works, run the example to see if the result you achieve on paper matches the output of the example.

A bitwise operator is used to change the value of a bit. Table 3-5 contains the bitwise operators available in Java.

Operation	Operator	Example
Bitwise AND	&	`a & b`
Bitwise inclusive OR	|	`a	b`
Bitwise exclusive OR	^	`a ^ b`
Left shift	<<	`a << b`
Right shift	>>	`a >> b`
Unsigned right shift	>>>	`a >>> b`
Bitwise complement	~	`a ^ b ~a`

Table 3-5 Bitwise Operators

Bitwise AND Operator (&)

Let's begin exploring bitwise operators with the bitwise AND operator (&). The bitwise AND operator compares two bits. If both bits are 1's, then the AND operator returns a binary 1. Otherwise, it returns a binary 0.

The best way to see how this works is to create an equation. For this example, we'll use the binary equivalent of decimal values 15 and 10. The actual numbers aren't important to learning how the AND bitwise operator works. The top value is 15, and the middle value is 10. The bottom value is determined by the AND operator by comparing the digits of the top and middle values. Notice that the bottom value is the same as the middle value. If you convert the bottom value from the binary numbering system to the decimal numbering system, you'll notice that the AND bitwise operator returns the value 10 in this example.

```
  00001111
& 00001010
  --------
  00001010
```

Bitwise operators are typically used in programs that exchange data, such as network communications software. Therefore, the result of a bitwise operation isn't displayed on the screen. However, we'll use the bitwise operator in examples that display the decimal value equivalent of the binary value returned by the bitwise operator.

Let's begin with the following example, which uses the AND bitwise operator to change the bit values described in the previous equation:

```
class Demo {
      public static void main (String args[]) {
         int a = 15, b = 10, c;
         c = a & b;
         System.out.println ("a & b = " + c);
        }
}
```

Bitwise OR Operators

The next bitwise operator we'll explore is the bitwise OR operator. Actually, there are two versions of the bitwise OR operator in Java—the inclusive OR operator (|) and the exclusive OR operator (^). Both of these operators are used to compare the value of two bits.

The bitwise inclusive OR operator returns a binary 1 if one of the bits is a binary 1. However, a binary 0 is returned if both bits are a binary 0. Let's set up our expression again to see how the inclusive OR operator works. The following expression uses the same binary numbers used to explain other bitwise operators in this chapter. Whenever both bits are 0, the bitwise inclusive OR operator returns a binary 0; otherwise, a binary 1 is returned.

```
   00001111
|  00001010
   --------
   00001111
```

The following example illustrates how to use the bitwise inclusive OR operator in a program. As with previous examples in this chapter, numbers are represented as decimal values. Java converts these to binary, and then applies the inclusive OR operator. The result is then converted from a binary value to a decimal value, which is then displayed on the screen. The example uses the same numbers as used in the previous expression. What number is displayed on the screen by this example? Run the example to verify that your answer is correct.

```
class Demo {
      public static void main (String args[]) {
         int a = 15, b = 10, c;
         c = a | b;
         System.out.println ("a | b = " + c);
        }
}
```

The bitwise exclusive OR operator (^), referred to as XOR, compares two bits. If either bit is a binary 1, then the XOR operator returns a binary 1. If both bits are a binary 1, then the XOR operator returns a binary 0. And if neither bit is a binary 1, then a binary 0 is returned. This is illustrated in the following expression.

```
  00001111
^ 00001010
  --------
  00000101
```

Here is how you use the bitwise exclusive OR operator in a Java program. This example uses the decimal equivalent of the numbers used in the previous expression. What number does this example display on the screen?

```
class Demo {
      public static void main (String args[]) {
         int a = 15, b = 10, c;
         c = a ^ b;
         System.out.println ("a ^ b = " + c);
        }
}
```

Bitwise Shift Operators

So far in this chapter, you learned that the value of a bit can be changed by using the AND bitwise operator and the OR bitwise operators to compare the values of two bits. Another way to change the value of a bit is to use *bit shifting.*

Bit shifting is the technique of moving (shifting) a bit to either the left or the right position in a binary number. Let's see how this works using the following binary number. This is equivalent to the decimal value 15:

```
00001111
```

We can change the value of each bit by shifting each bit to the right. In doing so, the rightmost bit is removed from the value and the leftmost bit is replaced with a zero. Here's the new value that results from shifting bits to the right. This is equivalent to the decimal value 7:

```
00000111
```

Keep in mind that the numeric value of these bits typically is irrelevant to an application that uses bitwise operators. For example, you won't shift bits to change a value from 15 to 7. In some applications, such as in network communications, programmers use a bit as a flag rather than a numeric value. A bit might be turned on (1) to signify that the program is ready to transmit a message, and a bit can be turned off (0), implying that the program isn't going to transmit a message.

Java has three bitwise operators used to shift bits:

- Left shift (<<) operator
- Signed right shift (>>) operator
- Unsigned right shift (>>>) operator

The left shift operator moves bits one position to the left, dropping the leftmost bit and replacing the rightmost bit with a zero. Here how this works. Let's shift the following number one bit to the left:

```
00001111
```

Here's the value after shifting is completed. This is equivalent to the decimal value 30:

```
00011110
```

The following example illustrates how to use the bitwise left shift operator in a Java program. This example begins by declaring two ints. One is initialized to the decimal value 15, and the other is initialized to 0.

Next, the left shift operator is used to shift bits to the left. The left shift operator requires two operands. The left operand contains the value whose bits are being shifted. The right operand is an integer that tells Java how many places to shift the bits. This example shifts the bits left one position; however, you can change the left operand to any integer. If your application needs to shift bits two places, then replace 1 in this statement with 2. After bits are shifted, the resulting value is assigned to a variable and then displayed on the screen.

```
class Demo {
      public static void main (String args[]) {
         int a = 15, c = 0;
         c = a << 1;
         System.out.println (" a << 1 = " + c);
        }
}
```

Two right shift operators are available in Java. These are the signed right shift operator (>>) and the unsigned right shift operator (>>>). Both of these operators shift bits to the right by one position, which leaves the leftmost bit position empty. The signed right shift operator fills the empty position with a bit whose value represents the sign. If the value is a positive number, then the leftmost position is filled with a 0. If the value is a negative number, then the leftmost position is filled with a 1. The signed right shift operator uses the same sign as is used in the value before the bits are shifted.

Let's use the signed right shift operator to change the value of the following binary value. The value of the leftmost bit is significant in this example because that value is a signed value. The leftmost bit is 1, which means that this is a negative value:

```
10001111
```

Here's the same value after the bits are shifted to the right one position. The leftmost bit must remain 1 because this bit signifies that this is a negative value:

```
10000111
```

The following example shows how to use a signed right shift operator in a Java program. Similar to the left shift operator, the right shift operator also requires two operands. The left operand is the value whose bits are being shifted to the right. The right operand is an integer that indicates the number of positions the value is being shifted. In this example, bits are being shifted one place to the right:

```
class Demo {
      public static void main (String args[]) {
         int a = -15, c = 0;
         c = a >> 1;
         System.out.println (" a >> 1 = " + c);
        }
}
```

The unsigned right shift operator performs nearly the same operation as the signed right shift operator, except the unsigned right shift operator fills the leftmost empty space(s) with 0 because the value isn't a signed value.

Here's the unsigned right shift operator version of the previous program:

```
class Demo {
      public static void main (String args[]) {
         int a = 15, c = 0;
         c = a >>> 1;
         System.out.println (" a >>> 1 = " + c);
        }
}
```

Bitwise Complement Operator

Still another way programmers change the value of bits is by using the complement operator (~) to flip each bit. The complement operator changes a binary 0 to a binary 1, and it changes a binary 1 to a binary 0.

Let's see how this works on the following value:

```
00001111
```

By using the complement operator, we reverse each bit and end up with the following value. This is equivalent to the decimal value –16 because the leftmost bit is a binary 1, which symbolizes a negative sign:

```
11110000
```

Here's how to use the complement operator in a Java program. The complement operator requires one operand, which is the value whose bits are being flipped. The resulting value is then assigned to a variable and displayed on the screen.

```
class Demo {
      public static void main (String args[]) {
         int a = 15, c = 0;
         c = ~a;
         System.out.println (" ~a = " + c);
        }
}
```

Two's Complement

There are times when you'll come across a situation where you'll need to change the sign of a binary number from a positive to a negative or from a negative to a positive. You can change the sign by using a technique called *two's complement.* The two's complement technique adds 1 to the one's complement value that results in the sign being changed.

One's complement, two's complement. These are confusing terms. You might be scratching your head asking yourself, "What is a complement?" Let's return to the example in the previous section to get a better understanding of what a complement is. The example used the complement operator (~) to reverse each bit in a binary number. A 0 became a 1, and a 1 became a 0. Programmers call this *one's complement.*

Two's complement requires you to first perform one's complement on a number (that is, change all the 0's to 1's, and all the 1's to 0's) and then add 1 to the result.

Let's see how this works in the following example. As in the previous example, we'll use decimal values instead of binary values to make it easier to understand how two's complement works. The example starts by assigning the value 15 to variable `a`, which is later displayed on the screen. Next, the sign of the value 15 is changed from positive, which is implied, to negative by using two's complement. The complement operator tells Java to flip the bits and then add 1 to the value to change the sign from positive to negative. The result is assigned to variable `c` and is then displayed on the screen.

```
class Demo {
      public static void main (String args[]) {
         int a = 15, c = 0;
         c = ~a+1;
         System.out.println (" a = " + a);
         System.out.println (" ~a + 1 = " + c);
        }
}
```

Statements

The purpose of learning Java is to be able to take control of a computer. In order to do this, you must learn how to use Java keywords, operators, and operands to create expressions. You can think of keywords, operators, and operands as words understood by Java, and you can think of an expression as the way to organize those words to convey your request to Java. That request must be placed into a statement before Java will fulfill your request. Think of a statement as a sentence.

A statement is a sentence that consists of an expression that gives an instruction to Java. Every statement must end in a semicolon. Java doesn't recognize an expression as an instruction unless the expression is in a statement that terminates with a semicolon.

Think of this as a period at the end of a sentence. If you leave off the period, the reader won't know where one thought ends and another begins. The reader will quickly become confused. The same is true about Java. Java becomes confused if you leave out a semicolon.

By now you should be very familiar with writing statements because statements were used throughout every example in this chapter.

Quiz

1. What is a compound expression?
2. What is a unary operator?
3. What is the difference between an operator and an operand?
4. What is the purpose of parentheses in a compound expression?
5. What is precedence?

6. What does the modulus operator return?
7. Why is the position of the increment and decrement operators important?
8. What does a relational operator do?
9. What does a bitwise operator do?
10. What does the || operator do?

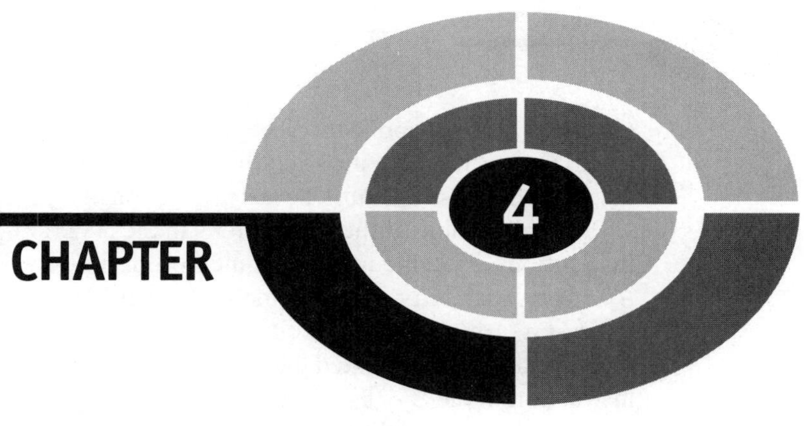

Control Structures

Some people believe that computers are smarter than humans, but that's giving computers more credit than they are due. Computers are as smart as the programmers who write instructions that computers follow. In many of those programs, a computer executes some instructions only if certain conditions exist. This requires the computer to make a decision. Programmers tell computers how to make decisions by using control statements in their programs. In this chapter, you'll learn how to tell a computer to make a decision and how to use various Java control statements in your program.

Program Flow

A computer executes instructions sequentially, beginning with the first instruction in the program and continuing until no more instructions exists. As you learned in

Chapter 1, all Java applications begin with the first instruction in the definition of the `main()` method. The program then flows to the second instruction, then the third instruction, and so on, until the last instruction in the `main()` method is executed.

Typically, some of the instructions in the `main()` method call groups of other instructions contained within a method definition. For example, each time the `System.out.println()` method is called, the flow of the program jumps from the `main()` method to the `System.out.println()` method. The flow returns to the instruction that called the `System.out.println()` method after the last instruction in the `System.out.println()` method definition executes.

Regardless of whether all the instructions are contained in the `main()` method or are divided among other methods, the flow of a program remains sequential. That is, all instructions are executed at some point.

In the real world, rarely do all instructions contained in a program execute. Some instructions execute all the time, whereas other instructions execute only when certain conditions are met. Therefore, all instructions within a program do not execute sequentially. Instead, some instructions are skipped.

This happens in a program used to register students for courses. Whenever a student registers for a course, the program determines whether the student has fulfilled prerequisites. If this condition is true, the program executes instructions that register the student for the course. If the condition is false, the instructions that register the student for the course are skipped.

Programmers change the flow of a program by using control statements that tell the computer to evaluate an expression and, based on the evaluation, either execute or skip one or more instructions.

Control Statements

A *control statement* tells Java to alter the sequence in which statements are executed within a program. There are three kinds of control statements: selection statements, iteration statements, and jump statements.

A selection control statement tells Java to evaluate an expression. If the expression is true, Java is told to execute one or more statements. If the expression is false, Java is told either to skip those statements or to execute a different set of statements. The `if...else` control statement briefly discussed in the previous chapter is an example of a selection control statement.

An iteration statement tells Java to execute one or more statements repeatedly. Programmers refer to an iteration statement as a *loop* because, after the last statement is executed within the iteration statement, Java automatically returns to the top of the iteration statement (the top of the loop) and begins executing the instructions again.

A jump statement transfers control to another part of the program. The `return` statement is a jump statement used in many programs to transfer control from a method back to the statement that called the method.

Selection Statements

A selection statement tells Java to evaluate a condition and then decide whether or not to execute one or a set of statements, depending on whether the condition is true. There are two types of selection statements: the `if` statement and the `switch` statement.

The `if` statement tells Java that if an expression is true, then execute these statements. Some programming languages call the `if` statement an `if...then` statement. Both have the same effect on a program. Typically, the `if` statement is combined with an `else` statement. The `else` statement contains another set of statements that are executed if the expression isn't true. Programmers call this combination an `if...else` statement.

The `switch` statement tells Java to compare the value in the `switch` statement to values stored in one or more `case` statements. If there is a match, the statements defined in the corresponding `case` statement are executed. The `switch` statement is also known as the `switch...case` statement.

The *if* Statement

The `if` statement is the most commonly used control statement to have Java make a decision. The `if` statement directs Java to evaluate an expression. If the expression is true, Java is told to execute one or more statements within the `if` statement. Otherwise, if the expression is not true, those statements are skipped.

The expression evaluated in an `if` statement is called a *conditional expression*. A conditional expression must evaluate to a Boolean value. That is, the expression must evaluate to either a true or false value. An expression used as a conditional expression for the `if` statement that evaluates to something other than a Boolean value will cause a compiler error.

A conditional expression is typically a relational expression. As you'll recall from the last chapter, a relational expression determines whether two values are the same or different by using a relational operator. The result can be only true or false.

A conditional expression can also be the keyword true or false without any operators and operands. For example, if you place the keyword true in the conditional expression of the if statement, the statements within the if statement will be executed. You'll see how this is done later in this chapter. You could also use the keyword false in the conditional expression, but that wouldn't make any sense because statements within the if statement will never execute.

Forms of the if Statement

The if statement has two forms: One form is an if statement without a code block, and the other form is an if statement with a code block. Let's take a look at the first form of the if statement.

The first form of the if statement has three parts, as shown in the following example. The first part is the keyword if. The second part is the conditional expression. The conditional expression must be contained within parentheses. The third part is one statement that is executed if the conditional expression is true. Only one statement can be executed in the first form of the if statement. The second form of the if statement must be used if multiple statements need to be executed if the conditional expression is true.

In this example, Java is told to compare the value of variable a and variable b. If they match, Java executes the statement that displays a message on the screen. If they are different, the statement is skipped.

```
class Demo {
   public static void main (String args[]) {
      int a = 80, b = 80;
      if (a==b)
          System.out.println("Hello world!");
   }
}
```

Some programmers find that the first form of the if statement can cause confusion when a program is being read because there isn't any symbol that tells you where the end of the if statement is. This becomes evident in the next example, where another statement appears below the statement within the if statement. What is displayed on the screen when this program executes?

```
class Demo {
   public static void main (String args[]) {
      int a = 80, b = 90;
      if (a==b)
          System.out.println("Hello world!");
      System.out.println("Goodbye!");
```

```
    }
}
```

If you quickly read this program, you might think that the statement that displays the "Goodbye!" message is part of the `if` statement because there isn't anything in the program that tells you where the `if` statement ends.

Actually, the statement that displays the "Hello world!" message is the only statement contained within the `if` statement. "Hello world!" is displayed only if the conditional expression is true. "Goodbye!" is displayed regardless of whether the conditional expression in the `if` statement is true or false because the statement that displays the "Goodbye!" message is not part of the `if` statement.

The second form of the `if` statement is nearly identical to the first form; however, the second form uses opening and closing braces to designate statements that are to be executed if the conditional expression is true.

Here is the previous example using the second form of the `if` statement. The second form of the `if` statement has four parts. The first part is the keyword `if`. The second part is the conditional expression contained within parentheses. The third part is the body of the `if` statement that is defined by the opening and closing braces. The fourth part is one or more statements executed if the conditional expression is true.

```
class Demo {
   public static void main (String args[]) {
      int a = 80, b = 90;
      if (a==b)
      {
          System.out.println("Hello world!");
      }
      System.out.println("Goodbye!");
   }
}
```

You have the option of using either form of the `if` statement if one statement is to be executed if the conditional expression is true. However, you *must* use the second form of the `if` statement if more than one statement is executed if the conditional expression is true, and those statements must be contained with the opening and closing braces.

TIP: *Here's a tip for avoiding a common compiler error when using the second form of the* `if` *statement. Always insert the opening and closing brace into your program before writing statements that are to execute if the conditional expression is true. This eliminates any chance that you will forget to include the closing brace in the* `if` *statement, which is an oversight that even professional Java programmers sometimes make.*

As previously mentioned in this chapter, the conditional expression can be as simple as the Boolean value true. This is illustrated in the next example. Although using the keyword `true` as the conditional expression is equivalent to a relational expression evaluating true, it really doesn't make any sense to use it in the `if` statement because the statements within the `if` statement will always execute. You could simply eliminate the `if` statement to achieve the same results. However, using the keyword `true` as the conditional expression does makes sense when it's used in an iteration control statement, which you'll learn about later in this chapter.

```
class Demo {
   public static void main (String args[]) {
      if (true)
      {
          System.out.println("Hello world!");
      }
      System.out.println("Goodbye!");
   }
}
```

The `else` Clause

Many times programmers combine an `if` statement with an `else` clause. An `else` clause provides one or more alternative statements that are executed when the conditional expression in the `if` statement is false. Think of the `else` clause as telling Java to execute one or more statements if Java doesn't execute the statements within the `if` statement.

The `else` clause has two forms that are nearly identical to the two forms of the `if` statement. The first form is without opening and closing braces and is used to execute only one statement. This is illustrated in the next example where the "Goodbye!" message is displayed only if the conditional expression in the `if` statement is evaluated false.

```
class Demo {
   public static void main (String args[]) {
      int a = 80, b = 90;
      if (a==b)
         System.out.println("Hello world!");
      else
         System.out.println("Goodbye!");
   }
}
```

The second form of the else clause uses opening and closing braces within which you place one or more statements that are executed if the conditional expression is not true. The following example shows how this form of the else clause is used in a Java program. You can include any number of statements within the braces of the else clause, although only one statement is shown in this example.

```
class Demo {
   public static void main (String args[]) {
      int a = 80, b = 90;
      if (a==b)
         System.out.println("Hello world!");
      else
      {
         System.out.println("Goodbye!");
      }
   }
}
```

You can mix and match forms of the if statement with forms of the else clause, depending on the nature of your program. There isn't any requirement that these forms match. For example, you can use an if statement without braces with an else statement that uses braces, and vice versa. Basically, if you have one statement to execute, don't use the braces; otherwise, use the braces.

The else if Clause

The else if clause is a combination of the else clause and the if statement. It lets you tell Java to evaluate another conditional expression. Think of the else if clause as saying, "If the first condition isn't true, evaluate the second condition. If the second condition is true, execute these statements."

The else if clause takes the same forms as the if statement. That is, the else if clause requires a conditional expression contained within parentheses and a statement that is executed if the condition is true. You also have the option of using opening and closing braces. As with the if statement and the else clause, the braces are optional if the else if clause executes one statement, and they are required if multiple statements are executed.

The following example shows you how to use the else if clause. This example uses a conditional expression in the if statement to tell Java to compare values of two variables. If they are the same value, the message "a and b match" is displayed on the screen. If they don't match, the condition in the else if clause tells Java to determine whether variable a is less than variable b. If this is true, the message "a is less than b" is displayed.

```
class Demo {
   public static void main (String args[]) {
      int a = 80, b = 90;
      if (a==b)
         System.out.println("a and b match");
      else if ( a < b)
         System.out.println("a less than b");
      }
   }
}
```

It is very common for programmers to include an `else` clause in whenever an `else if` clause is used in order to give Java instructions to follow if neither the `if` statement and `else if` clause conditional expressions are false. Think of the `else` clause as the default action Java should perform unless one of the previous conditions are met.

The next example illustrates how to use the `else` clause in this manner. This example displays the message a is greater than b. We make this the default action because this is the only condition that could exist if the previous two conditions are not true. If a is not equal to b and a is not less than b, then a must be greater than b. Therefore, we use an `else` clause instead of an `else if` clause to test the condition if a is greater than b.

```
class Demo {
   public static void main (String args[]) {
      int a = 80, b = 90;
      if (a==b)
         System.out.println("a and b match");
      else if ( a < b)
         System.out.println("a is less than b");
      else
         System.out.println("a is greater than b");
      }
   }
}
```

Too much of a good thing isn't good, and this is true about the `else if` clause. Using too many `else if` clauses makes a program difficult for other programmers to read, although the length doesn't impair Java's ability to carry out your instructions.

If you find yourself using a lot of `else` clauses in the same `if` statement, you should replace the `if` statement and all those `else` clauses with a `switch` control statement, which you'll learn about later in this chapter. The switch statement is easier for you to read and provides a similar functionality as the if...else clause of an if statement.

Nested if Statement

Sometimes you'll come across a situation when you need to make another decision if the first decision is true. For example, you might tell Java that if the student's ID is valid, it should determine whether the student's password is valid. If the student's ID isn't valid, you don't need to make a decision about the student's password.

You tell Java to make those decisions by using a nested if statement. A nested if statement is an if statement that exists within another if statement. This is illustrated in the next example. Programmers call a nested if statement an *inner* if statement, and they call the first if statement the *outer* if statement.

This example tells Java to determine whether the value of variable a is greater than zero. If this is true, Java is told to determine whether the value of variable a is the same as variable b. If this is the case, the message "a and b match" is displayed.

Notice that Java skips the second if statement if the conditional expression in the first if statement is false. Each if statement has an else clause in this example that displays an appropriate message when either conditional expression is false.

```
class Demo {
   public static void main (String args[]) {
      int a = 80, b = 90;
      if (a > 0 )
         if ( a == b)
            System.out.println("a and b match");
         else
            System.out.println("a and b are different");
      else
         System.out.println(
             "a is less than 0 or equal to 0 ");
   }
}
```

Don't confuse a nested if statement with the if...else clause of an if statement, which tells Java to evaluate the second conditional expression in the else if clause only if the conditional expression in the if statement is false. In a nested if statement, the second conditional expression is evaluated only if the conditional expression in the first if statement is true.

An outer if statement can have multiple nested if statements. These can take two forms. The first form is to have each nested if statement on the same level. The second form is to have each nested if statement on a different level. This means that each nested if statement has its own nested if statement.

The next example shows the first form of multiple nested if statements. This has one outer if statement and two inner if statements. Braces are used in this example to make it easier for you to see where the if statements begin and end. The outer if statement determines whether the value of variable a is greater than zero. If so, Java tests whether variable a is the same as the value of variable b. Regardless of the outcome of this test, Java then determines whether the value of variable a is greater than the value of variable b.

```
class Demo {
   public static void main (String args[]) {
      int a = 80, b = 90;
      if (a > 0 )
      {
         if ( a == b)
         {
            System.out.println("a and b match");
         }
         if (a > b)
         {
            System.out.println("a greater than b ");
         }
      }
   }
}
```

The next example shows the second form of nesting multiple if statements, where each if statement is on its own level. The outermost if statement tells Java to determine whether the value of variable a is greater than zero. If so, Java is told to determine whether the value of variable b is greater than zero. If this is the case, Java determines whether the values of both variables are the same.

The outermost if statement has only one inner (nested) if statement. The inner if statement also has one inner (nested) if statement.

```
class Demo {
   public static void main (String args[]) {
      int a = 80, b = 90;
      if (a > 0 )
      {
         if ( b > 0 )
         {
```

```
            if ( a == b)
            {
               System.out.println("a and b match");
            }
         }
      }
   }
}
```

Compound Conditions

Under certain situations, you can avoid using a nested `if` statement and use a compound conditional expression instead. A compound conditional expression consists of two relational expressions that are linked using a logical operator.

You'll recall from the previous chapter that there are two logical operators: the AND (&&) operator and the OR (||) operator. The AND operator returns a Boolean true if both relational expressions are true; otherwise, a Boolean false is returned. The OR operator returns a Boolean true if one of the relational expressions is true; otherwise, a Boolean false is returned.

The following example shows how to use a compound conditional expression in an `if` statement. The form is also used for the `else...if` clause and any other place where you use a conditional expression in your program.

This example uses a compound conditional statement in the first `if` statement where Java is told to determine whether the value of `a` is greater than zero. If so, Java evaluates the second relational expression to determine whether the value of `b` is greater than zero. If `a` isn't greater than zero, the second expression is not evaluated because the compound expression requires both relational expressions to be true for the compound expression to be true. (Refer to the previous chapter to learn how to force Java to evaluate both relational expressions.) Only if both relational expressions are true will the compound expression be true and the statement within the first `if` statement executed.

Compare this example with the previous example and you'll notice how we eliminated one nested `if` statement by using a compound expression. You should use a compound expression rather than a nested `if` statement wherever possible.

```
class Demo {
   public static void main (String args[]) {
      int a = 80, b = 90;
      if (a > 0 && b > 0)
      {
         if ( a == b)
         {
```

```
                System.out.println("a and b match");
            }
        }
    }
}
```

The *switch* Statement

An alternative to using a long series of `if...else` clauses in your `if` statements is to use the `switch` control statement, commonly referred to as a `switch...case` statement or simply the `switch` statement. The `switch` statement tells Java to compare a value to one of many values, each of which is contained in a `case` statement. If there is a match, Java executes the statements contained in the `case` statement.

The format of the `switch` statement is illustrated in the next example. A `switch` statement has seven parts. These are the keyword `switch`, the value used for comparison, braces that define the body of the `switch` statement, the `case` keyword, the `case` constant, the semicolon, and statements that are executed if the value matches the `case` value.

The `switch` keyword appears at the beginning of every `switch` statement and is followed by a value that is enclosed within parentheses. The value must be a char, byte, short, or int data type and can be either a literal or a variable. However, the value cannot be of any other data type or an expression.

The body of the `switch` statement should contain at least one `case` statement, but it can contain as many `case` statements as required by the program. A `case` statement consists of the `case` keyword followed by a `case` constant, and it ends with a colon. The `case` constant must be a literal that is of the char, byte, short, or int data type. The `case` statement also consists of one or more statements that are executed if the value of the `switch` statement matches the `case` constant.

Here's what happens when Java executes the `switch` statement. First, Java compares the value of the `switch` statement to the constant of the first `case` statement. If there isn't a match, Java compares the value to the constant of the next `case` statement. This continues until there is a match or until Java reaches the closing brace of the `switch` statement.

If there is a match, Java executes each statement contained beneath the `case` statement whose constant matches the `switch` value. If one of those statements is the `break` statement, Java immediately exits the body of the `switch` statement and executes the next statement below the closing brace.

However, if there isn't a `break` statement, Java continues to compare the `switch` value against the constants of all the `case` statements that follow the `case` statement that matched the `switch` statement value.

Let's see how this works in the next example. The switch value is 80. Java will compare the switch value to each of the case constants, beginning with the first case statement. There isn't a match until the third case statement. Java then executes the System.out.println() statement that displays "80" on the screen. Once "80" is displayed, Java executes the break statement, which causes Java to exit the switch statement.

```
class Demo {
   public static void main (String args[]) {
      switch (80) {
         case 100:
            System.out.println("100");
            break;
         case 90:
            System.out.println("90");
            break;
         case 80:
            System.out.println("80");
            break;
      }
   }
}
```

The next example is a modification of the previous one. The switch value is changed to 90 and the break statement is removed from the case statement whose constant is 90. Java behaves differently in this example than it does in the previous example.

Here's what is happening: Java compares the switch value to the first case constant, as was done in the previous example. Because the first case constant isn't a match, Java compares the second case constant, where there is a match. Java proceeds to execute the statement beneath this case constant, which displays "90" on the screen.

Afterward, Java moves to the next statement. Notice that the next statement is another case statement and not a break statement. A break statement tells Java to break out of the switch statement. Because there isn't a break statement, Java continues by comparing the switch value to the next case constant.

```
class Demo {
   public static void main (String args[]) {
      switch (90) {
         case 100:
            System.out.println("100");
            break;
         case 90:
```

```
            System.out.println("90");
        case 80:
            System.out.println("80");
            break;
      }
   }
}
```

Previously in this chapter, you learned that an `else` clause is used in an `if` statement to define statements that will execute if the condition in the `if` statement isn't true. The `switch` statement has a similar feature called a *default statement*.

The default statement is written similar to a `case` statement, and it's placed after the last `case` statement. The default statement doesn't have a constant or a `break` statement because it is the last statement within the `switch` statement. However, the default statement has other statements beneath it that are executed when Java reaches the default statement.

The following example illustrates how to use a default statement in your program. This example tells Java to examine the constant for each `case` statement, looking for a match for the `switch` value, which is 70. Because none match, Java executes the statement beneath the default statement, which displays a message on the screen.

```
class Demo {
   public static void main (String args[]) {
      switch (70) {
         case 100:
            System.out.println("100");
            break;
         case 90:
            System.out.println("90");
            break;
         case 80:
            System.out.println("80");
            break;
         default:
            System.out.println("No match.");
      }
   }
}
```

Something very interesting happens to the default statement when the `break` statement isn't used in a `case` statement whose constant matches the `switch` value. Java executes statements beneath the default statement if the `break` statement is excluded from a matching `case` statement.

Let's see how this works in the next example. Java is told to look at the case constants and find a match to the switch value, which is 80. When a match is found, Java displays "80" on the screen.

However, notice that the matching case statement doesn't have a break statement. This means that Java continues to the next line of the program below the statement that displays 80, which contains the default statement. When Java encounters a default statement, it always runs the statements contained within the default statement. Therefore, "No match" is also displayed on the screen.

```
class Demo {
   public static void main (String args[]) {
      switch (80) {
         case 100:
            System.out.println("100");
            break;
         case 90:
            System.out.println("90");
            break;
         case 80:
            System.out.println("80");
         default:
            System.out.println("No match.");
      }
   }
}
```

Nested switch Statements

As with if statements, you can also nest switch statements. A nested switch statement is a switch statement that is placed within a case statement or default statement of another switch statement. The purpose for nesting a switch statement is to tell Java to make another decision after making the first decision.

The next example shows how to nest a switch statement. The nested switch statement appears in the case 90 statement. Java begins by comparing the switch value to each case constant. Only one case statement matches the switch value. Java then compares the second switch value, which is the character *B*, to a second set of case statements.

You can include as many case statements as needed by your program in the nested switch statement. Likewise, you can also include a default statement.

```
class Demo {
   public static void main (String args[]) {
      char a = 'B';
```

```
            switch (90) {
               case 100:
                  System.out.println("100");
                  break;
               case 90:
                  switch (a){
                     case 'a':
                        System.out.println("A");
                        break;
                     case 'b':
                        System.out.println("B");
                        break;
                  }
                  break;
               case 80:
                  System.out.println("80");
                  break;
               default:
                  System.out.println("No match.");
            }
      }
}
```

Iteration Statements

An iteration statement is what programmers call a *loop*. It causes Java to continue to execute one or more statements as long as a condition exists. Think of an iteration statement as being a drill instructor who tells you to continue to do push-ups until you're told to stop.

Java has three kinds of iteration statements: the `for` loop, the `while` loop, and the `do...while` loop.

The *for* Loop

The `for` loop tells Java to executes one or more statements contained in the `for` loop as long as a specified condition is true. The condition is specified in a *control expression*, which is a relational expression that evaluates to either a Boolean true or a Boolean false.

If the control expression is false, Java moves to the statement that follows the `for` loop in the program. If the control expression is true, Java enters the `for` loop and executes statements contained in the for loop. After the last statement within the loop is executed, Java once again evaluates the control expression to determine whether it should enter the loop for another iteration.

The for loop has three expressions that are contained within parentheses and separated with a semicolon. Each expression is optional. However, the parentheses and the semicolon are required. You'll be including all three expressions in most of your programs.

The first expression is called the *initialization expression* and is used to declare and initialize a control variable that is typically used in the conditional expression. This is the first expression within the for loop that is evaluated by Java. Technically, the initialization expression and the control variable don't have to be used in the conditional expression, but for our examples they will be used this way.

The second expression is the conditional expression. This is the second expression in the for loop that is evaluated by Java. The conditional expression sets the threshold for when Java enters the for loop. You can use any relational expression and compound relational expressions that are linked together using a logical operator as the conditional expression for the for loop.

The third expression is the iteration expression, and it's the first expression evaluated by Java after executing statements within the loop. The iteration expression changes the value of the control variable. Typically, the change involves incrementing or decrementing the control variable.

The next example illustrates how to write a for loop in your Java program. Here's what Java is being told to do: The first time it encounters the for loop, Java evaluates the first expression. This expression declares the variable x and then initializes it to zero. Variable x is used as the control variable. A *control variable* is a variable whose value is used in the conditional expression to help control the number of iterations that Java executes in the for loop.

Next, Java evaluates the second expression, which is the conditional expression that determines whether Java should enter the for loop. The conditional expression tells Java to determine whether the value of x is less than 2. If so, the conditional expression is true, and Java enters the for loop. The value of x is zero, making the conditional expression true.

Java enters the loop and executes the System.out.println() statement that displays the value of variable x on the screen. After this statement executes, Java evaluates the third expression. The third expression increments the value of variable x. The value of variable x becomes 1.

Java then evaluates the second expression to determine whether it should reenter the loop. Because the value of x is still less than 2, Java again enters the for loop and displays the value of x on the screen.

Once again, Java evaluates the third expression and increments the value of x, changing its value to 2. The second expression is then evaluated. This time, the value

of x is 2, thus causing the conditional expression to be false. Java no longer enters the for loop and instead goes to the statement beneath the for loop. There isn't any, so the program ends.

```
class Demo {
   public static void main (String args[]) {
      for (int x = 0; x < 2; x++)
         System.out.println("Current value of x = " + x);
   }
}
```

Although the previous example has one statement within a for loop, you can include multiple statements within a for loop by using opening and closing braces, similar to how braces are used in the if statement.

Here is how to format the for loop to use multiple statements:

```
class Demo {
   public static void main (String args[]) {
      for (int x = 0; x < 2; x++)
      {
         System.out.println ("Current value of x:");
         System.out.println(x);
      }
   }
}
```

Alternative Initialization Expression

The for loop is very flexible because various forms of the three expressions can be used with the for loop. Also, as you'll see later in this chapter, a for loop doesn't require any expression.

For now, let's take a look at the first of two alternative forms of initialization expression. In the following example, the control variable is declared outside of the initialization expression of the for loop; however, the initialization expression still sets the initial value of the control variable:

```
class Demo {
   public static void main (String args[]) {
      int x;
      for (x = 0; x < 2; x++)
         System.out.println("Current value of x = " + x);
   }
}
```

This next example illustrates a second alternative to the initialization expression. In this example, the initialization expression is inserted in the program before the `for` loop. There isn't an initialization expression in the `for` loop; however, the `for` loop still needs the semicolon that follows what would normally be the initialization expression in the `for` loop.

The advantage of declaring and initializing the control variable outside the `for` loop is so that the control variable can be used by statements outside of the `for` loop.

```
class Demo {
   public static void main (String args[]) {
      int x = 0;
      for (; x < 2; x++)
         System.out.println("Current value of x = " + x);
   }
}
```

Alternative Conditional Expression

An alternative form of the conditional expression is also used with a `for` loop. This is to use a Boolean value instead of a relational expression that evaluates to a Boolean value.

For example, you could simply use the keyword `true` as the conditional expression. This transforms the `for` loop into an endless loop. An endless loop is a loop where a statement within the body of the loop controls when the loop ends.

There are three ways in which to create an endless `for` loop. The first way is to use a Boolean variable initialized to `true` as the conditional expression. A statement within the body of the `for` loop then changes the value of the variable to `false`. This is shown in the next example, which begins by declaring a Boolean variable called `y` and initializing it to `true`. Variable `y` is then used as the conditional expression in the `for` loop. The control variable `x` is initialized in the initialization expression and incremented in the iteration expression. However, it is not used in the conditional expression. Instead, the control variable is used in the conditional expression of an `if` statement within the body of the `for` loop. If the control variable is 5, the value of `y` is changed to `false` in the `if` statement, thus causing Java to break out of the loop.

```
class Demo {
   public static void main (String args[]) {
      boolean y = true;
      for (int x = 0; y ; x++ )
      {
         System.out.println("Current value of x = " + x);
         if (x == 5)
```

```
            y = false;
        }
    }
}
```

The second way to create an endless `for` loop is to simply use the keyword `true` as the conditional expression. In order to break out of the loop, you'll need to include a `break` statement within the body of the loop.

This method is illustrated in the next example. The body of the `for` loop contains an `if` statement that uses the control variable in its conditional expression. When Java detects that the conditional variable is 5, the `break` statement within the `if` statement is executed. This is the same `break` statement used in the `switch` statement. The `break` statement tells Java to exit the `for` loop.

```
class Demo {
   public static void main (String args[]) {
      for (int x = 0; true ; x++ )
      {
         System.out.println("Current value of x = " + x);
         if (x == 5)
            break;
      }
   }
}
```

The third way to create an endless `for` loop is to simply not include a conditional expression. Java assumes that the condition is true if the conditional expression is not found in a `for` loop.

The following example shows how to create this type of endless `for` loop. You'll notice that this example is practically the same as the previous example, except the conditional expression is empty in the `for` loop. Although there isn't a conditional expression, you are still required to include the semicolon.

```
class Demo {
   public static void main (String args[]) {
      for (int x = 0; ; x++ )
      {
         System.out.println("Current value of x = " + x);
         if (x == 5)
            break;
      }
   }
}
```

Some programmers prefer not to use a control variable in an endless `for` loop. Instead, they use statements within the body of the `for` loop to control when Java should break out of the loop.

Let's say that you've written a program that displays a menu. You could place statements that read the keyboard inside an endless `for` loop. When a valid menu item is received by one of those statements, you can break out of the loop and process the menu item. You can continue to loop until a valid menu item is entered.

Nested `for` Loops

You can place one or more `for` loops within the body of another `for` loop. Programmers call this *nesting* `for` loops. The nested `for` loop is referred to as the *inner* `for` loop and is placed inside the *outer* `for` loop.

Each time Java loops around the outer `for` loop, it loops around the inner `for` loop until it breaks out of the inner loop. Let's see how this works in the next example, which has two `for` loops. Statements in the outer loop are executed five times before the conditional expression is false. The statement in the inner loop is executed three times before the conditional expression in the inner loop is false. Each time the outer loop is looped, the inner loop is looped three times.

```
class Demo {
   public static void main (String args[]) {
      for (int x = 0; x < 5 ; x++ )
      {
         System.out.println("Current value of x = " + x);
         for (int y = 0; y < 3 ; y++)
            System.out.println(
                 "Current value of y = " + y);
       }
    }
}
```

The *`while`* Loop

Another kind of iteration statement is the `while` loop. The `while` loop tells Java to execute one or more statements contained in the body of the `while` as long as a conditional expression is true. Statements within the `while` loop are not executed if the conditional statement is false.

When Java sees a `while` loop in your program, it immediately evaluates the `while` loop's conditional expression, which is a relational expression. If the condition is false, Java skips the body of the while loop and continues by executing the first statement that appears below the body of the while loop in your program.

However, if the conditional expression is true, Java enters the body of the while loop and executes each statement within the body in sequence. If one of those statements is a break statement, Java immediately exits the body of the while loop and continues by executing the first statement below the body of the while loop.

If Java doesn't encounter a break statement, it continues executing statements within the while loop until the bottom of the loop is reached. At that time, Java returns to the top of the while loop and reevaluates the conditional expression. If the conditional expression is still true, Java reenters the body of the while loop and reexecutes those statements. If the conditional expression is false, Java jumps out of the while loop and executes the first statement after the bottom of the body of the while loop.

The while loop consists of four components: the keyword while, the conditional expression placed within parentheses, the body of the while loop defined by opening and closing braces, and one or more statements within the body of the while loop that are executed if the conditional expression is true.

The following example illustrates how to use a while loop in your program. This example begins by declaring an integer variable and initializing it to zero. The while loop uses the integer variable in the conditional expression x < 5. If variable x is less than 5, Java is told to execute the two statements within the body of the while loop. The first statement displays the value of x on the screen. The second statement uses the incremental operator to increase the value of x by 1.

After the value of x is incremented, Java returns to the top of the loop and reevaluates the conditional expression. The value of x is now 1 and is still less than 5, so the conditional expression is true and Java once again enters the body of the while loop to execute those two statements. Java continues to loop through the while loop until the value of x is 5, at which time Java exits the loop. Because there isn't another statement that follows the closing brace of the while loop, the program terminates.

```
class Demo {
   public static void main (String args[]) {
      int x = 0;
      while (x < 5)
      {
         System.out.println("Current value of x = " + x);
         x++;
       }
    }
}
```

In the previous section of this chapter, you learned how to create an endless `for` loop. An endless loop is one where the conditional expression is always true. The `break` statement is the only way to exit the loop.

You can create an endless `while` loop by using the keyword `true` as the conditional expression. Here's how to create an endless `while` loop: First, notice that the conditional expression consists of the keyword `true`. This causes Java to execute statements within the body of the `while` loop. The first statement displays the value of `x`. The second statement uses the incremental operator to increase the value of `x` by 1. You've seen both of these statements used in the previous example.

The next statement is an `if` statement. The conditional expression in the `if` statement determines whether the value of `x` is 5. If so, the `break` statement within the body of the `if` statement executes, causing Java to exit the `while` loop. If the value of `x` isn't 5, Java returns to the top of the `while` loop, where it finds the conditional expression to still be true, causing it to again enter the body of the `while` loop and execute those statements.

```
class Demo {
   public static void main (String args[]) {
      int x = 0;
      while (true)
      {
         System.out.println("Current value of x = " + x);
         x++;
         if (x == 5)
            break;
       }
    }
}
```

The *do while* Loop

The `do while` loop is another iteration statement that works nearly identically to a `while` loop, with one exception. As you learned in the previous section, the conditional expression in a `while` loop must be true for statements within the body of the `while` loop to execute at least once. If the conditional expression is never true, those statements will never be executed.

However, statements within a `do while` loop execute at least once, even if the conditional expression is false. Think of the `do while` loop as telling Java, "Execute these statements and then check to see if the condition is true."

The do while loop has six components: the keyword do, the body of the do while loop defined by opening and closing braces, statements within the body of the do while loop, the keyword while, the conditional expression contained within parentheses, and a semicolon.

The following example shows how to use a do while loop in your program. In this example, Java displays the value of x on the screen before evaluating the con ditional expression x > 0. Notice that the conditional expression is false, causing Java to exit the loop. However, the statement within the body of the do while loop executed once.

Programmers commonly use a do while loop to display a menu and then read the menu selection from the keyboard because the menu is displayed at least once before the conditional expression evaluates the menu selection.

```
class Demo {
   public static void main (String args[]) {
      int x = 0;
      do
      {
        System.out.println("Current value of x = " + x);
      } while (x > 0);
    }
}
```

Jump Statements

A jump statement is another control statement that transfers control to another part of the program. There are three kinds of jump statements: break, continue, and return.

break

You were introduced to the break statement when you learned about the switch statement, the for loop, and the while loop. The break statement tells Java to exit a code block defined by opening and closing braces and used in a loop or a switch statement.

continue

The `continue` statement is used within the body of a loop to tell Java to immediately return to the top of the loop without executing statements that appear below the `continue` statement. This has the same effect as Java reaching the end of the loop.

The following example shows how the `continue` statement works in a program. You'll notice that this example is a slight modification of the example used in the `while` loop section of this chapter. The example begins by initializing variable `x` to zero. Java is then told to enter the body of the `while` loop if the value of `x` is less than 5, which it is.

Inside the body of the `while` loop, Java displays the value of `x` before the `continue` statement has an opportunity to execute. The value of `x` is then incremented, and Java is then told to determine whether the value of `x` is 3. If it's not, Java displays the value of `x` again before returning to the top of the loop.

However, when the value of `x` is 3, Java enters the body of the `if` statement and executes the `continue` statement. The `continue` statement tells Java to return to the top of the loop and reevaluate the conditional expression of the `while` loop. The `while` loop conditional expression is true, so Java reenters the body of the `while` loop and continues to executes those statements. Notice that the second `System.out.println()` statement isn't executed when the value of `x` is 3 because Java is told to skip that statement and return to the top of the loop.

```
class Demo {
   public static void main (String args[]) {
      int x = 0;
      while (x < 5)
      {
          System.out.println ("Before continue x = " + x);
          x++;
          if (x == 3)
             continue;
          System.out.println ("After continue x = " + x);
      }
    }
}
```

Here is the output of this program:

```
Before continue x = 0
After continue x = 1
```

```
Before continue x = 1
After continue x = 2
Before continue x = 2
Before continue x = 3 //The continue statement executes
After continue x = 4
Before continue x = 4
After continue x = 5
```

return

The `return` statement is used in methods to return control back to the statement that called the method. The `return` statement may or may not return a value. You'll learn more about how to use the `return` statement in Chapter 6, where methods are introduced.

Quiz

1. What is the normal flow of a program?
2. What is an endless loop?
3. What is the purpose of a conditional expression?
4. Can a `switch` statement use a Boolean value as the `switch` variable?
5. How is a constant used in a `switch` statement?
6. What is the difference between a `while` loop and a `do while` loop?
7. What is the purpose of a default statement in a `switch` statement?
8. What does the term *nested* mean in relation to a control statement?
9. What does the `break` statement do?
10. What does the `continue` statement do?

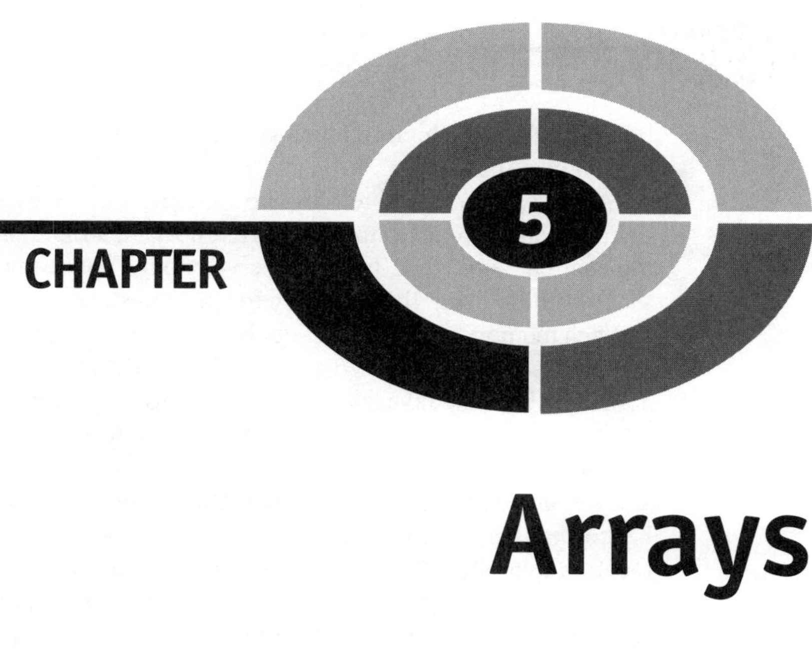

CHAPTER 5

Arrays

Reserving memory to store data is a no-brainer. You simply use a data type and a name to declare a variable. You learned how this is done in Chapter 2. However, suppose you have to reserve memory for 100 data elements. At first this may not seem challenging because all you need to do is declare 100 variables. However, try doing this, and you'll discover that you need to come up with 100 unique and meaningful names—one name for each variable. Some programmers find themselves doing a little head-banging trying to name 100 variables. Fortunately, there is a better way. You can use an array instead of a variable. An array requires one unique, meaningful name that can be used to reference all 100 data elements—or as many data elements that you need for your program. You'll learn about arrays in this chapter and see how to use them in your Java program.

Inside an Array

Previously in this book, you learned that before you can store data in computer memory you must first reserve memory. Think of this as making sure there is an empty bag available in which to place your groceries at the checkout counter before you begin checking out.

You use a data type to tell Java how much space to reserve in memory and the kind of data that you plan to store in that memory location. For example, you'll recall that the char data type tells Java to reserve enough space in memory to store a char and that you'll be using that memory location to store a character.

Each memory location is uniquely identified by a memory address that's similar to an address for a house in your town. You don't have to be concerned about memory addresses because Java takes care of them for you. However, you do have to tell Java what name you'll be using in your program to refer to each memory address you ask Java to reserve.

The name you give to a memory address should reflect the nature of the data you'll be storing there. For example, `finalGrade` might be a good name for a memory location that is used to store a student's final grade.

Java associates the name you provide with the memory address that is reserved for your data. Each time you reference the name in your program, Java automatically looks up the corresponding memory address and then uses that memory address to store or retrieve data.

You reserve memory by using a declaration statement in your program, as shown here:

```
int finalGrade;
```

This statement tells Java to reserve memory sufficient enough to store an integer and that you'll be storing an integer in that location. It also tells Java that you'll be calling that memory location by the name `finalGrade` within your program.

The name you give to a memory location is referred to as a *variable* primarily because you can change the value stored at that memory location countless times while your program runs. Therefore, the value of a memory location "varies."

An *array* is a collection of variables of the same data type, and the collection is assigned a name. This collection is referred to as an array. Each variable within the collection is called an *array element*. An array element is identified by combining the array name and a unique index. An *index* is an integer from zero to 1 minus the maximum number of elements in the array. The index is contained within opening and closing square brackets to the right of the array name.

Let's say that we have declared an array called `finalGrades` and want to reference the first element of that array within our program. Here's how you reference it:

```
finalGrades[0]
```

Notice that an array element is referenced nearly the same way you reference a variable, with one exception: Although both a variable and an array element have a unique and meaningful name, you reference the array element by specifying its index.

You can use an array element in the same way you use a variable in your program. Here are two common ways to use an array element. The first statement assigns the integer 90 to the array element, and the second statement assigns the value of the array element to a variable:

```
finalGrades[0] = 90;
myFinalGrade = finalGrades[0];
```

Allocating Memory for an Array

Similar to a variable, you must tell Java to reserve memory for an array. You do this by *declaring* an array. Programmers call declaring an array *allocating memory* for the array. Memory is allocated dynamically in a three-step process. The first step is to declare a reference to the memory allocated for the array. The second step is to reserve memory, and the third step is to assign the reserved memory location to the reference. All three steps are shown in the following example:

```
class Demo {
   public static void main (String args[]) {
      int finalGrades[] = new int[100];
   }
}
```

Here's what is happening. First, the `new` operator tells Java to reserve memory to hold 100 integers, as shown here:

```
new int[100]
```

The `new` operator then returns the address of the first memory location. Think of the other memory locations reserved by the `new` operator being laid side by side in sequence next to the first memory location.

Java is also told to create a reference to an array of integers, as shown here:

```
int finalGrades[]
```

Think of a reference as something that points to the first memory address of the block of memory that is reserved for the array. The reference is called `finalGrades[]`. Then, Java is told to assign the address of the first memory location to the reference, as shown here:

```
int finalGrades[] = new int[100];
```

Here's an important point to remember whenever you declare an array: Always specify the number of array elements you need in the declaration of an array. If you need 100 array elements, you place **100** in the declaration. However, remember that the first index of an array is 0, not 1. Some programmers get confused and place 0 as the array size or 1 when referencing the first array element. Both of these are incorrect.

Initializing Arrays

Initialization is the process of placing an initial value in memory by assigning the value to either a variable or an array element. In Chapter 2, you learned how to initialize a variable by assigning a value when the variable is declared, as shown here:

```
int myGrade = 0;
```

An array is initialized a little differently. You place the initial values of each array element within braces, as shown in the following example:

```
class Demo {
   public static void main (String args[]) {
      int finalGrades[]= {95, 87, 93, 84, 79};
   }
}
```

Notice that you don't explicitly specify the array size. Instead, the number of initial values implies the array size. The previous example implies that the array has five array elements because five values are used to initialize the array. A comma must separate each initial value, and all the initial values must be contained within braces.

Don't use the `new` operator to declare an array if you plan to initialize the array because Java dynamically allocates sufficient memory for the array using the initial values to determine the size of the array.

Multidimensional Arrays

The arrays you've seen so far in this chapter are called *one-dimensional* arrays because they consist of one list of array elements. Think of the pair of square brackets used to declare an array as a dimension.

Arrays can have more than one dimension. These are referred to as *multidimensional* arrays. Think of a multidimensional array as being declared within two or more pairs of square brackets, where each square bracket is a dimension.

Some programmers call a multidimensional array as *an array of an array*. For example, a two-dimensional array has two lists of array elements. Each element of the first list (first dimension) points to another array (second dimension).

Programmers use multidimensional arrays to organize lists of relation information so that these lists can be manipulated within a Java program. However, programmers usually work with a multidimensional array that has no more than two dimensions because an array of any more dimensions is difficult to work with.

Creating a Multidimensional Array

You declare a multidimensional array by using the new operator, which is very similar to the way you use the new operator for a single-dimensional array. The following example illustrates how this is done. This example declares a two-dimensional array. The first dimension consists of three array elements, and the second dimension consists of two array elements. Think of this as saying, each of the three array elements has two array elements of its own (see Figure 5-1).

```
class Demo {
   public static void main (String args[]) {
      int grades[][] = new int [3][2];
   }
}
```

You can declare additional dimensions by inserting a pair of square brackets for each additional dimension. For example, here's the declaration for a three-dimensional array:

```
      int grades[][][] = new int [5][2][3];
```

A three-dimensional array can be a little difficult to comprehend because we're not used to organizing data in three dimensions. Think of a three-dimensional array this way: Each array element in the first dimension has two array elements of its own, and each of those three array elements has two array elements of its own.

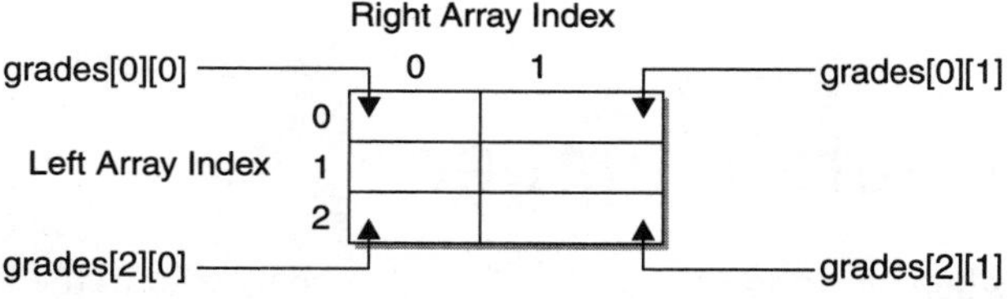

Figure 5-1 Each element of the first dimension has its own two elements.

Values Assigned to Array Elements

An element of an array is used in an expression similar to how a variable is used in an expression. The only difference between a variable and an array element is that you must specify both the array name and the index when using an array element.

You can assign a value to an array element by using the assignment operator, as shown here. This example assigns 90 to the first array element of the grades array:

```
grades[0] = 90;
```

The value assigned to an array element is used in an expression similar to how you use the value of a variable in an expression. This is illustrated in the following example, where the value of `grades[0]` is assigned to the second element of the array `grades`:

```
grades[1] = grades[0];
```

You assign a value to a multidimensional array practically the same way you do in a single-dimensional array, except you must use the index of both dimensions when referencing the array element.

The following example assigns a grade to the second element (second dimension) of the first array element (first dimension):

```
grades[0][1] = 90;
```

Likewise, you reference each dimension of a multidimensional array whenever you need to access the value stored in an array element. This is illustrated in the following example, where the value assigned to the second element (second dimension) of the first array element (first dimension) is assigned to the third element of the first array element:

```
  grades[0][2] = grades[0][1];
```

The same format is used for arrays that contain more than two dimensions, except that you'll need to include each dimension when referencing an array element in the expression.

The `Length` Data Member

Sometimes when working with arrays, you'll need to refer to the length of the array. For example, suppose you want to access each array element. You can do this quite easily by using a `for` loop. As you'll recall from the previous chapter, a `for` loop can use a control variable and a conditional expression that evaluates the value of the control variable. For each turn around the loop, the control variable is typically incremented using the incremental operator.

A `for` loop is a perfect way to step through array elements because with each iteration of the `for` loop, Java is told to move to the next array element. The conditional expression is set to evaluate false when the last array element is accessed by Java. And to do that, you must include the size of the array in the conditional expression. Programmers also call the size of the array, the *length* of the array.

You have two ways in which to reference the length of an array. You can explicitly place the length into the conditional expression, and you can reference the `length` data member of the array object. Before exploring the `length` data member, let's examine the explicit way of specifying the length of an array.

The following example shows how to use a `for` loop to access each array element. Notice that the length of the array is explicitly included in the `for` loop's conditional expression. This example declares an array of three elements. Therefore, the length of the array is 3. It also initializes the array.

```
class demo {
   public static void main (String args[]) {
      int myGrades[] = { 90, 70, 80 };
      for (int x = 0; x < 3; x++ )
      {
         System.out.println("The value of array element x is " +
                  myGrades[x]);
      }
   }
}
```

The `for` loop is then used to walk Java through each element of the array, printing the value of each array element on the screen. The control variable is used as the index for each array element. The `for` loop continues until the value of `x` is equal to the length of the array, at which time Java breaks out of the loop and the program ends.

Now that you have an idea of how to use a `for` loop to step through elements of an array, let's modify the previous example to use the `length` data member instead of explicitly placing the length of the array in the conditional expression of the `for` loop.

If you are familiar with other programming languages, such as C, you might become a little confused about the `length` data member, because an array in some programming languages does not have any methods associated with it. An array in other programming languages is a collection of variables of a specified data type.

Java treats an array as an instance of a class, which is called an *object*. You'll learn about classes in Chapter 7. For now, think of a *class* as a cookie cutter that defines data and methods. A cookie cutter isn't a cookie. Therefore, a class isn't real data and methods. That is, memory isn't reserved for the data and methods associated with a class.

When you press a cookie cutter into dough and then remove the cookie cutter, what remains is a real cookie (although you still need to bake it). When you declare an object of a class, what remains is a real object. That is, memory is reserved for the data and methods associated with the object of the class.

Therefore, when you declare an array, Java treats the array as if you declared an object of an array that has data members. Later in this chapter, we'll explore the methods associated with an array object. An array has data members: the array elements and the `length` data member. The value of the `length` data member is the length of the array. You can reference the `length` data member in your program any time you need to refer to the length of the array.

Let's see how this works. The next example is a modification of the previous example where the `length` data member of the array is used in the conditional expression in place of explicitly specifying the length of the array. Notice that you use the array name to reference the `length` data member.

```
class Demo {
   public static void main (String args[]) {
      int myGrades[] = { 90, 70, 80 };
      for (int x = 0; x < myGrades.length; x++ )
      {
         System.out.println("The value of array element x is " +
               myGrades[x]);
      }
   }
}
```

Passing an Array to a Method

As you learned in Chapter 1, a *method* is a block of statements that is identified by a unique name. You call the name of the method in your program whenever you want to execute those statements. Sometimes a method requires data in order to execute those statements. That data is provided to the method by the program when the method is called. This is called *passing data* to the method.

Let's say you have a method that calculates a grade based on the number of correct answers and the number of questions asked on the test. This method needs two data elements in order to calculate the grade: the number of correct answers and the total number of questions on the test. Both of these are provided to the method by the program that calls the method.

Data required by a method is called an *argument that is contained in an argument list*. An argument list consists of data elements, each represented as data type and name, which is very similar to the way you declare a variable.

Sometimes a method returns data to the program that called the method. This is called a *return value*. For example, the method that calculated the grade probably returns the grade to the program that asked for the grade to be calculated.

Now that you have an understanding of how a method works, let's see how you can pass an array to a method. The first step is to define a method that will receive the array. This is shown in the following example:

```
class Demo {
   public static void main (String args[]) {
      float grade;
      float rawTest[] = {70,100};
       grade = gradeCalc(rawTest);
      System.out.println("Your grade is:  " + grade );
   }
   static float gradeCalc(float test[])
   {
      return (test[0]/test[1]) * 100;
   }
}
```

The method is called `gradeCalc()` and is defined below the `main()` method. The purpose of the `gradeCalc()` method is to calculate a grade based on the number of responses the student correctly gave on the test and the number of test questions. Both these values are stored in elements of an array that is passed to the `gradeCalc()` method. After the calculation is completed, the grade is returned by the `gradeCalc()` method.

Let's see how this program works. The program begins in the `main()` method by declaring a float variable and an array called `rawTest`. The array has two array elements that store two float values. The first array element is the number of correct answers. The second array element is the number of questions on the test. Notice that the array is initialized when it is declared.

The program then calls the `gradeCalc()` method. The `gradeCalc()` method expects to receive a reference to the array that contains the data necessary to calculate the grade. You place the name of the array between parentheses in order to pass an array to a method.

Let's follow the array into the definition of the `gradeCalc()` method. The argument of the `gradeCalc()` method consists of `float test[]`. Notice that this doesn't declare the length of an array. Instead, it declares a reference to an array, which is similar to the reference that is declared when you dynamically declare an array. Think of a reference as a pointer to the first address of the block of memory that contains the array. It just so happens that the name of an array is also a pointer to the address of the block of memory that contains the array. Therefore, the argument is assigned the pointer to the array.

The `gradeCalc()` method then uses each element of the array to calculate the grade. The result of the calculation is then returned to the statement in the `main()` method that called the `gradeCalc()` method.

The grade returned by `gradeCalc()` is then assigned to the variable `a`, which is then displayed on the screen.

Returning an Array from a Method

Sometimes a method needs to return an array to the statement that calls the method. This is accomplished by placing the array name in the `return` statement of the method, as is shown in the following example:

```
class Demo {
   public static void main (String args[]) {
      float rawTest[];
      rawTest = testData();
      System.out.println("Correction Answers:   " +
           rawTest[0]);
      System.out.println("Total Questions:   " +
           rawTest[1]);
   }
   static float[] testData()
   {
      float rawTest[] = {70,100};
      return rawTest;
   }
}
```

Let's see how this program works. It begins in the `main()` method with a declaration of a reference to an array of floats. Remember that a declaration of a reference is not the same as declaring an array. A reference is simply a pointer to an array, and an array is actually a block of memory.

The reference is used to receive the return value from the `testData()` method. The `testData()` method returns the number of correct answers and the number of questions appearing on the test. You'll notice from looking at the definition of the

testData() method that there are no arguments because the testData() method doesn't require any additional information to complete its processing.

The testData() method declares an array of floats that consists of two array elements. This is the same array used in the previous example. The first array element contains the number of correct answers, and the second array element contains the number of questions appearing on the test. Notice that the name of the array is used as the return value. As you'll recall from the previous section, the array name points to the first address of the memory that contains the array. It is this address that is assigned to the array reference in the statement that calls the testData() method.

An array is returned by a method. That is, both the method and the statement that called the method have access to the array. Either one can change the elements of the array.

Alternate Ways of Creating an Array

In Java, you have several other ways to declare an array other than those discussed so far in this chapter. One of those ways is to place the square brackets on the left side of the array name. In the examples so far, we've placed the square brackets on the right side of the array. Either way is acceptable, as shown here. There is no advantage or disadvantage to using one way over the other.

```
float rawTest []
float rawTest [] []
float [] rawTest
float [] [] rawTest
```

Another alternative is to declare an array reference in two different statements. Previously in this chapter, we declared the array reference in the same statement that declared the array. Here are examples of both ways:

```
float rawTest = new float [4];
```

and

```
float rawTest;
rawTest = new float [4];
```

Also, you can declare a multidimensional array by specifying only one dimension rather than all dimensions. This is referred to as an *irregular* array because all the dimensions of the array are not created in the same statement. There is no advantage or disadvantage to declaring an irregular array.

Here's how this works: The first statement in the following example declares a two-dimensional array where only the dimension is defined in the statement that declares the array. Subsequent statements declare the second dimension.

```
float rawTest[][] = new float[3][];
rawTest [0] = new float [2];
rawTest [1] = new float [2];
rawTest [2] = new float [2];
```

The `Arrays` Class

Previously in this book you learned that a class is like a cookie cutter. A cookie cutter defines all the parts of a cookie, and a class defines all the parts of an object of that class. Think of the object of the class as the cookie made by a cookie cutter.

As you'll recall, parts of a class are called *members* of a class, and they fall within two categories: data members and method members. A *data* member is like the `length` data member for an array, which you were introduced to earlier in this chapter. A *method* member is a method that is associated with the class.

You'll learn a lot more about classes in Chapter 7, but for now that's all you need to know in order to understand how to use the `Arrays` class in your program. The `Arrays` class is a class already defined for you in the `java.util` package that came with your Java compiler. Its purpose is to make it easy for you to work with arrays.

Typically, you'll want to search, sort, and otherwise manipulate elements of an array. You can use loops and a variety of statements and expressions to do these things. However, you can save a lot of time and reduce the amount of statements you have to write by using methods defined in the `Arrays` class.

The `Arrays` class defines a number of methods. We'll take a close look at how to use the more common methods: `equals()`, `fill()`, `sort()`, and `binarySearch()`.

`equals()`

The `equals()` method is used to compare elements of two arrays. Each array is passed as an argument to the `equals()` method, which then computes whether the arrays are equal to each other. If so, the `equals()` method returns a Boolean true; otherwise, a Boolean false is returned.

The following example shows how to use the `equals()` method in your program:

```
import java.util.*;
class Demo {
   public static void main(String args[]) {
      int student1Grades []= new int[3];
      student1Grades [0] = 90;
      student1Grades [1] = 80;
      student1Grades [2] = 70;
      int student2Grades []= new int[3];
      student2Grades [0] = 90;
      student2Grades [1] = 80;
      student2Grades [2] = 70;
      if (Arrays.equals(student1Grades, student2Grades))
         System.out.println("Match");
      else
         System.out.println("No Match");
   }
}
```

This example declares two arrays, both containing student grades. The `equals()` method is then called and passed the name of both arrays. The value returned by the `equals()` method becomes the conditional expression for the `if` statement. Remember that statements within an `if` statement are executed if the conditional expression is true; otherwise, statements within the `else` statement are executed. An appropriate message is displayed on the screen, depending on the value returned by the `equals()` method.

Two special things happen in this example because we are using the `equals()` method. The first thing is that the `java.util` package is imported into the program. Many of the packages you'll be using come with your Java compiler. Each package is given a name. In this example, `java.util` is the name of the package we're using in this program. You must import into your program the package that contains the classes your program uses; otherwise, you'll experience a compiler error. This is because Java needs to know the class definition before you can use the class in your program. The `java.util` package contains the definition of the `Arrays` class, which we use in this example.

Another special thing that is going on in this example is that the `equals()` method is called by referencing the name of the `Arrays` class. The class name must precede the member of the class that you want to use in your program, and the class name and the name of the class member must be separated by a period, which is called a *dot operator*. Think of this as telling Java, "Use the `equals()` method that is defined in the `Arrays` class."

fill()

The `fill()` method is a handy tool to use whenever you have to assign an initial value to an array that has a large number of array elements. Suppose you've declared an array of 2,000 integers and, following good programming practice, you decide to initialize each array element to zero. Previously in this chapter, you learned the two ways to accomplish this. First, you can assign an initial value when you declare the array. However, you'll end up with a very long statement consisting of 2,000 zeros. Alternatively, you can declare an array that has 2,000 elements and then write 2,000 statements to assign zero to each array element.

Neither of these options is appealing because both are time consuming and fraught with opportunities for you to make typographical errors. The best solution is to have the `fill()` method assign zero to all those array elements. The following example shows how this is done.

This example declares an array of 2,000 floats. The `fill()` method is then called to initialize each element of the array. The `fill()` method requires two arguments. The first argument is the array name, and the second argument is the value that will be assigned to each array element. It is critical that the initial value is of a data type that is compatible with the data type of the array; otherwise, you'll receive a compile error. After the `fill()` method is finished, this program displays the value of each array element.

```
import java.util.*;
class Demo {
   public static void main(String args[]) {
      int studentIDs[] = new int [2000];
      Arrays.fill(studentIDs, 0);
      for (int i = 0; i < studentIDs.length; i++)
        System.out.println(studentIDs [i]);
   }
}
```

Sometimes you'll have a need to reset the value of a range of array elements rather than the value for the entire array. Let's say that after initializing the array of 2,000 student IDs used in the previous example, you replaced the initialized value with real student IDs from a database. However, in doing so, you realized that a range of 100 of those student IDs is wrong and must be reset to zero.

You have three ways of addressing this problem. First, you could start over by using the `fill()` method to reset all the array elements to zero. Second, you could manually reset the range of the 100 incorrect IDs to zero. Third, you could use another version of the `fill()` method to reset only a specific range of array elements to a value. The third choice is obviously the best one.

The other version of the `fill()` method enables you to specify the range of array elements you want filled by the `fill()` method. Programmers call this *overloading* the method. You'll learn about overloading methods in Chapter 6. For now, simply think of overloading as a method that has the same name as another method but has different kinds of data passed to it within the parentheses, which is called an *argument list*.

This is illustrated in the next example. You'll notice that the first part of this example is the same as the previous example, except the `fill()` method assigns 1 instead of 0 to the array elements.

After the value of the array is displayed on the screen, the other version of the `fill()` method is called to reset the value of 100 array elements from 1 to 0. This version of the `fill()` method requires four arguments. The first argument is the array name, and the second argument is the index of the first array element whose value will be changed.

The third argument is the index of the array element that comes after the last array element whose value will be changed. This is a bit confusing, so let's take a closer look at this example. The second argument is 200. This tells the `fill()` method to change values beginning with `studentIDs[200]`. The third argument is 301, which refers to `studentIDs[301]`. This tells the `fill()` method to stop changing values when it reaches array element `studentIDs[301]`. In other words, the value of array element `studentIDs[301]` is not changed. The last array element that is changed by the `fill()` method is `studentIDs[300]`.

The fourth argument of the `fill()` method is the value that will be assigned to the range of array elements. In this example, array elements from `studentIDs[200]` to `studentIDs[300]` are changed from 1 to 0.

```
import java.util.*;
class Demo {
   public static void main(String args[]) {
      float studentIDs[] = new float [2000];
      Arrays.fill(studentIDs, 1);
      for (int i = 0; i < studentIDs.length; i++)
        System.out.println(studentIDs [i]);
      Arrays.fill(studentIDs,200,301, 0);
      for (int i = 0; i < studentIDs.length; i++)
        System.out.println(studentIDs [i]);
   }
}
```

sort()

Sorting values of array elements is one of the basic things you'll do with an array. The easiest way to sort an array is by calling the `sort()` method of the `Arrays` class. The `sort()` method requires that you pass it the name of the array. It then rearranges values of array elements so that they are sorted.

Let's see how this works in the next example. This example declares an array of Strings and then assigns a name to each of the array elements. Notice that these names are not in sorted order. The `sort()` method is called and is passed the name of the array. After the array is sorted, elements of the array are displayed on the screen—in sorted order.

```
import java.util.*;
class Demo {
   public static void main(String args[]) {
      String myArray[]= new String[4];
      myArray [0] = "Mary";
      myArray [1] = "Adam";
      myArray [2] = "Clark";
      myArray [3] = "Bob";
      Arrays.sort(myArray);
      for (int i = 0; i < 4; i++)
         System.out.println(myArray[i]);
   }
}
```

binarySearch()

That last commonly used method of the `Arrays` class that we'll discuss is the `binarySearch()` method. The `binarySearch()` method is used to locate an array element that contains a particular value. This is very useful when you have a very large array. Instead of having to examine each array element yourself looking for a particular value, you can call the `binarySearch()` method, and it will find the value in the array for you.

The `binarySearch()` method requires that the array be sorted before the search begins; otherwise, the `binarySearch()` method won't be able to find the search criteria. Therefore, you'll need pass the array to the `sort()` method before calling the `binarySearch()` method.

The `binarySearch()` method requires two arguments. The first argument is the array name, and the second argument is the search criteria. The search criteria

must be compatible with the data type of the array; otherwise, you'll receive a compiler error.

The `binarySearch()` method returns an integer. The integer can be a positive number or a negative number. A positive number represents the index of the array element that contains the search value. A negative number means that the search criterion isn't a value in the index.

The following example shows how to use the `binarySearch()` method in your program. You'll notice that this example is nearly the same as the previous example, and it uses the same array and array element values. Those values are sorted by the `sort()` method before the `binarySearch()` method is called.

Two arguments are passed to the `binarySearch()` method. The first ar gument is the array name, and the second argument is the search criteria. The `binarySearch()` method returns a 2 when this program runs because 2 represents the index of the array element that contains the value Clark. The index is then displayed on the screen.

```
import java.util.*;
class Demo {
   public static void main(String args[]) {
      int index;
      String myArray[]= new String[4];
      myArray [0] = "Mary";
      myArray [1] = "Adam";
      myArray [2] = "Clark";
      myArray [3] = "Bob";
      Arrays.sort(myArray);
      index = Arrays.binarySearch(myArray, "Clark");
      System.out.println("Clark is in array element: " + index);
   }
}
```

Quiz

1. What is an index?
2. What is a reference to an array?
3. What does the `new` operator return when an array is declared?
4. What is the index of the first element of an array?
5. How do you pass an array to a method?

6. How do you return an array from a method?
7. How do you determine the number of array elements of an array?
8. What does the third parameter of the `fill()` method (the second version of the method) represent?
9. What does it mean when the `binarySearch()` method returns a negative number?
10. What is a package?

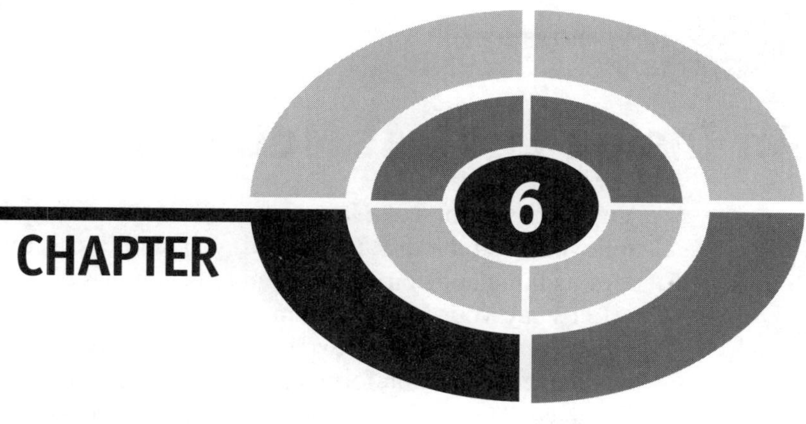

Methods and Polymorphism

The best part of calling is plumber to fix a leaky pipe is that you don't have to fix the pipe yourself. You don't even need to know how to fix a pipe. Instead, you simply say, "This pipe has a leak. Fix it." A few hours later, the plumber returns telling you that the pipe is fixed—and presents you with the bill. The plumber is like a method in a Java program because a programmer calls a method to perform a task, and then the method tells the programmer whether the task was successfully completed. Fortunately, a method doesn't present the programmer with a bill. In this chapter, you learn how to call a method from within your program and how to create your own methods.

An Inside Look at Methods

A method is the part of a Java program that contains the logic to perform a task. Each time you need the task performed, you simply call the method. The method then does its thing and comes back and tells you that the task is completed.

Let's say your Java program displays a course registration form on the screen whenever a student needs to register for a course. You can create a method to display the course registration form and then call the method whenever you need the form displayed. The method handles all the steps necessary to display the form.

A major reason for using methods is to drastically reduce the number of duplicated statements in a program. This can be seen in the example of the course registration form. Suppose that 15 statements are needed to display the course registration form. Also suppose that you didn't create a method to display the form. This means you'll need to write 15 statements each time you want to display the course registration form—a total of 150 statements if the form is displayed ten times in your program.

An alternative is to place these 15 statements in a method and then call the method ten times. Those 15 statements are written once in your program, saving you from having to write 135 statements.

Another reason for using a method is to make it easy for you to maintain the program. Changes are made in one place—in the method. You don't have to hunt down and change statements in all the places in your program. Instead, you look in one place in your program and make the change once.

Using a method also reduces the risk of errors. Typographical errors commonly occur when you type instructions into your program. By reducing the number of statements that are repeated in a program, you also reduce number of opportunities for making typographical errors.

Types of Methods

The two types of methods are nonstatic methods and static methods. A *nonstatic* method is a method that is a member of a class and can only be called by an instance of that class. A *static* method is also member of a class, but it can be called without having to be declared by an instance of the class.

Typically the task performed by a nonstatic method is dependent on data stored in an instance of the class. For example, suppose you have a class called `student` that has a nonstatic method called `display()`. The `display()` nonstatic method displays information about a student that's contained in the class. You'll learn all about classes in Chapter 7.

A static method usually performs tasks that are not directly associated with data members of the class. In fact, a static method may not have any relationship with the class other than being a static method of it.

Many of the methods you will use in your programs will be member methods.

The Method Definition

Before a method can be called within a program, it must be defined in a method definition within the definition of a class. A method definition contains all the statements necessary for the method to perform a task, and it's organized into two parts: the method header and the body of the method.

The Method Header

The method header consists of three basic elements, but it sometimes includes an access and behavioral modifier. We'll explore the basic elements in this section. You'll learn about the other elements in Chapter 7. The three basic elements are the method name, the method argument list, and the data type of the value returned by the method. The method name and method argument list are collectively referred to as the *method signature*, which uniquely identifies a method from other methods.

The method name is a name you give to the method. The name should reflect the task that the method performs. For example, `display()` is a good name for a method that displays data on the screen because the name implies the task performed by the method. Also, the name must conform to the Java Naming Convention (see Chapter 1).

The method argument list consists of the data the method needs to perform the task. You'll recall that in Chapter 5 we defined a method that calculates a grade based on the number of correct answers and the number of questions on a test. This method requires both of these data elements in order to calculate the grade. These are passed to the method's argument list by the statement that calls the method.

The method argument list is formed by specifying the data type and name of each data element passed to the method. This is shown in the next example. Two arguments are shown here. The first argument is the number of correct answers, and the second argument is the number of questions on the test. Both are of the int data type.

```
calcGrade( int correctAns, int numberTestQuestions)
```

The name of an argument should reflect the nature of the data stored in the argument. The name must also conform to the Java Naming Convention. You use the name of the argument within statements of the method whenever you need to refer to the data stored in the argument. For example, you would use correctAns to refer to the number of correct answers given by the student.

Any number of arguments can be included in an argument list as long as a comma separates the arguments and the name of each argument is unique. That is, you cannot have two arguments called correctAns.

The argument list is optional. Only a method that requires data from the statement that called the method needs to have an argument list. However, the method definition still requires the parentheses even if there isn't an argument list, as shown in the following example:

```
display ()
```

The remaining part of the method header is the data type of the return value. Some methods return data back to the statement that called the method after the method completes its task. Other methods don't return anything back.

If data is returned by the method, you must include the data type of that data in the method header. If data isn't returned by the method, you must use void as the data type. The keyword void infers nothing (that is, no return data type). Don't confuse void (nothing) with zero. Zero is a value, whereas void is the absence of a value.

The data type of the data returned by the method is placed to the left of the method name, as shown in this example, where the method returns a float:

```
float calcGrade( int correctAns, int numberTestQuestions)
```

However, if the calcGrade() method didn't return data, void is placed to the left of the method name, as shown here:

```
void calcGrade(int correctAns, int numberTestQuestions)
```

The Method Body

The body of the method is defined within the opening and closing braces and appears below the method header. This is where you place statements that are executed when the method is called. Java executes the first statement below the opening brace and continues to execute statements sequentially until the closing brace is reached or until a return statement is executed.

The following example illustrates how to construct the body of a method:

```
void calcGrade(int correctAns, int numberTestQuestions)
{
   //Place statements here
}
```

The Method Return Value

Depending on the task performed by a method, the method may return data to the statement that called it. For example, the `calcGrade()` method shown previously in this chapter calculates and returns a grade.

Programmers call data that is returned by a method a *return value*. The return value is placed to the right of the keyword `return` in a return statement. Java immediately exits the method and returns to the statement that called the method when the return statement executes. Statements below the return statement are not executed.

A return value can be a literal, a variable, or an object. Some programmers place an expression in the return statement. Java then evaluates the expression and returns the result of the expression. The return value must be compatible with the return data type specified in the method header; otherwise, you'll receive a compiler error.

A return statement can be placed anywhere in the body of a method. Keep in mind that no statement below the return statement is executed once Java executes the return statement. Typically programmers place a return statement immediately before the closing brace in the body of the method if the method has a return value. The return statement is excluded from a method if the method doesn't have a return value.

Multiple return statements can be used to return different return values, depending on conditions within the body of the method.

Say you created a method to validate a user password. The value 0 is returned if the password is valid. A value of 1 is returned if the password is invalid. Two return statements are used within an `if...else` statement. One within an `if` statement that is executed only if the password is valid, and the other in an `else` statement that is executed if the password is invalid. Only one ever executes. This is illustrated in the following code segment, where the password entered by the user is assigned to the variable `password`:

```
if (password == "Bob")
   return 0;
else
   return 1;
```

Some programmers always use a return statement in a method, even if the method doesn't require a return value. They do so to signal whether or not the method successfully performed the task. A zero is returned if the task was performed successfully.

A nonzero number is returned if the method had problems performing a task. Some programmers return a negative number to signal that a problem has occurred. Other programmers return a positive value that corresponds to the error that helps them identify the problem. This is commonly referred to as an *error code*.

Let's return to the method that validates a user password and see how error codes are used. The validation task consists of three subtasks. The first subtask is to open the database that contains valid passwords. The second subtask is to search for the user password passed by the statement that called the method. The third subtask is to report back the password's status.

We could return –1 if the first subtasks fails because the method couldn't open the database. Likewise, we could return –2 if there is a problem searching the database. If both subtasks are successfully completed, we could return 0 if the user password is valid and 1 if it isn't valid.

Error codes are commonly used only in complex programs and methods, where it is difficult and time consuming to track down problems occurring in the program.

The following example is a complete method definition that illustrates how to return a value to the statement that called the method. This example calculates and returns a test grade. You'll notice that the return statement contains an expression rather than a return value. Remember that Java evaluates the expression before executing the return statement. The result of the expression replaces the expression in the return statement, and the result is returned.

```
float calcGrade(int correctAns, int totalQuestions)
{
   return (correctAns / totalQuestions) * 100;
}
```

The Argument List

Now that you know how to define a method, let's take a closer look at the method argument list. Previously you learned that some methods require data in order to perform a task and that the data is supplied by the statement that calls the method. This data is referred to as an *argument* and is passed to a method in the form of an argument list. Think of an argument list as the collection of data a method needs to perform a task.

The statement that calls the method places data between the parentheses of the *method call*, as shown in this example, which passes two integer literals to the `calcGrade()` method defined in the previous section of this chapter:

```
calcGrade(70, 100)
```

Some programmers call data passed to a method a *parameter list*. Each data element in the parameter list is referred to as a *parameter*. Therefore, 70 and 100, collectively, comprise the parameter list, and each is a parameter. Other programmers use the terms *argument list* and *arguments* as synonymous for *parameter list* and *parameters*. We'll use the terms *argument list* and *arguments* throughout this book.

You have three things to remember when using an argument list. First, the data passed to a method by the statement must be compatible with the data type of the method's argument list, as specified in the method definition.

Second, the order in which data is passed to a method must be the same order as the method's argument list.

Third, you must pass the method the correct number of arguments. That is, the number of arguments in the argument list in the method definition must be the same as the number of data elements passed to the method.

Failure to do these three things might result in a compiler error or cause the method to process erroneous data. For example, switching the position of the data passed to the `calcGrade()` method results in the method calculating an erroneous grade.

Elements of an Argument List

An argument list consists of two elements: the argument data type and the argument name. An argument data type is the same as a data type of a variable. It tells Java the amount of memory to reserve for the argument and the kind of data that will be stored there.

An argument name is similar to a variable name. It is an alias for the memory address that contains the data passed by the statement that calls the method. You use the argument name within the method the same as you use a variable name.

How an Argument List Works

Before data is passed to a method, it is stored in memory. When the method is called, Java allocates memory based on the data types of the arguments specified in the method definition. Java then makes available to the method the data passed by the statement that called the method.

Data is made available to a method in two way: pass by value and pass by reference. *Pass by value* makes a copy of the data available to the method. That is, Java makes a copy of the data passed to the method and stores the copy in memory that is allocated for the argument. Statements with the method can change the value of the data passed to it, but that change isn't available to the statement that called the method because each has its own copy of the data.

The following is an example of how data is passed by value to a method. This example declares three ints. One stores the value returned by the method, and the other two store values passed to the method, which are initialized to 70 and 100, respectively. A copy of these values are assigned to the arguments `correctAns` and `totalQuestions` by Java. The values 70 and 100 appear twice in memory—once for the `calcGrade()` method, and the other for the `main()` method.

```
class Demo {
   public static void main (String args[]) {
      float a;
      int b = 70, c = 100;
      a = calcGrade (b, c);
      System.out.println("Your grade is:  " + a);
   }
   static float calcGrade(int correctAns, int totalQuestions)
   {
      return (correctAns / totalQuestions) * 100;
   }
}
```

Command-Line Arguments

A command-line argument is data that is passed to your Java program from the command line when you run the program. The command line is also called the *command prompt*. (You can display the command prompt in Windows by selecting Start | Programs | Accessories | Command Prompt.)

Sometimes programmers use a command-line argument to override a default setting in the Java program. For example, a Java program might use the system's date as today's date throughout the program unless a date is passed in a command-line argument, which overrides the default date.

A Java program receives data from the command line in the `main()` method's argument list. You probably noticed the `main()` method's argument list in examples throughout this book, as shown here:

```
void main (String args[])
```

The `main()` method's argument list consists of one argument, which is a reference to an array of String objects called `args`. You'll learn about String objects in Chapter 7. For now, think of a String object as one or more words, such as "Bob Smith" or "121 Main Street."

As you'll recall from the previous chapter, a reference to an array isn't an array. Instead, it is something that points to the memory address that contains the first element of the array. Data passed to a program is placed in memory, and the memory address of the first data element is assigned to the `args` reference. You've seen this done previously in this chapter when an array is passed to a method.

The number of data elements placed on the command line determines the number of array elements in the `args` array. You can determine the number of array elements by using the `length` member of the array, which you learned about in the previous chapter. The following example will refresh your memory on how this is done:

```
class Demo {
   public static void main (String args[]) {
      System.out.println("
          The number of command line arguments is:  " + args.length);
   }
}
```

Data passed on the command line is assigned to each of the `args` array elements, and you can access that data from within your program by referencing the array element the same way you reference any array element (see Chapter 5).

Let's see how this is done. The following example begins by determining whether there are any command-line arguments. If there aren't any, an appropriate message is displayed. If there are, a `for` loop is used to display each element of the array pointed to by the `args` reference.

```
class Demo {
   public static void main (String args[]) {
      if ( args.length > 0)
      {
         for (int x = 0; x < args.length; x++)
         {
           System.out.println(
               "Command line argument " + x + " :  " + args[x]);
          }
      }
      else
      {
            System.out.println(
               "There are no command line arguments.");
       }
   }
}
```

Passing Command-Line Arguments

Now that you know how to use command-line arguments within your program, let's turn our attention to how arguments are passed from the command line to your program. If you are using Windows, you may not have had the opportunity to use the command line because many programs running in Windows are started by double-clicking an icon or selecting the program from a menu.

In order to run a program from the command line and pass it command-line arguments, you'll need to display a command line on the screen. You do this in Windows by selecting Start | Programs | Accessories | Command Prompt in many versions of Windows.

We'll use the example in the previous section to illustrate how to pass a command-line argument. Type the following on the command line and press ENTER to run the program:

```
java demo Amber
```

Here's what is happening: The first word, java, is used to run the Java Virtual Machine. The second word, `demo`, is the name of the Java program, which is the program shown in the previous section. The third word, `Amber`, is the command-line argument.

When you press ENTER, your operating system runs the Java Virtual Machine and passes it the name of your program and the command-line argument. The Java Virtual Machine then uses the command-line argument as it executes your program.

You can pass multiple command-line arguments to your program by typing them on the command line and separating them with a space. Arguments are assigned to the `args` array in the order in which those arguments appear on the command line. For example, the first argument is assigned to the first array element, the second argument is assigned to the second array element, and so on.

The following command line shows you how to use multiple command-line arguments. Notice there are two command-line arguments: `Amber` and `Joanne`. When the program runs, `Amber` is assigned to `args[0]` and `Joanne` is assigned to `args[1]`.

```
java demo Amber Joanne
```

There might be an occasion when you need to pass a command-line argument that consists of two or more words, such as "Amber Leigh." There's a problem. These words are separated by a space, which will confuse Java because it interprets these words as two command-line arguments instead of as one command-line argument.

The solution to this problem is to place all the words that comprise the command-line argument within double quotation marks. This causes Java to interpret the space as part of the argument rather than the beginning of a new argument. The following command line illustrates how this is done. There are two command-line arguments in this example (`"Amber Leigh"` and `Joanne`):

```
java demo "Amber Leigh" Joanne
```

On other occasions, you may want quotation marks to be part of the command-line argument. For example, the command-line argument might be `"Amber"` including the quotation marks. The problem is that the operating system shell interprets the

quotation marks as a signal to make everything between them the command-line argument—excluding the quotation marks.

The solution is to precede each quotation mark with a backslash (\). The backslash tells the operating system shell that the quotation mark is part of the command-line argument. The following command-line argument shows you how this works. When the program runs, `args[0]` is assigned `"Amber"` and `args[1]` is assigned `Joanne`.

```
java demo \"Amber\" Joanne
```

Calling a Method

Previously in this chapter, you saw how to call a method within a statement. You simply use the method name followed by any arguments. The arguments must be contained within parentheses. Empty parentheses are used if the method doesn't require any arguments. You need to consider a number of factors when calling a method. We'll discuss those factors in this section.

The first thing to consider is that Java is case sensitive. Therefore, you must be careful to use exactly the name of the method that appears in the method definition when calling it. Otherwise, Java will think you want to use a different method, and it will then display a compiler error if that method isn't found.

Second, make sure you include all the arguments in the method call that are found in the method definition. The method call must have the same number of arguments. Arguments passed by the method call must be of a data type that is compatible with arguments in the method definition. Also, those arguments must appear in the method call in the same order as the arguments appear in the method definition. You'll receive a compiler error if there is a mismatch of arguments.

Some methods return a value; however, the statement that calls the method can ignore the return value without experiencing a compile error. Here's a modified version of the example used earlier in this chapter to call a method to calculate a grade:

```
class Demo {
   public static void main (String args[]) {
      float rawTest[] = {70,100};
      calcGrade (rawTest);
   }
   static float calcGrade (float test[])
   {
      return (test[0]/test[1]) * 100;
   }
}
```

You'll notice that a statement calls the `calcGrade (rawTest)` method and passes it the name of an array. The `calcGrade()` method calculates and returns the grade back to this statement. However, the statement does nothing with the grade. Although this isn't a Java error, it is illogical to call the `calcGrade()` method without doing something with the grade returned by the method. Therefore, you need to make sure it makes sense to your program to ignore the return value of a method.

A common practice among programmers is to call a method from within an expression when the return value of the method is used in the expression. This is illustrated in the next example. This example applies a curve to the grade calculated by `calcGrade()`, which you've seen used in the previous example. The call to the `calcGrade()` method is made within the expression that calculates the curve. Java calls the method before evaluating the expression.

```
class Demo {
   public static void main (String args[]) {
      float  rawTest[] = {70,100};
      double finalGrade, curve = 1.2;
      finalGrade = curve * calcGrade (rawTest);
      System.out.println(
            "Your final grade is:  " + finalGrade );
   }
   static float calcGrade (float test[])
   {
      return (test[0]/test[1]) * 100;
   }
}
```

Polymorphism

The Greeks coined a term to refer to something that has multiple forms—*polymorphism*. This term is also used by programmers to describe Java's capability to have a method take on different meanings (forms), depending on the context in which the method is called within a program.

Java implements polymorphism by enabling a programmer to overload a method. A programmer "overloads" a method by defining two or more methods using the same name but defining different argument lists for each method.

You are probably wondering why any programmer would want to use the same name for two methods. On the surface, this seems as if it would confuse anyone calling the method. However, overloading actually makes it easier to use methods because the programmer doesn't have to remember a lot of method names. The programmer only needs to remember the method name and the appropriate argument lists.

The next example illustrates the benefits of overloading a method. This example defines a method called `displayError()`, which displays an error message on the screen. The error message is contained in the `System.out.println()` statement within the body of the `displayError()` method.

You'll notice that this is a generic error message that doesn't provide any clue as to the nature of the error. In some circumstances, this error message is fine. In other circumstances, a programmer may want a more informative error message.

Therefore, we overloaded the `displayError()` method with another method called `displayError()`. The other version of the `displayError()` method has one argument: the text of the error message that will be displayed on the screen.

A programmer has the option to call the `displayError()` method and use the generic error message or to call the other version and provide the `displayError()` method the error message to display on the screen. In either case, the programmer still calls the `displayError()` method and either includes an argument in the method call or excludes the argument, depending on whether the programmer wants a generic error message or a custom error message displayed.

```
class Demo {
   public static void main (String args[]) {
      displayError();
      displayError("Your printer is out of paper.");
   }
   static void displayError()
   {
      System.out.println("An error has occurred." );
   }
   static void displayError (String errorMsg)
   {
      System.out.println(errorMsg);
   }
}
```

The Method Signature

Although we tend to use a method name to identify a method, Java identifies a method by its signature. As you'll recall from earlier in this chapter, a method's signature is the combination of the method name and the method argument list.

This means that the programmer sees both versions of the `displayError()` method as the same method. However, Java sees these versions as different methods because their argument lists are different.

An argument list can be different in several ways. You can have a different number of arguments, the same number of arguments but different data types, or the same number arguments and the same data types but in a different order in the argument lists.

Some of these differences can be seen in the next example. Notice that the third and fourth versions of the `displayError()` method contain basically the same arguments, except the order in which they appear in the argument lists are reversed. Java considers each a different method.

```
class Demo {
   public static void main (String args[]) {
      displayError();
      displayError("Your printer is out of paper.");
      displayError("ver3", 1);
      displayError(1, "ver4");
   }
   static void displayError()
   {
      System.out.println("An error has occurred." );
   }
   static void displayError (String errorMsg)
   {
      System.out.println(errorMsg);
   }
   static void displayError (String errorMsg,
          int errorNum)
   {
      System.out.println("ver 3");
   }
   static void displayError (int errorNum,
          String errorMsg )
   {
      System.out.println("ver 4");
   }
}
```

Quiz

1. What are the components of a method header?
2. What are the components of a method signature?
3. What is the purpose of a return statement?
4. What are the two components of an argument?
5. What is a command-line argument?
6. How can a quotation mark be passed as a command-line argument?
7. What is polymorphism?
8. What is overloading a method?
9. What is a method?
10. What are the two kinds of methods available in Java?

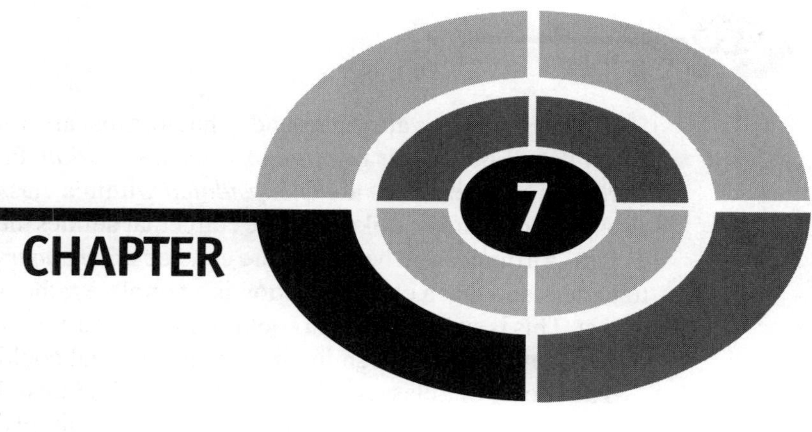

CHAPTER 7

Classes

Some programming languages lack class, but that can't be said about Java because Java has more class than the British Royals (although Java's class is a bit more technical than the class spawned by the upper crust). Java's class is used to mimic a real-world item in a Java program, such as a student, a course registration form, or a transcript. Real-world things consist of attributes and behaviors, such as a student's name and a student registering for a course. A Java class also has attributes and behaviors, known as *data* and *methods*. You'll learn how to create and use Java classes in this chapter.

Class Definition

A primary objective of object-oriented programming languages such as Java is to emulate real-world things—which we'll call *objects*—by defining a class within a program. You can also think of a class as a new data type that you define and that is used to create instances of the class.

A class combines attributes and behaviors that are associated with an object into a new data type. This is referred to as *encapsulation*. Programmers like to say that attributes and behaviors are *encapsulated* within a class definition.

A class definition is like a cookie cutter that defines the attributes and behaviors of a class. Attributes and behaviors are considered *members* of the class. It is important to understand that a class definition is a template rather than the emulation of a real object. This is similar to how a cookie cutter isn't a cookie. The cookie cutter must be pressed into cookie dough in order to make a real cookie.

The cookie of a class is called an *instance* of the class. Many programmers refer to an instance of a class as an *object of the class* or simply as an *object*. We'll use the term *instance* throughout this book so that you don't confuse *object* (the term that refers to a real-world object) with an object created by a class.

Think of a class in this way: A cookie cutter makes a cookie, and a class makes an instance or object. You'll learn how to create an instance of a class later in this chapter. For now, we'll focus on defining a class.

A class definition consists of three components: the keyword `class`, the class name, and the class body. The `class` keyword is used to tell Java that you are defining a class. The class name is the name you'll be calling the class within your Java program. The class name must conform to the Java Naming Convention, which is presented in Chapter 1. The class body is defined by an opening and closing brace and is the place where you declare attributes and define behaviors.

Here is the form of a Java class definition. This class is called `myClass`.

```
class myClass {
}
```

An *attribute* of a class is data that is associated with the class. Programmers call an attribute an *instance variable*. In Chapter 2, you learned about instance variables of the program class. Each instance of a class has its own copy of the data that is assigned to an instance variable. More about this in a moment.

A *behavior* of a class is a method that is associated with the class. Programmers call this a *method member*. In Chapter 6, you learned about method members of the program class. Each instance of a class shares method members of the class.

If you create two instances of `myClass`, each instance has its own instance variable but shares the same member method.

In Chapter 1, you learned that a Java application is a class referred to as an *application class*. The Java application class must define the `main()` method, which is the entry point into the application. The Java application is actually a class definition, and the `main()` method is a member method of that class. However, you do not need to have a `main()` method in other classes that you define in your program because there is only one `main()` method in a Java program.

You place class definitions of other classes outside of the Java application class definition. Here's an example of how this is done. This example is a valid Java application. It will compile, but nothing happens when you run it because the `main()` method doesn't contain any statements.

```
Class Demo {
   public static void main (String args[]) {
   }
}
class myClass {

}
```

Defining a Method Member

A member method is defined nearly identically to the way a method is defined, which you learned how to do in Chapter 6. However, there are two differences. First, the definition of a method member must be placed within the body of a class definition. The other difference is that you must include an access specifier, which tells Java how the method member can be called within the Java program (see "Access Specifiers" next in this chapter).

As you'll recall from Chapter 6, a method definition consists of a method name, an argument list, a return value, and the body of the method. The method name is used to call the method within your Java program. The argument list is used to provide the method with information needed for it to perform a task. An argument list is optional. If a method has all the information necessary to perform a task, an argument list isn't necessary. If a method needs information to perform the task, an argument list is required.

The return value is information returned by the method to the statement that called the method. The return value is also optional because not every method needs to return a value. The body of the method is defined using an opening and closing brace within which you place the statements to be executed when the method is called by a statement in your program.

Access Specifiers

Each member of a class has an access specifier that tells Java how that member can be accessed by other parts of the program. The three types of access specifiers are public, private, and protected.

A class member designated as *public* can be accessed by any part of the program as long as an instance of the class is created before the member is accessed. Many methods are designated as public in order for parts of the program to call those methods. The exception to this rule involves public static members of a class. You can access a public static member of a class without first creating an instance of the class.

A class member designated *private* can be accessed only by members of the same class. A private member cannot be accessed by other parts of the program. Many instance variables are designated as private in order to protect them from other parts of the program. Typically, only method members of the class can access instance variables.

A class member designated *protected* can be accessed by method members of the same class and by method members of a class that inherits the class. It can also be accessed by classes in the same package (see "Packages" later in this chapter). You'll learn about inheritance in Chapter 8. Other parts of the program cannot access a protected member of a class. Some method members and maybe a few instance variables are designed as protected, depending on the nature of the program.

You place the access specifier to the left of the data type of a method member definition and to the left of the data type when declaring an instance variable, which you'll see later in this chapter.

You do not have to include the access specifier. If you exclude an access specifier, Java assumes that the member is designated public, making it available to all parts of the program that are in the same package as the class.

The following example shows how to define a method member called `print()`, which is a member of the `myClass` class. This method displays text that is received from the statement that calls the method. There isn't a return value, and the method can be accessed by any part of the program. You'll notice that the body of the `main()` method contains no statements, so nothing happens when this program runs.

```
class Demo {
   public static void main (String args[]) {

   }
}
class myClass {
  public void print(String str){
     System.out.println(str);
   }
}
```

Declaring Instance Variables

Previously in this chapter, you learned that an instance variable is data that is associated with a class, such as a student's ID number for the class that emulates a student. An instance variable is declared similarly to how you declare a variable (Chapter 2), with three exceptions.

You'll recall that a variable is declared by specifying a data type followed by the name of the variable in a statement. The following statement declares a student ID. The variable is an int data type and is called `student`.

```
int student;
```

The same statement is used to declare an instance variable. However, an instance variable must be declared within the body of the class and should be preceded by an access specifier. Remember that Java designates an instance variable as available to classes within the same package as this class if you don't use an access specifier.

The following example shows how to declare an instance variable. Instance variables are usually designated as private, thus limiting the access to these variables to only method members of the same class.

```
class Demo {
   public static void main (String args[]) {

   }
}
class myClass {
   private int student;

}
```

The third difference between declaring a variable and declaring an instance variable is in the way both are initialized. You'll recall that *initialization* is the process of assigning a variable an initial value. You can initialize a variable when the variable is declared, as shown in this next statement:

```
int student = 12345;
```

However, some programmers initialize an instance variable by using the class constructor (see the next section).

Keep in mind that changes to an instance variable of one instance don't have any effect on the instance variable of a different instance. This means that if we declare two instances called `student` of the `myClass` class, each instance has its own `student` instance variable. A change to one instance variable doesn't change the other.

Constructor

A constructor is automatically called whenever an instance of the class is created. Technically, the constructor is called before the new operator completes its operation when declaring an instance of the class (see the section "Declaring an Instance of a Class"). Programmers use the constructor to initialize instance variables as well as to perform other tasks when an instance of the class is created.

A constructor is defined nearly the same way as how you define a method member of a class, with three exceptions. First, the name of the constructor must be the same name as the class. Second, the constructor has an implicit return value, which is the class type. That is, you are not permitted to define a return value for a constructor. Third, the constructor must be designated with any access specifier or no access specifier.

The following example illustrates how to define a constructor. This example defines the myClass class that contains an instance variable called student and a method member called myClass(). This method member is the constructor for the class because it has the same name as the class. The constructor is designated as having public access. The constructor in this example initializes the instance variable student with a student ID number.

```
class Demo {
   public static void main (String args[]) {

   }
}
class myClass {
   private int student;
   myClass (){
      student = 12345;
   }
}
```

You don't have to define a constructor for your program unless there is a need to execute statements when an instance is created. If you don't define a constructor, Java uses a default constructor.

You can define multiple constructors for your program, with each one having a different argument list. For example, a constructor without an argument list might initialize instance variables with default values. Another constructor with an argument list might initialize instance variables with values passed to the constructor when the instance is declared.

Declaring an Instance of a Class

Remember that a class definition is like a cookie cutter and not a cookie. This means that you must use the class definition to make a real copy of the class, which is called an *instance* of the class. You do this by declaring an instance of the class within your program.

When an instance is declared, Java reserves memory for all instance variables and then calls the constructor. Initial values are then stored in memory, if the constructor initializes instance variables. Also, any other statements within the constructor are executed.

Here's how to declare an instance of a class. This statement probably looks familiar because it is basically the same statement used to declare an array (see Chapter 5).

```
myClass x = new myClass();
```

Three tasks occur in this statement. First, the `new` operator tells Java to reserve a block of memory for the instance. This block of memory is large enough to store instance variable(s). The `new` operator returns the address of that block of memory.

Second, a reference to an instance of `myClass` is declared, which is called `x`. The reference is declared by using the name of the class. This is called the *class type*. Finally, the third task is to assign the first address of the block of memory of the instance to the reference. The reference (in this case, `x`) is used anytime you want to refer to the instance within the program.

Although the previous example declared a reference and an instance of a class in one statement, these declarations can be placed in two statements, as shown in the next example. The first statement declares the reference, and the second statement assigns the instance to the reference.

```
myClass x;
x = new myClass();
```

Programmers declare a reference separately from the declaration of an instance of a class in order to assign different instances to the same reference, unless the reference is declared final. Any reference declared final cannot be reassigned a value. You'll see how this is done in the next example.

Notice that the next example begins by declaring three references to `myClass`. The next two statements declare an instance of `myClass`, which is assigned to reference `x` and reference `y`, respectively.

Next, the reference `x` is assigned to the reference `current`. Both `x` and `current` refer the same instance of the class because the value of `x` points to the memory block that contains the instance. This memory address, stored in reference `x`, is copied (assigned) to reference `current`. This mean that both `x` and `current` can be used to access members of the same instance because both point to the same address in memory.

The last statement assigns the value of reference `y` to `current`. The value of `y` is the memory address of the second instance of `myClass`. Both `y` and `current` point to the same memory address, which contains the second instance of the class. Programmers use this technique to switch between instances of classes.

```
myClass x,y,current;
x = new myClass();
y = new myClass();
current = x;
current = y;
```

In the previous examples, the `new` operator is followed by the class name. The class name actually calls the constructor of the class (see the section titled "Constructor"). The `new` operator dynamically allocates memory for the instance of the class. *Dynamic allocation* means that Java reserves memory at run time rather than at compile time. However, it is possible that sufficient memory isn't available in the computer that runs your program. If this occurs, an exception is thrown by the `new` operator (see Chapter 9).

Accessing Members of a Class

Once an instance of a class is declared, a reference to the instance is used to access members of the class. To access a member of the class, you use the name of the reference followed by the dot operator and then the name of the member. You can see how this is done in the next example.

The following example defines the `myClass` class, which has three members. These are an instance variable called `student`, a constructor, and a method member called `print()`. The instance variable is assigned a student ID by the constructor when an instance is declared. The instance is then used to call the `print()` method member. The `print()` method member displays the student ID on the screen.

```
class Demo {
   public static void main (String args[]) {
      myClass x = new myClass();
       x.print();
   }
}
class myClass {
```

```
      int student;
      myClass(){
         student = 1234;
      }
      public void print(){
         System.out.println("Hello, student: " + student);
   }
}
```

Overloading Member Methods

In Chapter 6, you learned that Java identifies a method by its method signature, which is a combination of the method name and argument list. This means that two methods can have the same name and different arguments.

The same is true about the method members of a class. That is, a class can have multiple methods that have the same name as long as each method member's argument list is unique within the class definition. Two method members of the same class cannot have the same method signature. However, methods that are members of different classes can have the same method signature. When there are two method members of the same class that have the same method name, programmers say that the second method *overloads* the first method.

As you'll recall from Chapter 6, programmers overload methods to reduce the number of methods that need to be learned. Typically, methods that have the same name perform variations of the same task. Instead of remembering a different name for each variation, a programmer only needs to remember one method name and the appropriate argument list.

This is illustrated in the next example, where two method members have the name `print()`. One version doesn't have an argument list and displays a default greeting whenever it is called. The other version enables the programmer to enter text that will be incorporated into the message. As you can see, the programmer has the option to use the default greeting or to use a personal greeting.

```
class Demo {
   public static void main (String args[]) {
      myClass x = new myClass();
       x.print();
       x.print("Bob");
   }
}
class myClass {
```

```
  public void print(){
     System.out.println("Hello.");
   }
  public void print(String str){
     System.out.println("Hello, " + str);
   }

}
```

Overloading a Constructor

A common use of overloading a method is to overload a constructor. Previously in this chapter, you learned that a constructor is used with the `new` operator to create an instance of a class. The default constructor doesn't have an argument list. Programmers overload a constructor by defining a constructor that has a parameter list. This is called a *parameterized constructor*. You can use any number and type of arguments in the argument of a constructor.

There are many reasons for overloading a constructor. A common reason is to enable a programmer to override values used to initialize instance variables. This is illustrated in the next example, where two constructors are defined. One constructor initializes the instance variable to zero, and the other constructor initializes the instance variable to whatever value is passed to the constructor by the programmer.

Two instances of `myClass` are created in this example. The first instance is declared using the default value to initialize the instance variable. The second instance uses the parameterized constructor, which is passed the number 354. The value of the instance variable is then displayed on the screen.

```
class Demo {
   public static void main (String args[]) {
      myClass x = new myClass();
      myClass y = new myClass(354);
       x.print();
       y.print();
   }
}
class myClass {
     int student;
     myClass(){
        student = 0;
     }
     myClass(int ID){
        student = ID;
```

```
        }
        public void print(){
            System.out.println("Hello, student: " + student);
    }
}
```

The `this` Keyword

A method member of a class has implicit access to instance variables and other method members of the class that defines a method member. In previous examples throughout this book, you've seen how a method member of a class is used to initialize an instance variable of the same class.

There will likely be occasions when you'll need to declare a variable in the definition of a method member that has the same variable name as an instance variable. A variable that is declared within a method member is called a *local variable*. Whenever a statement in a method member references a variable name, Java uses the local variable before an instance variable if both variables have the same name.

However, you can tell Java to use an instance variable rather than a local variable of the same name by using the `this` keyword. The `this` keyword is a way to refer to the object of the class within the class definition.

Using the `this` keyword can be confusing to understand. However, remember how you access a class member in your program. First, you declare a reference to an instance of the class, and then you use the name of the reference whenever you want to refer to a member of the class.

For example, suppose we created an instance of a class and assigned it to the reference `newClass`. Here's how you would access the `display()` method member of `newClass`, assuming such method member was defined in the class definition:

```
newClass.display()
```

In essence, you do the same thing when you want to access a class member from a method member of the same class. However, the reference to the class is implied. That is, you don't need to make reference to the instance of the class when accessing another member of the class. Java assumes that you want to use a member of the class.

However, when there is a conflict, such as two variables having the same name, you must explicitly tell Java which one you want to use. If you want to use the local variable, simply use the name of the variable. If you want to use the instance variable, you'll need to reference the instance in the statement that accesses the instance variable.

No doubt you see a problem. There can be many instances of the class, each having a different reference. Therefore, you cannot refer to the reference of the instance in the class definition. The solution is to use the `this` keyword in place of the reference name. The `this` keyword tells Java to use the current instance.

The following example illustrates how to use the `this` keyword in a Java program. This example defines a class called `myClass` that has three members: the instance variable `student` and two method members. The first method member is a constructor that is used to initialize the instance variable. The second method member is called `display()`. The `display()` method member declares a local variable also called `student`, which is initialized with a value that is different from the value of the instance value. Also in the `display()` method are two statements that display each variable on the screen. One statement displays the local variable, and the other uses the `this` keyword to display the instance variable.

```
class Demo {
   public static void main (String args [] ) {
        myClass x = new myClass ();
         x.display();
    }
}
class myClass {
    int student;
    myClass(){
       student = 1234;
    }
    void display() {
       int student = 12;
       System.out.println("Hello, student " + student);
       System.out.println("Hello, student " +
this.student);
    }
}
```

Garbage Collection

Your program can access members of a class as long as the instance of the class remains in scope, which you learned about previously in this chapter. Although an instance may go out of scope, the instance remains in memory until Java *garbage collection* removes it.

In some computer languages, such as C and C++, a programmer can remove any instance or data type from memory that is declared dynamically, such as you do using the new operator in Java. For example, the delete keyword instructs C and C++ to remove an object or data type from memory and make that memory available for other use.

You cannot explicitly direct Java to remove from memory an instance or anything else that is declared dynamically. Instead, Java removes it behind the scenes without your intervention. The good thing about garbage collection is that you won't forget to release unneeded memory. The not-so-good thing is that you have no control over when memory is released. This can become problematic if you have a memory-intense program and a limited amount of available memory on the computer that runs your program. Simply said, you cannot release memory for use by another part of your program. Only Java can release memory at Java's own schedule.

The finalize() Method

The finalize() method is another special method member of a class. The finalize() method member is called immediately before memory allocated for an instance is released by Java's garbage collection. You might be asking yourself whether the finalize() method member is an alternative to using a destructor in your class definition. The answer is no.

A destructor, as you'll recall, is a special method member that is called when an instance of a class goes out of scope. Although an instance goes out of scope, the instance remains in memory until it is picked up by Java's garbage collection.

The finalize() method member is called after the instance goes out of scope and immediately before the instance is picked up by Java's garbage collection. That is, the finalize() method member is called after the destructor is called and before the instance is removed from memory.

Programmers place statements within the finalize() method member that release resources, such as those acquired to connect the program to a network or to a file.

The following example shows how to define a finalize() method member of a class. You must designate the finalize() method member as having protected access by using the protected access specifier, and you must use void as the return type because finalize() does not return any value after it executes. Any statement that you want executed when finalize() is called must be placed within the body of the finalize() method member.

```
class Demo {
   public static void main (String args[]) {
      myClass x = new myClass();
   }
```

```
}
class myClass {
     int student;
     myClass(){
        student = 0;
     }
     protected void finalize (){
        //Place statements here
   }
}
```

Inner Classes

A class definition can contain the definition of another class. This is called *nested classes*. The two kinds of nested classes are static nested classes and nonstatic nested classes.

A static nested class is one that is designed with a static modifier and cannot directly access members of its enclosing class. Instead, it must create an instance of the enclosing class and use the instance to access members of the enclosing class. Nested classes are rarely used.

A nonstatic class is called an *inner* class and is commonly used by programmers. An inner class is defined within an enclosing class. The enclosing class is referred to as an *outer* class. An inner class has access to all members of the outer class directly without having to declare an instance of the outer class.

The inner class can contain instance variables and method members. However, only the inner class knows those members. The outer class can access members of an inner class by declaring an instance of the inner class and then using the instance to access members of the inner class. The inner class is not accessible from outside the outer class definition. This means that you cannot declare an instance of an inner class within your program. An instance of an inner class can only be declared within the definition of the outer class.

The following example illustrates how this is done. This example defines a class called `Outer`. Within the `Outer` class definition is the definition of the `Inner` class. You'll notice there isn't anything unusual about these definitions. They look similar to other class definitions used in this chapter.

However, notice how the instance variable `student` is displayed on the screen in this example. The instance variable `student` is declared as a member of the `Outer` class, as is the `display()` member method. The `display()` method member doesn't contain statements that directly display the instance variable on the screen. Instead, the `display()` method member declares an instance of the `Inner` class and calls the `Inner` class's `print()` member method, which directly displays the instance variable. The `Inner` class can directly access the `Outer` class's instance variable.

```
class Demo {
    public static void main (String args [] ) {
        Outer outer = new Outer();
        outer.display();
    }
}
class Outer {
    int student = 1234;
    void display() {
        Inner inner = new Inner();
        inner.print();
    }
    class Inner {
        void print() {
            System.out.println("Hello, student " + student);
        }
    }
}
```

Static Initializers

Sometimes, programmers define a class whose sole purpose is to initialize variables that are used by other classes in the program. Programmers call such a class a *static initializer*. A static intitalizer class contains static variables that can be used within a program directly without declaring an instance of the class. This is Java's way of effectively enabling a program to create a global variable, which is a variable that can be used throughout the program.

You reference a static variable by using the class name and the name of the static variable separated by a dot, as shown in the following example. This example defines the `DefaultValues` class. This class contains the static variable `passingGrade`, which is initialized within the class. The `passingGrade` variable is then called within the `main()` method and displayed on the screen.

```
class DefaultValues {
   static int passingGrade = 70;
}
```

```
class demo {
  public static void main(String args[]) {
       System.out.println(
            "The value of the passing grade is : " + DefaultValues.
 passingGrade);
  }
}
```

Packages

Programmers organize classes into groups, and each group is stored in a package. The package provides naming and visibility control in addition to being an efficient way to manage classes. Programmers reference a package at the top of their source code whenever a class contained in the package is used in the source.

Before showing you how to access classes stored in a package, let's explore how to define your own package. You create a package by including the `package` statement as the first statement in your Java source file. Classes defined within the source file become members of the package.

The `package` statement looks like this:

```
package MyPackage;
```

This statement creates a package called `MyPackage` and places any classes defined in the source code into this package when the source code is compiled. If you exclude the `package` statement in your source code, Java uses the default package to store your classes, which is the package used in examples throughout this book. The default package has no name. Programmers use the default package for sample programs, but they create their own packages for real-world applications.

You can use the same `package` statement in multiple source code files in order to have the classes stored in those files placed in the same package. Programmers typically have many source code files whose classes are stored in the same package.

Java stores a package in a directory of the same name on your disk drive. This means that the `MyPackage` package is stored in the directory MyPackage. The name of the directory must exactly match the name of the package, and the package must always reside in that directory.

It is not unusual for programmers to create a hierarchy of packages, where a parent package is associated with a child package. You will see this done all the time with the Java class library. The Java class library consists of many hierarchical packages. For example, Java GUI classes are stored with the following hierarchy:

```
java.awt.image
```

In this case, `java` is the parent package, and `awt` is the child package, which is also a parent package to `image`.

You can create your own hierarchy of packages by specifying the package hierarchy in the `package` statement. Each package in the hierarchy must be separated by a dot, as shown here:

```
package MyPackage.MyDaughter.MyGranddaughter
```

A directory structure is created to replicate the package hierarchy. Each package in the hierarchy gets its own directory/subdirectory. For example, the `MyPackage` hierarchy is stored in the following directory structure:

```
C:\MyPackage\MyDaugher\MyGraddaughter
```

The names of these directories must exactly match the names of these packages.

Using a Package

You access classes stored in a package by using an `import` statement at the top of your source code. The `import` statement must contain the name of the package and the class(es) you want to use in your source code.

Let's say that you want to use the `Student` class that is contained in the `MyPackage` package. You'd write the following `import` statement at the top of your source code:

```
import MyPackage.Student
```

The `import` statement tells Java where to reference the class. Once a class is imported into your source code, you can use the name of the class to reference it. You don't need to reference the package name.

In real-world applications, you'll probably want to import all the classes of a package rather than a few classes. You do this by using an asterisk rather than a class name in the `import` statement. Using the asterisk may increase compile time, but it will have no effect on run-time performance. Here's how you import all the classes in the `MyPackage` package:

```
import MyPackage.*
```

You can reference a class within a package without having to import the package by using the fully qualified class name in a statement within your source code. A fully qualified class name consists of the package name, a dot, and the class name. Let's say that the `Student` class in `MyPackage` has a method member called `display()`, and we want to call that method within our source code. Here's how this is done:

```
MyPackage.Student.display();
```

Notice that the fully qualified class name is used rather than an `import` statement. Using the `import` statement or using the fully qualified class name produces the same results.

You reference a package hierarchy in the `import` statement the same way you reference a single package, except you use all the package names in the hierarchy, separating each one with a dot.

CLASSPATH

Packages can cause you problems when compiling and running a program because of the way Java locates packages. Java uses the `CLASSPATH` environment variable to locate packages. If the directory containing a package is not referenced in the `CLASSPATH`, the package won't be found by Java.

An environment variable is a memory location allocated by an operating system whose contents are available to programs running within the operating system. Some environment variables are defined automatically by the operating system. Other environment variables are defined by a program when the program is installed. And still other environment variables are defined by a programmer. The `CLASSPATH` environment variable is defined when you install Java on your computer.

Previously in this chapter, you learned that the default package is used whenever you don't specify a package in your source code. The default package is stored in the default current working directory, and the default current working directory is on the `CLASSPATH`. This is why you can compile and run programs without explicitly specifying a package.

As you'll recall, each package is stored in its own directory. That directory must be included on the `CLASSPATH` in order for your source code to use the package; otherwise, you won't be able to compile your source code because the compiler won't know where to look for the package.

The `CLASSPATH` sets the top of the class hierarchy, so you must include the top directory of your package hierarchy in the `CLASSPATH`. You do so by editing the `CLASSPATH`. In Windows, you create or edit an environment variable by following these steps:

1. Select the Control Panel.
2. Select Systems.
3. Select the Advanced tab.
4. Select Environment Variables.
5. Select New to insert the `CLASSPATH` environment variable, if it doesn't exist. You do this by entering a variable name (`CLASSPATH`) and a value, which is the path to the package.

6. If CLASSPATH already exists, highlight CLASSPATH and select Edit. Then place the path to the package at the end of the CLASSPATH.
7. Click OK.

Packages and Access Protection

Previously in this chapter, you learned how access specifiers are used to control access to members of a class. Packages provide a mechanism for controlling access, too. A class is a container that encapsulates members of the class. A package is also a container that encapsulates classes and subordinates packages.

Packages provide four kinds of access control to classes contained in a package:

- Control of subclasses in the same package
- Control of no subclasses in the same package
- Control of subclasses in a different package
- Control of classes that are not in the same package or not a subclass

The following table shows the effect access specifiers have on packages.

	Same Package	**Same Package, Subclass**	**Same Package, No Subclass**	**Different Package, Subclass**	**Different Package, No Subclass**
No Modifier	Yes	Yes	Yes	No	No
Public	Yes	Yes	Yes	Yes	Yes
Protected	Yes	Yes	Yes	Yes	No
Private	Yes	No	No	No	No

Quiz

1. What is an instance variable?
2. What is the difference between an instance and an object?
3. What is a class?
4. What is a constructor?
5. What is the difference between a destructor and the `finalize()` method member of a class?
6. What does overloading a method member mean?

7. How do you declare an instance of a class?
8. What is the purpose of an access specifier?
9. Can a constructor have an argument list?
10. What is a common reason for overloading a constructor?

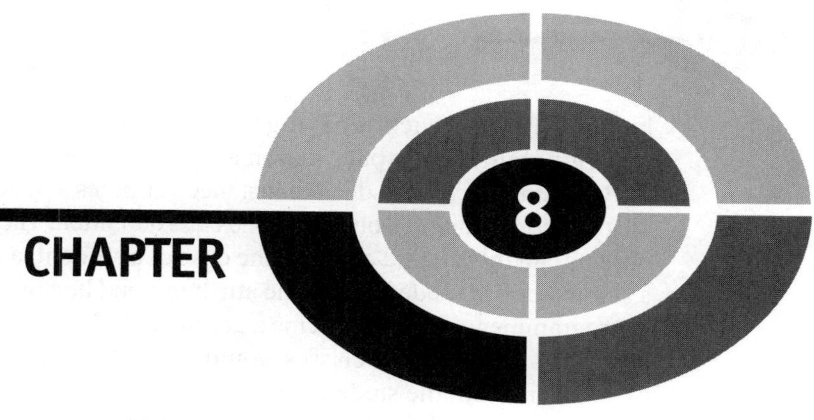

Inheritance

Some say that inheriting wealth is the best thing that can happen to you, because you don't have to scrimp and save to get what you want. Instead, someone else has done that for you, letting you focus on spending the money. Inheritance has a similar effect when you're writing a Java program. Although you'll still need to count your pennies, you can utilize someone else's classes. Instead of writing all the classes for yourself, you can focus on creating only classes that no one else has written. You'll learn how to inherit classes in this chapter.

What Is Inheritance?

In the previous chapter, you learned that a class definition defines attributes and behaviors of a real-world object. Attributes are represented as instance variables, and behaviors are represented as method members of a class.

Some objects have some things in common yet other things that are unique to each kind of object. For example, a graduate student and an undergraduate student are both students. That is, they have the same attributes and behaviors of all students. Yet a graduate student also has attributes and behaviors that are different from other kinds of students, such as paying tuition based on the graduate per-credit rate. An undergraduate student pays tuition at the undergraduate per-credit rate.

Programmers tend to declare instance variables and define method members that are common to multiple objects in one class definition. Then, classes that define related objects can inherit that class. In the case of a student, a programmer would define a student class that defines all the attributes and behaviors common to all students. A programmer would also define a graduate student class and an undergraduate student class. Both of these classes would inherit the common attributes and behaviors of a student from the student class.

From a practical viewpoint, a programmer would have to replicate attributes and behaviors common to all students in both the graduate student class and the undergraduate student class if the student classes were not inherited. This amounts to redundant code, which is something to avoid because it unnecessarily makes your program complex and requires you to maintain the same code in more than one place in the program.

When to Use Inheritance

Programmers follow a simple rule to determine when inheritance is appropriate for a program. The rule is called "is a," and it requires an object to have a relationship with another object before it can inherit the object.

The "is a" rule asks the question, Is object A an object B? If so, then object A can inherit object B. If not, then object A should not inherit object B. Technically, there is nothing prohibiting one class from inheriting another class, but each inheritance should pass the "is a" rule.

Let's apply the "is a" rule to the student example discussed in the previous section of this chapter. The three objects in this example are student, graduate student, and undergraduate student.

First, apply the "is a" rule to the graduate student object. You do this by asking the question, Is a graduate student a student? Sure is! Therefore, the graduate student can inherit the student object.

Next, apply the "is a" rule to the undergraduate student object by asking, Is an undergraduate student a student? That's also true. Therefore, the undergraduate student can inherit the student object.

Now let's look at a slightly different example. Suppose you want to have the graduate student object inherit the undergraduate student object. Will this pass the "is a" test? In order to answer this question, you need to ask, Is a graduate student an undergraduate student? The answer is no. Therefore, you know that the graduate student should not inherit the undergraduate student.

Inside Inherence

You cause a class to inherit another class by using the keyword `extends` in the class definition. Think of this as telling Java that the second class is extending the class definition of the first class. The class that is being inherited is called a *superclass*. Some programmers also call this a *parent*. The class doing the inheriting is called a *subclass* or a *child*.

The keyword `extends` is placed in the class definition of the subclass. Here is the form for using the `extends` keyword. Class `B` is inheriting some or all the attributes and behaviors of class `A`, depending on the access specifier (see Chapter 7).

```
class B extends class A {
}
```

The following example illustrates how to inherit a class. This example contains two class definitions. First is the `Student` class definition and the second is the `GraduateStudent` class definition. The `GraduateStudent` class is a subclass and inherits the `Student` class by using the `extends` keyword, which is placed to the right of the class name.

```
class Student {

}

class GraduateStudent extends Student {

}
```

Accessing Members of an Inherited Class

As you'll recall from Chapter 7, members of a class can be accessed based on its access specifier. There are three access specifiers: public, private, and protected. A member of any class can access a member designated as public. A member designated as private can only be accessed by a method member of its own class. A member designated as protected can be accessed by method members of its own class and by method members of subclasses that inherit the superclass.

This may seem confusing, so let's take a look at an example so you can see how this works. This example declares two classes other than the Java application class called demo. These are the Student class and the GraduateStudent class. The GraduateStudent class inherits the Student class.

```
class Demo {
   public static void main (String args[]) {
      GraduateStudent gs = new GraduateStudent();
      gs.display();
   }
}
class Student {
   private int studentID;
   Student (){
      studentID = 12345;
   }
   protected void display(){
      System.out.println("Student ID: " + studentID);
   }
}

class GraduateStudent extends Student {

}
```

There are two members of the Student class besides the constructor. These are an instance variable called studentID and a display() method member that displays the value of the instance variable on the screen. The constructor (see Chapter 7) is used to initialize the instance variable.

The GraduateStudent class doesn't have any members, but it can access public and protected members of the Student class because the GraduateStudent class inherits the Student class. This means that an instance of the GraduateStudent class can access the display() member method of the Student class, just as if the display() method member was a member of the GraduateStudent class.

This is illustrated in statements within the main() method of the application. The first statement declares an instance of the GraduateStudent class. The second statement uses the instance to call the display() method member. Looking at the main() method, you'd think that the display() method is a member of the GraduateStudent class, when in fact the display() method is a member of the Student class.

The Superclass Can Be Instantiated

There is practically no difference between a superclass and a subclass class, except that a subclass has access to public and protected members of the superclass. This means you can declare an instance of the superclass without having to declare an instance if the subclass.

Let's modify the previous example to illustrate how this is done. This example is practically the same as the previous one. The `GraduateStudent` class inherits the `Student` class. However, we don't declare an instance of the `GraduateStudent` class in the `main()` method. Instead, we declare an instance of the `Student` class. We then proceed to call the `display()` method to display the value of the `studentID` instance variable on the screen.

```
class Demo {
   public static void main (String args[]) {
      Student s = new Student();
      s.display();
   }
}
class Student {
   private int studentID;
   Student (){
      studentID = 12345;
   }
   protected void display(){
      System.out.println("Student ID: " + studentID);
   }
}

class GraduateStudent extends Student {

}
```

One-way Inheritance

Inheritance is a one-way street. That is, a subclass can access public and protected members of the superclass, but the superclass cannot access members of the subclass. In fact, the superclass doesn't know the existence of the subclass.

This is important to keep in mind whenever you use inheritance in your program; otherwise, you might use a method member of the superclass to interact with members of the subclass, only to discover that you receive an error when you compile your program.

Calling Constructors

At least two constructors are involved whenever a subclass inherits a superclass. Both of these classes have a constructor. As you'll recall from Chapter 7, every class has a default constructor that is automatically called when you create an instance of a class. This is true even if you don't define a constructor in your class. A default constructor is defined for every class as part of the Java language. It has no arguments. However, if a constructor is declared in a class, then the default constructor doesn't exist.

Java calls the constructor of the subclass and the superclass when you declare an instance of the subclass. That is, both constructors execute. Java calls the constructor of the superclass first and then calls the constructor of the subclass. Only if a constructor does not explicitly invoke another constructor does Java implicitly invoke the superclass constructor automatically. The implicit call is `super()`, so the superclass must define a constructor with no arguments.

As you'll see later in this chapter, you use multilevel inheritance in your program. This means a superclass is inherited by a subclass, and the subclass is inherited by another subclass. Each class has at least one default constructor, and all of them are executed whenever an instance of the lowest subclass is declared.

Java executes each constructor beginning with the constructor of the superclass, followed by the constructor of the first subclass, and then the constructor of the second subclass. This is true only if all classes in the inheritance chain have constructors that have no arguments.

Using the `super` Keyword

On occasion, you'll need to explicitly reference the members of the superclass from a method member of a subclass. For example, the superclass may have overloaded constructors. As you'll recall from Chapter 7, a class definition can define two or more constructors, each of which has a different method signature. One constructor might not have an argument list, whereas another constructor may have an argument list.

Typically, the constructor of a superclass is called from within a constructor of a subclass using the following statement:

```
super ();
```

This statement tells Java to run the constructor of the superclass that doesn't contain an argument list. Here's a similar statement that tells Java to run a constructor of the superclass that has an argument list that consists of one integer:

```
super (5555);
```

The `super` keyword is used to refer to a member of a superclass other than the constructor. Let's suppose you want to call the superclass's `display()` method from within a subclass's `display()` method. Here's how this is written:

```
super.display();
```

You'll notice that the keyword `super` is used in the same way a reference to an instance is used to refer to a member of a class within your program.

The following example illustrates how to use the `super` keyword within a Java program. This example defines the `GraduateStudent` class and `Student` class, which you've seen used in previous examples in this chapter.

The `Student` class defines two constructors, both of which initialize the instance variable. The first constructor uses a default value for the initialization. The second constructor uses the value of the argument list as the initialization value. The second constructor is said to *overload* the first constructor. The `Student` class also defines a `display()` method member that is used to display the value of the instance variable on the screen.

The `GraduateStudent` class defines a constructor and defines a `display()` method member. The `GraduateStudent` constructor contains one statement that uses the `super` keyword to call the overloaded constructor of the `Student` class, passing it the value 5555. The `GraduateStudent` display member method also has one statement. This statement uses the `super` keyword to tell Java to run the `display()` member method of the `Student` class, which displays the value of the instance variable on the screen. Here's the value displayed on the screen:

```
Student ID: 5555
```

```
class Demo {
   public static void main (String args[]) {
      GraduateStudent gs = new GraduateStudent ();
      gs.display();
   }
}
class Student {
```

```
    private int studentID;
    Student (){
       studentID = 12345;
    }
    Student (int sID){
       studentID = sID;
    }
    protected void display(){
       System.out.println("Student ID: " + studentID);
    }
}
class GraduateStudent extends Student {
  GraduateStudent(){
     super (5555);
  }
  public void display() {
    super.display();
  }
}
```

Multilevel Inheritance

As mentioned previously in this chapter, you can use multilevel inheritance in your program. Multilevel inheritance enables a subclass to inherit members of more than one superclass. Programmers use multilevel inheritance to group together simpler objects into more complex objects.

Some programming languages, such as C++, have various kinds of multiple inheritance. However, Java has one kind of multiple inheritance called *multilevel inheritance*. Multilevel inheritance limits a subclass to inherit from one superclass. However, that superclass can itself be a subclass of another superclass.

Let's take a look at an example so you can clearly see this relationship. We'll define three classes: the `Person` class, the `Student` class, and the `GraduateStudent` class. Notice that each of these classes pass the "is a" test. That is, a graduate student is a student, and a student is a person. This means that we can relate together these classes using inheritance. Classes that don't pass the "is a" test shouldn't be related together.

Multilevel inheritance limits a subclass to inherit from one superclass. However, we need the `GraduateStudent` class to inherit members of both the `Student` class and the `Person` class. We can work around the limits of multilevel inheritance by first creating an inheritance relationship between the `Person` class and the

Student class. That is, the Student class will inherit the Person class. The Student class has access to all its own members and access to the public and protected members of the Person class.

Next, we create an inheritance relationship between the Student class and the GraduateStudent class. The GraduateStudent class inherits the public and protected members of the Student class, which includes access to the public and protected members of the Person class, because the Student class has already inherited access to those members by inheriting the Person class.

This example creates a two-level inheritance. The first level consists of the Person class and the Student class. The Person class is the superclass, and the Student class is the subclass. The second level consists of the Student class and the GraduateStudent class, where the Student class is the superclass and the GraduateStudent class is the subclass.

You can have any number of levels of inheritance in your program as long as each class passes the "is a" test. However, programmers try to avoid using more than three levels because each level adds a degree of complexity to the program and makes it a little more difficult to maintain and update.

The following program illustrates the previous example. This program defines the Person class, the Student class, and the GraduateStudent class. The Person class contains an instance variable called name, a constructor that initializes the instance variable, and a method member that displays the instance variable on the screen. The Student class is similar to the Person class, but its instance variable stores a student ID. The GraduateStudent class has one member—a method member called display(). The display() method member calls display() method members of the Person class and the Student class.

Statements in the main() method declare an instance of the GraduateStudent class and call the display() method member of that class to display the name and student ID of the student. Each of these are processed behind the scenes by the corresponding class.

```
class Demo {
   public static void main (String args[]) {
      GraduateStudent gs = new GraduateStudent ();
      gs.display();
   }
}
class Person {
  private String name;
  Person(){
     name = "Bob Smith";
  }
  protected void displayName(){
```

```
        System.out.println("Student Name: " + name);
    }
}
class Student extends Person {
    private int studentID;
    Student (){
        studentID = 12345;
    }
    protected void displayStudentID(){
        System.out.println("Student ID: " + studentID);
    }
}
class GraduateStudent extends Student {
    protected void display(){
        displayName();
        displayStudentID();
    }
}
```

Overriding Method Members Using Inheritance

Previously you learned that a method member enables an instance of a class to perform a specific kind of behavior, such as displaying instance variables on the screen. A subclass inherits behavior from a superclass when a subclass can access method members of the superclass. You saw this in the previous example, where the `GraduateStudent` class called method members of its superclass to display instance variables.

Sometimes the behavior of a method member of a superclass doesn't meet the needs of a subclass. For example, the manner in which a superclass's method member displays an instance variable isn't exactly the way the subclass wants the instance variable displayed.

In this case, a programmer defines another version of the superclass's method member within the subclass and includes statements that enhance the original behavior of the superclass's method member. Programmers referred to this as *overriding* a method member.

Don't confuse overriding a method member with overloading a method, which you learned about in Chapter 6. Overloading a method requires you to define a method that has the same method name but a different argument list than a method that is already defined. That is, each method has a different signature. Overriding a method member requires you to use the same method name and the same argument list as a method member defined in a subclass's superclass.

You might think that having two method members with the same signature will confuse Java. It won't, and here's why: Java uses method members of the class whose instances call the method. Therefore, if you use an instance of the subclass in your program to call the method member, Java uses the subclass's version of the method member.

Let's take a look at an example to see how this works. The following program is a variation of the program used in the previous example. Here's what is happening in this program: three classes are defined. They are the `Person` class, the `Student` class, and the `GraduateStudent` class. The `Person` class and the `Student` class both declare an instance variable, initialize the instance variable, and define a method member called `display()` that displays its instance variable. Notice that these instance variables are designed with the protected access specifier. This means they can be accessed directly by the subclass.

Neither version of the `display()` method member is suitable for the `GraduateStudent` class. Therefore, the `GraduateStudent` class overrides the `display()` method member. Statements within the new version of the `display()` method directly access instance variables of the `Person` class and the `Student` class.

An instance of the `GraduateStudent` class is declared in the `main()` method, and the instance is used to call the `display()` method. Java uses the `display()` method member defined in the `GraduateStudent` class.

```
class Demo {
   public static void main (String args[]) {
      GraduateStudent gs = new GraduateStudent ();
      gs.display();
   }
}
class Person {
   protected String name;
   Person(){
      name = "Bob Smith";
   }
   void display(){
     System.out.println("Person Class: " + name);
  }
}
class Student extends Person {
   protected int studentID;
```

```
   Student (){
      studentID = 12345;
   }
    void display(){
     System.out.println("Student Class: " + studentID);
   }
}
class GraduateStudent extends Student {
   void display(){
     System.out.println("Graduate Student Class:");
     System.out.println("Name:" + name);
     System.out.println("Student ID: " + studentID);
   }
}
```

Dynamic Method Dispatch

Dynamic method dispatch might seem to be a term you need four years at MIT to understand. However, the concept of dynamic method dispatch is rather simply to understand. Let's begin by translating this term into everyday English.

The word *dynamic* refers to doing something when the program runs as opposed to when the program is compiled. You've seen this word used previously in this book when you learned how to dynamically declare an object (that is, declaring memory for an object at run time rather than compile time). *Method dispatch* simply means the program is calling a method member of a class. Therefore, dynamic method dispatch means deciding which method member to call when your program runs rather than making that decision when your program is compiled.

The method member that we're talking about is a method member of a subclass that overrides a method member of a superclass. You learned how to override method members in the previous section of this chapter.

You call a method member by using a reference to its instance, the dot operator, and the name of the method member, which you learned how to do in this chapter. For example, here is how to call the `display()` method member of the `Person` class:

```
Person p = new Person ();
p.display();
```

Suppose that the `Person` class is a superclass, and its subclass (called the `Student` class) needs to modify the behavior of the `display()` method member. The `Student` class does this by overriding the `display()` method member. You saw how to do this in the previous section of this chapter. You determine which version of the `display()` method member to call by referencing the appropriate instance.

For example, you'd reference the instance of the Person class when calling the Person class's display() method member. Likewise, you'd reference the instance of the Student class when calling its display() method member. These calls are made at compile time.

Dynamic method dispatch enables you to use the same reference to call different versions of an overridden method member. These calls are made at run time. Let's discuss how this works.

In Chapter 7, you learned how to assign an instance of a class to a reference and then use the reference to call members of the instance. Typically, programmers declare a reference, declare an instance, and assign the instance to the reference all in one statement, as shown here:

```
Person p = new Person();
```

Alternatively, a reference can be declared in one statement, and the assignment of the instance to the reference happens in another statement, as illustrated here:

```
Person p;
p = new Person();
```

Java uses dynamic method dispatch when you declare a reference and then assign the reference with the reference of an instance whose method member you want to call. Throughout the program, you can switch references and thus call different versions of the overridden method member.

The following example illustrates how to call method members this way by using dynamic method dispatch:

```
class Demo {
   public static void main (String args[]) {
      Person temp;
      Person p = new Person ();
      Student s = new Student ();
      GraduateStudent gs = new GraduateStudent ();
      temp = p;
      temp.display();
      temp = s;
      temp.display();
      temp = gs;
      temp.display();
   }
}
class Person {
   protected String name;
   Person(){
      name = "Bob Smith";
```

```
    }
    void display(){
      System.out.println("Person Class: " + name);
   }
}
class Student extends Person {
    protected int studentID;
    Student (){
       studentID = 12345;
    }
     void display(){
      System.out.println("Student Class: " + studentID);
    }
}
class GraduateStudent extends Student {
    void display(){
      System.out.println("Graduate Student Class:");
      System.out.println("Name:" + name);
      System.out.println("Student ID: " + studentID);
    }
}
```

As you can see, the example defines three classes—the `Person` class, the `Student` class, and the `GraduateStudent` class. All three are the same classes used in the previous example in this chapter. The `Person` class defines a `display()` method member, and the other two classes override the `display()` method member.

Dynamic method dispatch occurs within the `main()` method, where the first statement declares a reference of the `Person` class called `temp`. The `temp` reference is later assigned references to instances of the `Person` class, the `Student` class, and the `GraduateStudent` class.

Remember that a reference points to the first member address of the instance. When a reference to an instance is assigned to the `temp` reference, the `temp` reference also points to the same instance. This is illustrated in the following statement of the preceding program:

```
temp = p;
```

Prior to this assignment, the program declares `p` as a reference to an instance of the `Person` class and assigns it an instance. Likewise, the program declares `temp` as a reference to an instance of the `Person` class. However, `temp` is not assigned an instance of the class. Instead, `temp` is a reference to nothing—that is until the program assigns it the reference `p`, at which time both the reference `temp` and `p` point to the same instance.

Once the `temp` reference is assigned another reference, the `temp` reference is used to access members of the instance, which in this program is calling the `display()` method member of the instance.

Abstract Classes

So far in this chapter, you have seen how a subclass can override a method member of its superclass. However, overriding the method member is optional for a subclass. There will be occasions when the superclass requires that a subclass override a method member.

Let's say that you want any class that inherits the `Person` class to define a `display()` method in order to display a person's name. Each subclass has it own way of displaying a person's name. For example, the `Student` class might use the student's first name, whereas the `GraduateStudent` class might use the graduate student's first name.

You could define a `display()` method member in the `Person` class with statements that display a person's name, but none of the subclasses will use this method member because each overrides the method with its own way of displaying this information to the user.

Another option is not to define the `display()` method member in the `Person` class and leave each subclass to define its own method member. The problem with this option is that the programmer writing a subclass has the option not to define such a method member.

The third and preferred alternative is to define a general `display()` method member in the `Person` class and let each subclass provide its own details within the `display()` method member in order to retrieve a person's name. A general method member is a method definition that contains a method name, and argument list, and return value, but no method body. Each subclass overrides this method member and provides its own method body. A subclass must override this method member. It cannot simply use the method member of the superclass.

The superclass that defines a general method member is called an *abstract* class, and the general method is called an *abstract* method member. You cannot declare an instance of an abstract class. All abstract classes must be superclasses.

You define an abstract class similarly to how you define any class, except you precede the class name with the keyword `abstract`. Within the abstract class definition, there must be at least one abstract method member. You declare an abstract method member similarly to how you define a method member, except the definition

begins with the keyword `abstract`. The following example shows how to define an abstract class and abstract method member:

```
abstract Person {
   abstract void display();
}
```

Notice there isn't a body defined for the `display()` method member because this version of the `display()` method member can never be called. Therefore, it doesn't make sense to place statements within the body of the method member.

The following example shows how to use an abstract class and abstract method member in a program. This example is very similar to other examples used throughout this chapter in that it defines a `Person` class, a `Student` class, and a `GraduateStudent` class.

What is different in this program is that the `Person` class is an `abstract` class, and the `display()` method member of that class is an abstract method. Another difference is that an instance of the `Person` class is not declared within the program. If we tried to declare an instance of the `Person` class, we'd receive a compiler error. Likewise, if the `Student` class and `GraduateStudent` class fail to define a `display()` method member, we'd also receive a compiler error.

```
class Demo {
   public static void main (String args[]) {
      Student s = new Student ();
      GraduateStudent gs = new GraduateStudent ();
      s.display();
      gs.display();
   }
}
abstract class Person {
   abstract void display();
}
class Student extends Person {
   protected int studentID;
   Student (){
      studentID = 12345;
   }
    void display(){
     System.out.println("Student Class: " + studentID);
   }
}
class GraduateStudent extends Student {
   void display(){
     System.out.println("Graduate Student Class:");
```

```
      System.out.println("Student ID: " + studentID);
   }
}
```

Although you cannot declare an instance of an abstract class, you can declare a reference to an abstract class and use the reference to point to instances of other appropriate classes. For example, the following statement is illegal because the Person class is an abstract class:

```
Person p = new Person();
```

However, the following statement is legal because you can declare a reference to the Person class even though the Person class is an abstract class:

```
Person p;
```

An abstract class can define nonabstract members. A nonabstract member can be accessed by a subclass of the abstract class. This is illustrated in the next example, where an instance variable called name is declared in the Person class, and the constructor of the Person class initializes the instance valuable. The Student class inherits the Person class and has access to the initialized instance variable.

```
abstract class Person {
   protected String name;
   Person(){
      name = "Bob Smith";
   }
   abstract void display();
}
class Student extends Person {
   protected int studentID;
   Student (){
      studentID = 12345;
   }
    void display(){
      System.out.println("Student Class: " + studentID);
      System.out.println("Student Class: " + name);
   }
}
```

The `final` Keyword and Inheritance

The final keyword has two uses in inheritance. First, the final keyword is used with a method member of a superclass to prevent a subclass from overriding the method member. The second use is to use the `final` keyword with a class to prevent the class from becoming a superclass (that is, to prevent another class from inheriting it).

Let's begin exploring the `final` keyword by using it to prevent a subclass from overriding a superclass's method member. Suppose that a superclass defines a method member that displays a warning message on the screen. In order to prevent subclasses from overriding this superclass's method member, we designate the method member as *final*. The keyword `final` tells Java that this is the final definition of the method member.

You designate a member method as final by preceding the method member definition with the keyword `final`, as shown here. Any attempt by a subclass to override the `warningMsg()` method member will result in a compiler error.

```
class Person {
   final void warningMsg(){
      System.out.println("Invalid Entry.");
   }
}
```

A class can inherit any other class. However, you can prevent your class from being inherited by preceding the name of the class with the keyword `final`. The keyword `final` tells Java that no class can inherit this class. This means that the only way to access members of the class is to declare an instance of the class within a program and use the instance to access its members.

The following example shows how to use the `final` keyword to prevent the `Person` class from being inherited by other classes:

```
final class Person {
   void warningMsg(){
      System.out.println("Invalid Entry.");
   }
}
```

The `Object` Class and Subclasses

Java defines a master superclass called the `Object` class that is automatically inherited by all other classes, including classes you define in your program. This means that your class is a subclass of the `Object` class without you having to inherit the `Object` class by using the `extends` keyword. This also means that your class can access method members defined in the `Object` class.

The `Object` class defines 11 member methods that are available to all classes you define. These are shown in Table 8-1.

Method Member	Description
`Object clone()`	Creates a new object of the object being cloned
`boolean equals(Object obj)`	Determines whether two objects are equal
`void finalize()`	Called before the garbage collector recycles an object
`Class getClass()`	Retrieves the class of an object at run time
`int hashCode()`	Returns the hash code of an object
`void notify()`	Resumes execution of a thread that is waiting for an object to be called
`void notifyAll()`	Resumes execution of all threads that are waiting for an object to be called
`String toString()`	Returns a string of the object

`void wait()`
`void wait(long milliseconds)`
`void wait(int nanoseconds)`
	Waits for another thread in order to call an object

Table 8-1 Method Members of the `Object` Class

Quiz

1. What is an abstract method member of a class?
2. Explain the "is a" rule of inheritance.
3. What is the purpose of the keyword `extends`?
4. What effect does the keyword `final` have on a method member?
5. What is a superclass?
6. What is an abstract class?
7. What is the `Object` class?
8. How can you prevent a class from being inherited?
9. What is the purpose of the keyword `super`?
10. What is multilevel inheritance?

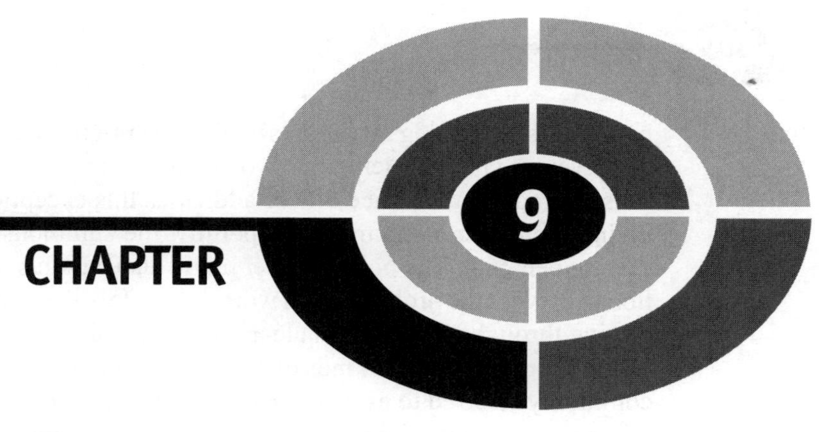

Exception Handling

It might be wishful thinking to suppose that every program you write will work perfectly each time it runs. The fact of the matter is, well-designed and craftily coded programs run nearly perfectly all the time, but that's not good enough for many applications that can't afford to have an error cause them to crash. There isn't any way to guarantee that errors won't occur. However, there is a way to have your program handle errors when they happen—by writing code that handles those exceptions to normal operations of your program. Programmers call this *exception handling*, which is the topic of this chapter.

What Is an Exception?

An exception is something other than what occurs normally. For example, most cars stop at red lights. A car that passes through a red light is an exception. Exception handling is something that addresses the exception, by either correcting the problem or preventing the problem from worsening. In the case of the erratic motorist who runs the red light, a police officer addresses this exception by stopping the car and giving the driver a summons. Hopefully, the summons corrects the driver's poor driving behavior. The police officer might also park his police car near the intersection to prevent the problem from worsening. Only the foolhardy would tempt fate by driving through a red light in clear view of a police officer.

In programming, two kinds of exceptions might occur with a program. These are commonly referred to as *compile errors* and *run-time errors*. A compile error usually occurs because the programmer made a fundamental mistake in the program, such as failing to include a semicolon at the end of a statement or mistyping the name of a variable. The compiler catches these kinds of errors.

A run-time error occurs when the program runs and is caused by a number of reasons, such as the program anticipating something that doesn't happen. Let's say that a program calculates the average grade of students who take a test. The instructor first enters into the program the number of students who sat for the test and then enters the test scores. The program tallies the scores and divides by the number of students who sat for the test. Suppose the instructor entered zero as the number of students who took the test, but entered the test scores. The program tries to divide by zero when calculating the average grade. This is illegal and causes a run-time error. In this case, the program anticipated that the instructor would enter a number greater than zero, which didn't happen.

Run-time errors are more serious than compile errors because the programmer is around to address a compiler error, but is likely not available when a run-time error occurs. Therefore, programmers must anticipate run-time problems and build into a program ways to address those problems automatically.

Exception Handlers

Programmers build into their programs *exception handlers* designed to react to run-time errors. An exception handler is a portion of the program that contains statements that execute automatically whenever a specific run-time error occurs while the program runs. Including an exception handler in a program is referred to as *exception handling*.

Not all computer languages support exception handling. Therefore, programmers are left to their own vices to handle run-time errors, usually by testing conditions that might generate a run-time error. For example, a programmer is likely to test whether an instructor input a valid entry (for example, zero number of students sitting for the

test) before processing the input. The program traps an invalid entry before the entry causes the run-time error.

A lot of conditions need to be tested for in a typical program, which makes this approach to exception handling complex and cumbersome for many programs to enact. Fortunately, Java supports exception handling, enabling a programmer to avoid having to identify conditions that have the potential of causing run-time errors and having to devise and code a test to catch errors before an error impacts the operation of the program.

Basic Exception Handling

Certain statements within a program are susceptible to causing a run-time error. These statements typically depend on a source outside of the control of the program, such as input from the person using the program or processing that could generate a run-time error.

Rather than test input received from outside sources and from processing, programmers tell Java to monitor those statements and then throw an exception if a run-time error occurs. Programmers provide Java with statements that are to be executed if an exception is thrown. This is referred to as *catching* an exception.

Statements that you want monitored by Java must appear within a try block. A try block consists of the keyword `try` followed by opening and closing braces, which define the block itself. Statements appearing within the opening and closing braces are monitored by Java for exceptions.

Statements that are executed when an exception is thrown by Java are placed within a catch block. A catch block consists of the keyword `catch` followed by opening and closing braces. Statements within the opening and closing braces are executed when an exception is thrown. A catch block responds to one kind of exception, which is specified within the catch block's parentheses. Multiple catch blocks are used to respond to multiple exceptions.

Every try block must have at least one catch block or a finally block. The catch block must appear immediately following its corresponding try block. Failure to pair them causes a compiler error.

Let's see how the try and catch blocks are used in a program. The following example uses a try block to monitor statements in the `main()` method. These statements declare and initialize variables and then perform division. Notice that the value of variable `b` is zero and that variable `b` is used as the divider in the division expression, which generates a run-time error.

At the end of the try block is a catch block. The catch block is said to catch an `ArithmeticException` that is represented by the variable `e`. Think of `ArithmeticException` as a type of exception and the variable `e` as the specific exception within this exception type. Exceptions of the `ArithmeticException` variety are errors in arithmetic. Therefore, `catch` catches arithmetic errors.

Code that is being monitored by the try block generates an arithmetic error when it tries to divide by zero. When Java detects this error, it throws a "divide by zero" exception and assigns it to variable `e`. The content of variable `e` is then used by the statement within the body of the catch block to display the exception on the screen. The following message is displayed on the screen when you run this program:

```
Error: java.lang.ArithmeticException: / by zero
```

```
class Demo {
   public static void main (String args[]) {
      try {
         int a = 10, b = 0, c;
         c = a/b;
      } catch (ArithmeticException e) {
           System.out.println("Error: " + e);
      }
   }
}
```

Multiple Catch Blocks

In the real world, a series of statements might generate more than one kind of runtime error. Therefore, programmers use multiple catch blocks, each one designed to catch a specific type of exception.

Multiple catch blocks must immediately follow the try block where the exception might be thrown. Also, each of those catch blocks must follow one another, which is illustrated in the next example.

When an exception occurs, Java throws the exception to each catch block in the order the catch blocks appear beneath the related try block. Let's say there are two catch blocks. If the first catch block catches the exception, the second catch block isn't thrown the exception because the first catch block handles it.

The following example shows how to use multiple catch blocks within your program. This example is nearly the same as the previous example, except an array is used instead of variables. We do this in order to demonstrate how the second catch block works. The second catch block catches the exception

ArrayIndexOutOfBoundsException, which is thrown if the program uses an index that is out of bounds of the array. Notice that the program references a[3] in the calculation. However, there isn't an index 3. Therefore, Java throws an out-of-bounds exception, causing the second catch block to display the following message on the screen:

```
Error: java.lang.ArrayIndexOutOfBoundsException: 3
```

```
class Demo {
   public static void main (String args[]) {
      try {
         int a[] = new int[3];
         a[0] = 10;
         a[1] = 0;
         a[2] = a[0]/a[3];
      } catch (ArithmeticException e) {
            System.out.println("Error: " + e);
      } catch (ArrayIndexOutOfBoundsException e) {
            System.out.println("Error: " + e);
      }
   }
}
```

The Finally Block

The finally block is used to place statements that must execute regardless of whether an exception is or is not thrown. That is, statements within the finally block execute all the time. Typically, programmers place statements within a finally block that release resources reserved by the program.

For example, a connection to a database might have been opened at the beginning of the program. If an exception is thrown before the program properly terminates, the database connection might still be open. Programmers resolve this problem by placing statements that close the database connection in the finally block, because statements in the finally block are executed whether there is or isn't an exception thrown.

The following example illustrates how to use the finally block in your program. You'll notice that this example is the same as the previous example, except we included the finally block. The finally block contains one statement that displays a message on the screen, showing you that the statement executed:

```
class Demo {
   public static void main (String args[]) {
```

```
        try {
            int a[] = new int[3];
            a[0] = 10;
            a[1] = 0;
            a[2] = a[0]/a[3];
        } catch (ArithmeticException e) {
            System.out.println("Error: " + e);
        } catch (ArrayIndexOutOfBoundsException e) {
            System.out.println("Error: " + e);
        } finally {
            System.out.println(
                "The finally block executed.");
        }
    }
}
```

Working with Uncaught Exceptions

Although there are many exceptions that can occur when your program executes, you don't have to write a catch block to catch all of them. It is simply not feasible to do so. Instead, any exception that doesn't have a catch block in your program is caught by Java's default catch block, which is called the *default handler*.

The default handler displays two kinds of information on the screen whenever it catches an exception: a string that describes the exception and a stack trace. A stack trace shows you what has been executed, beginning with a point in your program where the exception was thrown to the point when the program terminated.

This is clearly illustrated in the next example, which causes a "divide by zero" exception to be thrown. Notice that this example does not contain a try block or a catch block. Therefore, all exceptions are caught by the default handler.

```
class Demo {
    public static void main (String args[]) {
        int a = 10, b = 0, c;
        c = a/b;
    }
}
```

Here's what the default handler displays on the screen when it encounters the exception:

```
Exception in thread "main" java.lang.ArithmeticException:
            / by zero at demo.main(demo.java:4)
```

The first line is the string message that describes the exception. The second line is the stack trace. The stack trace is saying that the exception occurred at line 4 in the `main()` method of the demo.java program. If you look at line 4 of the previous example, you'll notice that it's the line that contains the calculation. This is where the program terminated once the exception is thrown.

If the exception is caused by a statement within a method called from the `main()` method, the stack trace includes both methods, showing you the path toward the statement that caused the exception. You can see this in the next example, where the calculation that causes the "divide by zero" error is placed in a method called by a statement within the `main()` method:

```
class Demo {
   public static void main (String args[]) {
      myMethod();
   }
   static void myMethod() {
      int a = 10, b = 0, c;
      c = a/b;
    }
}
```

Here is the stack trace that is displayed when the previous example is executed:

```
Exception in thread "main" java.lang.ArithmeticException: / by zero
        at demo.myMethod(demo.java:7)
        at demo.main(demo.java:3)
```

The first line is the message that describes the exception. The second line begins the stack trace. Beginning by reading the stack trace from the last line, here's what the stack trace is saying: First, the `main()` method of the demo.java program is called. Then, in line 3 of the program, `myMethod()` is called. Line 7 of the program, which is within the `myMethod()` definition, is where the program terminated because of an exception.

Nested Try Statements

Sometimes programmers combine two or more try blocks by placing one try block within another try block. This is referred to as *nesting* a try block, where the inner try block is considered the nested try block (that is, nested within the outer try block). Collectively they are called a *nested pair* of try blocks.

Each try block in the nested pair should have one or more catch blocks or a finally block that catch exceptions thrown by Java. The catch blocks are placed following the corresponding try block identically to the way single try blocks and catch blocks are written.

When a statement in an inner try block causes an exception to be thrown, the catch blocks associated with the inner try block are the first to be matched to the exception. If none of those catch blocks catches the exception, the catch blocks associated with the outer try block are matched. If the exception still isn't caught, the default handler catches the exception.

The following example illustrates how a nested try block works. This example is similar to the previous example used to show you how to use two catch blocks in your program. There is one error in this program. We are trying to access array element `a[3]`, which doesn't exist. Therefore, the array index is out of bounds.

This example contains two try blocks. The inner try block contains statements that cause the error. The catch block associated with the inner try block catches only arithmetic exceptions. This means that it does not catch the "out of bounds" exception. The outer try block contains only the inner try block. However, the catch block associated with the outer try block does catch arithmetic exceptions. Therefore, it is this catch block that catches the arithmetic exception thrown by the inner try block.

It is important to understand that although the outer try block in this example does not contain any statements other than the inner try block, you can include statements within the outer try block.

```
class Demo {
   public static void main (String args[]) {
      try {
         try {
            int a[] = new int[3];
            a[0] = 10;
            a[1] = 0;
            a[2] = a[0]/a[3];
         } catch (ArithmeticException e) {
              System.out.println("Error: " + e);
         }
      } catch (ArrayIndexOutOfBoundsException e) {
           System.out.println("Error: " + e);
      }
   }
}
```

Throwing an Exception

Sometimes programmers find it advantageous to throw an exception explicitly from the program whenever the program encounters an error that can be addressed by a catch block. Let's say that user input is used as the divisor for a calculation. The program determines that the input is zero and therefore would lead to a "divide by zero" error if the expression is calculated. Rather than perform the calculation, the programmer could write statements to have the program explicitly throw a "divide by zero" exception.

Programmers also explicitly throw an exception to test the function of catch blocks. Think about this for a second. You can write catch blocks to process exceptions, but there isn't any way to test these catch blocks until an exception occurs—and the exception may never occur during testing. Programmers throw an exception during testing in order to determine how successful a catch block handles an exception.

You explicitly throw an exception by using the `throw` keyword in a statement within your program. The `throw` keyword must be followed by the exception that is being thrown. The exception is specified using the `new` operator, the name of the exception, and the error message that is to be displayed when the exception is caught by a catch block.

The following example illustrates how to explicitly throw an `ArithmeticException`. This example evaluates the divisor before performing a calculation. If the divisor is zero, the exception is thrown rather than the calculation being performed.

The statement that calls the `throw` keyword uses the `new` operator to create an instance of the `ArithmeticException` exception. In this example, `ArithmeticException()` is a constructor that accepts a parameter that is used as the error message. There is also a constructor that does not accept a parameter. It is used if you don't want to create your own exceptions message.

The catch block matches the exception and therefore catches it. The parameter `e` contains the following value:

```
java.lang.ArithmeticException: Divide by zero.
```

The first part is provided by Java and the "Divide by zero." portion is the parameter of the `ArithmeticException` constructor. The catch block also corrects the problem by assigning zero to variable `a`, which is then displayed on the screen by the statement following the catch block.

```
class Demo {
   public static void main(String args[]) {
    int a = 10, b = 0, c;
    try {

       if (b == 0)
         throw new ArithmeticException (
              "Divide by zero.");
       else
```

```
            c = a/b;
        } catch (ArithmeticException e ) {
          System.out.println("Error: " + e);
          a = 0;
        }
        System.out.println("a = " + a);
    }
}
```

It is important to understand that the throw keyword must use an instance of a throwable object or a subclass of a throwable object. This means that you must use an exception and cannot use an int, char, or String.

Methods That Don't Handle Exceptions

A method that can cause an exception does not have to handle the exception. However, the method header must specify the exceptions that the method can cause. In this way, a programmer who calls the method can provide a catch block to handle any exceptions that are not caught by the method.

You specify exceptions by using the keyword throws in the method header to the right of the parameter list. Programmers call this the *exception list*. A comma must separate each exception in the exception list. The programmer who calls the method does not have to provide any catch blocks to catch the exceptions the method throws. The default handler provided by Java catches exceptions that are not caught by the program.

The following example shows how to specify exceptions that are thrown but not caught by a method. Two exceptions can be thrown by myMethod(). These are ArithmeticException and ArrayIndexOutOfBoundsException. However, myMethod() does not catch either of them. The main() method does catch the ArithmeticException exception, but it leaves Java's default handler to catch the ArrayIndexOutOfBoundsException exception.

```
class Demo {
    static void myMethod()
             throws ArithmeticException,
                    ArrayIndexOutOfBoundsException {
             int a[] = new int[3];
             a[0] = 10;
             a[1] = 0;
             a[2] = a[0]/a[1];
             System.out.println("Inside myMethod.");
    }
```

```
    public static void main(String args[]) {
       try {
          myMethod();
       }catch (ArithmeticException e) {
          System.out.println("Error: " + e);
       }
    }
}
```

Checked and Unchecked Exceptions

The two groups of exception classes are *checked* and *unchecked*. Checked exception classes must be included in a method's throw list if the method can throw the exceptions and doesn't catch the exceptions. This is because the Java compiler checks to see whether a catch block will handle these exceptions. That is, a checked exception must be explicitly handled either by being caught or by being declared as thrown.

Unchecked exception classes are exceptions that you don't need to include in a method's throw list because the compiler does not check to see whether a catch block will handle those exceptions. Both checked and unchecked exceptions are defined in the `java.lang` package, which is implicitly imported into all Java programs.

Table 9-1 contains a list of unchecked exception classes, and Table 9-2 contains a list of checked exception classes.

Exception	**Description**
`ArithmeticException`	Arithmetic error, such as divide by zero.
`ArrayIndexOutOfboundsException`	Array index is out of bounds.
`ArrayStoreException`	Assignment to an array element of an incompatible type.
`ClassCastException`	Invalid cast.
`IllegalArgumentException`	Illegal argument used to invoke a method.
`IllegalMonitorStateException`	Illegal monitor operation, such as waiting on an unlocked thread.
`IllegalStateException`	Environment or application is in incorrect state.

Table 9-1 Java Unchecked Exception Classes

Exception	Description
`IllegalthreadStateException`	Requested operation not compatible with current thread state.
`IndexOutOfBoundsException`	Some type of index is out of bounds.
`NegativeArraySizeException`	Array created with a negative size.
`NullPointerException`	Invalid use of a null reference.
`NumberFormatException`	Invalid conversion of a string to a numeric format.
`SecurityException`	Attempt to violate security.
`StringIndexOutOfBounds`	Attempt to index outside the bounds of a string.
`UnsupportedOperationException`	An unsupported operation was encountered.

Table 9-1 Java Unchecked Exception Classes *(continued)*

Exception	Description
`ClassNotFoundException`	Class not found.
`CloneNotSupportedException`	Attempt to clone an object that does not implement the `Cloneable` interface.
`IllegalAccessException`	Access to a class is denied.
`InstantiationException`	Attempt to create an object of an abstract class or interface.
`InterruptedException`	One thread has been interrupted by another thread.
`NoSuchfieldException`	A requested field does not exist.
`NoSuchMethodException`	A requested method does not exist.
`IOException`	An exception occurred during an input/output process.
`SQLException`	An exception occurred when interacting with a database management system using SQL.

Table 9-2 Java Checked Exception Classes

Creating an Exception Subclass

Many programmers define their own exception classes rather than use Java's built-in exception classes. This enables them to tailor exceptions to the specific needs of their Java programs. You, too, can define your own exception class by creating a

subclass of Java's `Exception` class. That is, you must extend the `RuntimeException` class.

As you'll recall from Chapter 8, a subclass is a class that inherits another class. The class that is being inherited is called a *superclass*. The superclass of all exception subclasses is Java's `Exception` class. The `Exception` class is itself a subclass of the `Throwable` class. The `Throwable` class defines several very useful methods that help to handle an exception. Your subclass inherits these methods. This means you can use those methods as if you defined them in your subclass. Table 9-3 contains a listing of the methods defined in the `Throwable` class. You can override any of them (see Chapter 8).

Method	Description
`Throwable fillInStackTrace()`	Returns a throwable object that contains a complete stack trace. This object can be rethrown.
`String getLocalizedMessage()`	Returns a localized description of the exception.
`String getMessage()`	Returns a description of the exception.
`void printStackTrace()`	Displays the stack trace.
`void printStackTrace(PrintWriter stream)`	Sends the stack trace to the specified stream.
`String toString()`	Returns a String object containing a description of the exception. This method is called by `println()` when outputting a `Throwable` object.

Table 9-3 Methods Defined in the `Throwable` Class

The name of your new exception is the name of the class that defines the exception. Suppose we wanted to create an exception called `DivideByZero`. We'll use this in place of `ArithmeticException`, the exception used in the examples throughout this chapter.

In order to create the `DivideByZero` exception, we need to define a class called `DivideByZero` and then inherit the `Exception` class. You'll recall from Chapter 8 that we inherit a superclass by using the keyword `extends` followed by the name of the superclass, as shown here:

```
class DivideByZero extends Exception
```

The class definition contains statements that handle the exception. You can place any statements you want in the class definition. Some programmers simply have their exception class display a message on the screen, which is what we'll do in the following exception class definition. The DivideByZero class contains three members: an integer variable, a constructor, and a method member. The program explicitly throws the exception by calling the DivideByZero constructor and passes it an integer that represents details about the exception. The constructor assigns the integer to the detail variable. The toString() method member then returns the message displayed on the screen by the program.

```
class DivideByZero extends ArithmeticException {
   private int detail;
   DivideByZero () {
     detail = 0;
   }
   DivideByZero (int a) {
     detail = a;
   }
   public String toString() {
    return "DivideByZero [" + detail + "]";
  }
}
```

The following example shows how to use your own exception within a program. The example begins by defining the DivideByZero class. It then defines the program class. The program class defines two methods: calc() and main(). The calc() method uses its parameter as the divisor in a calculation. However, the calc() method determines whether parameter is zero before performing the division. If it is, a DivideByZero exception is thrown. If it isn't, the expression is calculated and the results are returned to the statement that calls the calc() method. Notice that throws DivideByZero is used in the method header. We need this because the calc() method can throw a DivideByZero exception and doesn't have a catch block to handle the exception. Also notice that the DivideByZero exception is your exception and not an exception class defined by Java. Once you define your own exception class, you use the name of the exception class as if you were using a Java-defined exception class.

The main() method calls the calc() method twice within a try block. The first time the method is called, it is passed a one, which doesn't cause an exception to be thrown. The second time that the method is called, it is passed a zero, which does cause a DivideByZero exception. The catch block associated with the try block

catches this exception and handles it the same way it handles a Java-defined exception. Here's what is displayed on the screen when an exception is thrown:

```
Result: 1
Error: DivideByZero[0]
```

```
class DivideByZero extends ArithmeticException {
   private int detail;
   DivideByZero () {
     detail = 0;
   }
   DivideByZero (int a) {
     detail = a;
   }
   public String toString() {
    return "DivideByZero [" + detail + "]";
  }
}
class Demo{
   static void calc(int a) throws DivideByZero {
      int b = 10, c;
      if (a == 0 )
      {
        throw new DivideByZero (a);
      }
      else
      {
        c = b/a;
        System.out.println("Result: " + a);
      }
   }
   public static void main(String args[]) {
      try {
           calc(1);
           calc(0);
        } catch (DivideByZero e) {
          System.out.println("Error: " + e);
        }
   }
}
```

Quiz

1. What is an exception?
2. What is the purpose of a try block?
3. What is the purpose of a catch block?
4. What happens if an exception is thrown and you didn't catch it within your program?
5. What is the parent of the `Exception` class?
6. How can you create your own exception class?
7. What should you do if you define a method that might throw an exception but you don't catch the exception within the method definition?
8. How many exceptions can be caught by a catch block?
9. What is the purpose of the finally block?
10. Can you override methods inherited by your exception class?

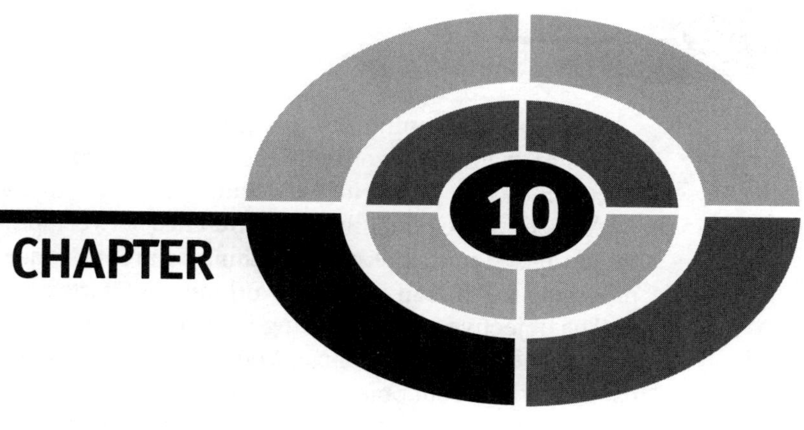

Multithreading

Marathon runners sometimes are faced with a dilemma when two major races fall during the same week because they have to choose which race to run in. They probably wish there was a way a part of them could go to one race and another part to the other race. That can't happen—that is, unless the runner is a Java program, because two parts of the same Java program can run concurrently by using multithreading. You'll learn about multithreading and how to run parts of your program concurrently in this chapter.

Multitasking

Multitasking is performing two or more tasks at the same time. Nearly all operating systems are capable of multitasking by using one of two multitasking techniques: process-based multitasking and thread-based multitasking.

Process-based multitasking is running two programs concurrently. Programmers refer to a program as a *process*. Therefore, you could say that process-based multitasking is program-based multitasking.

Thread-based multitasking is having a program perform two tasks at the same time. For example, a word processing program can check the spelling of words in a document while you write the document. This is thread-based multitasking.

A good way to remember the difference between process-based multitasking and thread-based multitasking is to think of process-based as working with multiple programs and thread-based as working with parts of one program.

The objective of multitasking is to utilize the idle time of the CPU. Think of the CPU as the engine of your car. Your engine keeps running regardless of whether the car is moving. Your objective is to keep your car moving as much as possible so you can get the most miles from a gallon of gas. An idling engine wastes gas.

The same concept applies to the CPU in your computer. You want your CPU cycles to be processing instructions and data rather than waiting for something to process. A CPU cycle is somewhat similar to your engine running.

It may be hard to believe, but the CPU idles more than it processes in many desktop computers. Let's say that you are using a word processor to write a document. For the most part, the CPU is idle until you enter a character from the keyboard or move the mouse. Multitasking is designed to use the fraction of a second between strokes to process instructions from either another program or from a different part of the same program.

Making efficient use of the CPU may not be too critical for applications running on a desktop computer because most of us rarely need to run concurrent programs or run parts of the same program at the same time. However, programs that run in a networked environment, such as those that process transactions from many computers, need to make a CPU's idle time productive.

Overhead

The operating system must do extra work to manage multitasking. Programmers call this extra work *overhead* because resources inside your computer are used to manage the multitasking operation rather than being used by programs for processing instructions and data.

Process-based multitasking has a larger overhead than thread-based multitasking. In process-based multitasking, each process requires its own address space in memory. The operating system requires a significant amount of CPU time to switch from one process to another process. Programmers call this *context switching*, where each process (program) is a context. Additional resources are needed for each process to communicate with each other.

In comparison, the threads in thread-based multitasking share the same address space in memory because they share the same program. This also has an impact on context switching, because switching from one part of the program to another happens within the same address space in memory. Likewise, communication among parts of the program happens within the same memory location.

Threads

A thread is part of a program that is running. Thread-based multitasking has multiple threads running at the same time (that is, multiple parts of a program running concurrently). Each thread is a different path of execution.

Let's return to the word processing program example to see how threads are used. Two parts of the word processor are of interest: The first is the part of the program that receives characters from the keyboard, saves them in memory, and displays them on the screen. The second part is the portion of the program that checks spelling. Each part is a thread that executes independently of each other, even though they are part of the same program. While one thread receives and processes characters entered into the keyboard, the other thread sleeps. That is, the other thread pauses until the CPU is idle. The CPU is normally idle between keystrokes. It is this time period when the spell checker thread awakens and continues to check the spelling of the document. The spell checker thread once again pauses when the next character is entered into the keyboard.

The Java run-time environment manages threads, unlike in process-based multitasking where the operating system manages switching between programs. Threads are processed asynchronously. This means that one thread can pause while other threads continue to process.

A thread can be in one of four states:

- **Running** A thread is being executed.
- **Suspended** Execution is paused and can be resumed where it left off.
- **Blocked** A resource cannot be accessed because it is being used by another thread.
- **Terminated** Execution is stopped and cannot be resumed.

All threads are not equal. Some threads are more important than other threads and are giving higher priority to resources such as the CPU. Each thread is assigned a thread priority that is used to determine when to switch from one executing thread to another. This is called *context switching*.

A thread's priority is relative to the priority of other threads. That is, a thread's priority is irrelevant if it is the only thread that is running. A lower-priority thread runs just as fast as a higher-priority thread if no other threads are executing concurrently.

Thread priorities are used when the rules of context switching are being applied. These rules are as follows:

- A thread can voluntarily yield to another thread. In doing so, control is turned over to the highest-priority thread.
- A higher-priority thread can preempt a lower-priority thread for use of the CPU. The lower-priority thread is paused regardless of what it's doing to give way to the higher-priority thread. Programmers call this *preemptive multitasking*.
- Threads of equal priority are processed based on the rules of the operating system that is being used to run the program. For example, Windows uses *time slicing*, which involves giving each high-priority thread a few milliseconds of CPU cycles, and keeps rotating among the high-priority threads. In Solaris, the first high-priority thread must voluntarily yield to another high-priority thread. If it doesn't, the second high-priority thread must wait for the first thread to terminate.

Synchronization

Multithreading occurs *asynchronously*, meaning one thread executes independently of the other threads. In this way, threads don't depend on each other's execution. In contrast, processes that run synchronously depend on each other. That is, one process waits until the other process terminates before it can execute.

Sometimes the execution of a thread is dependent on the execution of another thread. Let's say you have two threads—one handles gathering login information, and the other validates a user's ID and password. The login thread must wait for the validation thread to complete processing before it can tell the user whether or not the login is successful. Therefore, both threads must execute synchronously, not asynchronously.

Java enables you to synchronize threads by defining a synchronized method. A thread that is inside a synchronized method prevents any other thread from calling another synchronized method on the same object. You'll learn how to do this later in the chapter.

The Thread Classes and the Runnable Interface

You construct threads by using the `Thread` class and the `Runnable` interface. This means that your class must extend the `Thread` class or implement the `Runnable` interface. The `Thread` class defines the methods you use to manage threads. Table 10-1 contains the commonly used methods of the `Thread` class. You'll see how these are used throughout the examples in this chapter.

Method	Description
`getName()`	Returns the name of the thread.
`getPriority()`	Returns the priority of the thread.
`isAlive()`	Determines whether the thread is running.
`join()`	Pauses until the thread terminates.
`run()`	The entry point into the thread.
`sleep()`	Suspends a thread. This method enables you to specify the period the thread is suspended.
`start()`	Starts the thread.

Table 10-1 Commonly Used Methods Defined in the **`Thread`** Class

The Main Thread

Every Java program has one thread, even if you don't create any threads. This thread is called the *main* thread because it is the thread that executes when you start your program. The main thread spawns threads that you create. These are called *child* threads. The main thread is always the last thread to finish executing because typically the main thread needs to release a resource used by the program such as network connections.

Programmers can control the main thread by first creating a Thread object and then using method members of the Thread object to control the main thread. You create a Thread object by calling the `currentThread()` method. The `currentThread()` method returns a reference to the thread. You then use this reference to control the main thread just like you control any thread, which you'll learn how to do in this chapter.

Let's create a reference to the main thread and then change the name of the thread from main to Demo Thread. The following program shows how this is done. Here's what is displayed on the screen when the program runs:

```
Current thread: Thread[main,5,main]
Renamed Thread: Thread[Demo Thread,5,main]
```

```
class Demo {
   public static void main (String args[] ) {
      Thread t = Thread.currentThread();
      System.out.println("Current thread: " + t);
      t.setName("Demo Thread");
      System.out.println("Renamed Thread: " + t);
   }
}
```

As you previously learned in this chapter, a thread is automatically created when you execute a program. The objective of this example is to declare a reference to a thread and then assign that reference a reference to the main thread. This is done in the first statement of the `main()` method.

We declare the reference by specifying the name of the class and the name for the reference, which is done in the following line of code:

```
Thread t
```

We acquire a reference to the main thread by calling the `currentThread()` method member of the `Thread` class using the following method call:

```
Thread.currentThread()
```

The reference returned by the `currentThread()` method is then assigned to the reference previously declared in the opening statement. We then display the thread on the screen:

```
Thread[main,5,main]
```

Information within the square brackets tells us something about the thread. The first appearance of the word *main* is the name of the thread. The number 5 is the thread's priority, which is normal priority. The priority ranges from 1 to 10, where 1 is the lowest priority and 10 is the highest. The last occurrence of the word *main* is the name of the group of threads with which the thread belongs. A thread group is a data structure used to control the state of a collection of threads. You don't need to be concerned about a thread group because the Java run-time environment handles this.

The `setName()` method is then called to illustrate how you have control over the main thread of your program. The `setName()` method is a method member of the `Thread` class and is used to change the name of a thread. This example uses the

setName() method to change the main thread's name from main to Demo Thread. The thread is once again displayed on the screen to show that the name has been changed. Here's what is displayed:

```
Renamed Thread: Thread[Demo Thread,5,main]
```

Creating Your Own Thread

Remember, your program is the main thread, and other portions of your program can also be a thread. You can designate a portion of your program as a thread by creating your own thread. The easiest way to do this is to implement the Runnable interface. Implementing the Runnable interface is an alternative to your class inheriting the Thread class.

An interface describes one or more method members that you must define in your own class in order to be compliant with the interface. These methods are described by their method name, argument list, and return value.

The Runnable interface describes the method classes needed to create and interact with a thread. In order to use the Runnable interface in your class, you must define the methods described by the Runnable interface.

Fortunately, only you need to define one method described by the Runnable interface—the run() method. The run() method must be a public method, and it doesn't require an argument list or have a return value.

The content of the run() method is the portion of your program that will become the new thread. Statements outside the run() method are part of the main thread. Statements inside the run() method are part of the new thread. Both the main thread and the new thread run concurrently when you start the new thread, which you'll learn how to do in the next example. The new thread terminates when the run() method terminates. Control then returns to the statement that called the run() method.

When you implement the Runnable interface, you'll need to call the following constructor of the Thread class. This constructor requires two arguments. The first argument is the instance of the class that implements the Runnable interface and tells the constructor where the new thread will be executed. The second argument is the name of the new thread. Here's the format of the constructor:

```
Thread (Runnable class, String name)
```

The constructor creates the new thread, but it does not start the thread. You explicitly start the new thread by calling the start() method. The start() method calls the run() method you defined in your program. The start() method has no argument list and does not return any values.

The following example illustrates how to create and start a new thread. Here's what is displayed when this program runs:

```
Main thread started
Child thread started
Child thread terminated
Main thread terminated
```

Note: *The output of this program may be different when you run this program. Some Java run-time environments terminate the main thread before the child thread, whereas others terminate the child thread before the main thread. Therefore, the text shown here might appear in a different order when you run this program.*

```
class MyThread implements Runnable {
   Thread t;
   MyThread () {
      t = new Thread(this,"My thread");
      t.start();
   }
   public void run() {
      System.out.println("Child thread started");
      System.out.println("Child thread terminated");
  }
}
class Demo {
   public static void main (String args[]){
      new MyThread();
      System.out.println("Main thread started");
      System.out.println("Main thread terminated");
    }
}
```

This example begins by defining a class called `MyThread`, which implements the `Runnable` interface. Therefore, we use the keyword `implements` to implement the `Runnable` interface. Next, a reference to a thread is declared. Defining the constructor for the class follows this. The constructor calls the constructor of the `Thread` class. Because we are implementing the `Runnable` interface, we need to pass the constructor reference to the instance of the class that will execute the new thread and the name of the new thread. Notice that we use the keyword `this` as ref erence to the instance of the class. The keyword `this` is a reference to the current instance of the class.

The constructor returns a reference to the new thread, which is assigned to the reference declared in the first statement in the `MyThread` class definition. We use

this reference to call the start() method. Remember that the start() method calls the run() method.

Next, we define the run() method. Statements within the run() method become the portion of the program that executes when the thread executes. There are only two displayed statements in the run() method. Later in this chapter, we'll expand the run() method to include more interesting statements.

Next, we define the program class. The program class explicitly executes the new thread by creating an instance of the MyThread class. This is done by using the new operator and calling the constructor of MyThread.

Finally, the program finishes by displaying two lines on the screen.

Creating a Thread by Using extends

You can inherit the Thread class as another way to create a thread in your program. As you'll recall from Chapter 8, you can cause your class to inherit another class by using the keyword extends when defining your class. When you declare an instance of your class, you'll also have access to members of the Thread class.

Whenever your class inherits the Thread class, you must override the run() method, which is an entry into the new thread. The following example shows how to inherit the Thread class and how to override the run() method.

This example defines the MyThread class, which inherits the Thread class. The constructor of the MyThread class calls the constructor of the Thread class by using the super keyword and passes it the name of the new thread, which is My thread. It then calls the start() method to activate the new thread.

The start() method calls the run() method of the MyThread class. As you'll notice in this example, the run() method is overridden by displaying two lines on the screen that indicate that the child thread started and terminated. Remember that statements within the run() method constitute the portion of the program that runs as the thread. Therefore, your program will likely have more meaningful statements within the definition of the run() method than those used in this example.

The new thread is declared within the main() method of the Demo class, which is the program class of the application. After the thread starts, two messages are displayed, indicating the status of the main thread.

```
class MyThread extends Thread {
   MyThread(){
      super("My thread");
      start();
   }
```

```
  public void run() {
     System.out.println("Child thread started");
     System.out.println("Child thread terminated");
  }
}

class Demo {
   public static void main (String args[]){
      new MyThread();
       System.out.println("Main thread started");
       System.out.println("Main thread terminated");
     }
}
```

Note: *As a rule of thumb, you should implement the* `Runnable` *interface if the* `run()` *method is the only method of the* `Thread` *class that you need to override. You should inherit the* `Thread` *class if you need to override other methods defined in the* `Thread` *class.*

Using Multiple Threads in a Program

It is not unusual to need to run multiple instances of a thread, such as when your program prints multiple documents concurrently. Programmers call this *spawning* a thread. You can spawn any number of threads you need by first defining your own class that either implements the `Runnable` interface or inherits the `Thread` class and then declaring instances of the class. Each instance is a new thread.

Let's see how this is done. The next example defines a class called `MyThread` that implements the `Runnable` interface. The constructor of the `MyThread` class accepts one parameter, which is a string that is used as the name of the new thread. We create the new thread within the constructor by calling the constructor of the `Thread` class and passing it a reference to the object that is defining the thread and the name of the thread. Remember that the `this` keyword is a reference to the current object. The `start()` method is then called, which calls the `run()` method.

The `run()` method is overridden in the `MyThread` class. Two things happen when the `run()` method executes. First, the name of the thread is displayed on the screen. Second, the thread pauses for 2 seconds when the `sleep()` method is called. The `sleep()` method is defined in the `Thread` class can accept one or two parameters. The first parameter is the number of milliseconds the thread is to pause. The second parameter is the number of microseconds the thread pauses. In this example, we're only interested in milliseconds, so we don't need to include the second parameter (2,000 nanoseconds is 2 seconds). After the thread pauses, another statement is displayed on the screen stating that the thread is terminating.

The `main()` method of the `Demo` class declares four instances of the same thread by calling the constructor of the `MyThread` class and passing it the name of the thread. Each of these is treated as a separate thread. The main thread is then paused 10 seconds by a call to the `sleep()` method. During this time, the threads continue to execute. When the main thread awakens, it displays the message that the main thread is terminating.

Here's what is displayed on the screen when this example runs:

```
Thread: 1
Thread: 2
Thread: 3
Thread: 4
Terminating thread: 1
Terminating thread: 2
Terminating thread: 3
Terminating thread: 4
Terminating thread: main thread.
```

```
class MyThread implements Runnable {
  String tName;
  Thread t;
  MyThread (String threadName) {
     tName = threadName;
     t = new Thread (this, tName);
     t.start();
  }
  public void run() {
     try {
        System.out.println("Thread: " + tName );
        Thread.sleep(2000);
     } catch (InterruptedException e ) {
       System.out.println("Exception: Thread "
               + tName + " interrupted");
     }
     System.out.println("Terminating thread: " + tName );
  }
}
class Demo {
```

```
    public static void main (String args []) {
       new MyThread ("1");
       new MyThread ("2");
       new MyThread ("3");
       new MyThread ("4");
       try {
          Thread.sleep (10000);
       } catch (InterruptedException e) {
         System.out.println(
                  "Exception: Thread main interrupted.");
       }
       System.out.println(
                   "Terminating thread: main thread.");
    }
 }
```

Using isAlive() and join()

Typically, the main thread is the last thread to finish in a program. However, there isn't any guarantee that the main thread won't finish before a child thread finishes. In the previous example, we told the main method to sleep until the child threads terminate. However, we estimated the time it takes for the child threads to complete processing. If our estimate was too short, a child thread could terminate after the main thread terminates. Therefore, the sleep technique isn't the best one to use to guarantee that the main thread terminates last.

Programmers use two other techniques to ensure that the main thread is the last thread to terminate. These techniques involve calling the `isAlive()` method and the `join()` method. Both of these methods are defined in the `Thread` class.

The `isAlive()` method determines whether a thread is still running. If it is, the `isAlive()` method returns a Boolean true value; otherwise, a Boolean false is returned. You can use the `isAlive()` method to examine whether a child thread continues to run. The `join()` method works differently than the `isAlive()` method. The `join()` method waits until the child thread terminates and "joins" the main thread. In addition, you can use the `join()` method to specify the amount of time you want to wait for a child thread to terminate.

The following example illustrates how to use the `isAlive()` method and the `join()` method in your program. This example is nearly the same as the previous example. The difference lies in the `main()` method of the `Demo` class definition.

After the threads are declared using the constructor of the `MyThread` class, the `isAlive()` method is called for each thread. The value returned by the `isAlive()` method is then displayed on the screen. Next, the `join()` method is called for each thread. The `join()` method causes the main thread to wait for all child threads to complete processing before the main thread terminates.

Here is what is displayed on the screen when this program runs:

```
Thread Status: Alive
Thread 1: true
Thread 2: true
Thread 3: true
Thread 4: true
Threads Joining.
Thread: 1
Thread: 2
Thread: 3
Thread: 4
Terminating thread: 1
Terminating thread: 2
Terminating thread: 3
Terminating thread: 4
Thread Status: Alive
Thread 1: false
Thread 2: false
Thread 3: false
Thread 4: false
Terminating thread: main thread.
```

```
class MyThread implements Runnable {
  String tName;
  Thread t;
  MyThread (String threadName) {
     tName = threadName;
     t = new Thread (this, tName);
     t.start();
  }
  public void run() {
     try {
          System.out.println("Thread: " + tName );
          Thread.sleep(2000);
     } catch (InterruptedException e ) {
       System.out.println("Exception: Thread "
               + tName + " interrupted");
```

```
      }
      System.out.println("Terminating thread: " + tName );
   }
}
class Demo {
   public static void main (String args []) {
      MyThread thread1 = new MyThread ("1");
      MyThread thread2 = new MyThread ("2");
      MyThread thread3 = new MyThread ("3");
      MyThread thread4 = new MyThread ("4");
      System.out.println("Thread Status: Alive");
      System.out.println("Thread 1: "
                 + thread1.t.isAlive());
      System.out.println("Thread 2: "
                 + thread2.t.isAlive());
      System.out.println("Thread 3: "
                 + thread3.t.isAlive());
      System.out.println("Thread 4: "
                 + thread4.t.isAlive());
      try {
         System.out.println("Threads Joining.");
         thread1.t.join();
         thread2.t.join();
         thread3.t.join();
         thread4.t.join();
      } catch (InterruptedException e) {
        System.out.println(
              "Exception: Thread main interrupted.");
      }
      System.out.println("Thread Status: Alive");
      System.out.println("Thread 1: "
            + thread1.t.isAlive());
      System.out.println("Thread 2: "
            + thread2.t.isAlive());
      System.out.println("Thread 3: "
            + thread3.t.isAlive());
      System.out.println("Thread 4: "
            + thread4.t.isAlive());
      System.out.println(
            "Terminating thread: main thread.");
   }
}
```

Setting Thread Priorities

Previously in this chapter, you learned that each thread has an assigned priority that is used to let more important threads use resources ahead of lower-priority resources. Priority is used as a guide for the operating system to determine which thread gets accesses to a resource such as the CPU. In reality, an operating system takes other factors into consideration. Typically, programmers have little or no control over those other factors. Therefore, they establish a priority for their threads without further concern over those other factors.

A priority is an integer from 1 to 10 inclusive, where 10 is the highest priority, referred to as the *maximum priority*, and 1 is the lowest priority, also known as the *minimum priority*. The normal priority is 5, which is the default priority for each thread.

In general, a thread with a higher priority bumps a thread with a lower priority from using a resource. The lower-priority thread pauses until the higher-priority thread is finished using the resource. Whenever two threads of equal priority need the same resource, the thread that accesses the resource first has use of the resource. What happens to the second thread depends on the operating system under which your program is running. Some operating systems force the second thread to wait until the first thread is finished with the resource. Other operating systems require the first thread to give the second thread access to the resource after a specified time period. This is to ensure that one thread doesn't hog a resource and prevent other threads from utilizing it.

In the real world, the first thread usually pauses while using the resource because another resource it needs isn't available. It is during this pause that the operating system has the first thread relinquish the resource. The problem is, you don't know if and when the pause will occur. It is best to always cause a thread to pause periodically whenever the thread is using a resource for a long period time. In this way, the thread shares the resource with other threads. You learn how to pause a thread in the "Suspending and Resuming a Thread" section of this chapter.

You need to keep in mind that there is a downside to periodically pausing a thread. Pausing a thread diminishes the performance of your program and could cause a backlog for use of the resource. Therefore, you need to monitor the performance of your program regularly to make sure you are not experiencing this negative aspect of pausing a thread.

For now let's focus on something you do have control over—setting the priority of a thread. You set a thread's priority by calling the `setPriority()` method, which is defined in the `Thread` class. The `setPriority()` method requires one parameter, which is the integer representing the level of priority. You have two ways in which to represent the priority. You can use an integer from 1 to 10, or you can use final variables defined in the `Thread` class. These variables are `MIN_PRIORITY`, `MAX_PRIOIRTY`, and `NORM_PRIOIRTY`.

You can determine the priority level of a thread by calling the `getPriority()` method, which is also defined in the `Thread` class. The `getPriority()` method does not requires an argument, and it returns the integer representing the level of priority for the thread.

The following example illustrates how to use the `setPriority()` and `getPriority()` methods. This example creates two child threads and sets the priority for each. First, the low-priority thread starts, followed by the high-priority thread. Here's what is displayed when you run this program (notice that the high-priority thread runs ahead of the low-priority thread, even though the low-priority thread started first):

Note: *The results displayed on your screen might be different from the results shown here because of the way your operating system handles thread priorities.*

```
low priority started
high priority started
high priority running.
low priority running.
low priority stopped.
high priority stopped.
```

```
class MyThread implements Runnable {
  Thread t;
  private volatile boolean running = true;
  public MyThread (int p, String tName) {
     t = new Thread(this,tName);
     t.setPriority (p);
  }
  public void run() {
     System.out.println(t.getName() + " running.");
  }
  public void stop() {
     running = false;
     System.out.println(t.getName() + " stopped.");
  }
  public void start() {
    System.out.println(t.getName() + " started");
     t.start();
  }
}
```

```
class Demo {
  public static void main(String args[] ) {
     Thread.currentThread().setPriority(10);
     MyThread lowPriority =
                  new MyThread (3, "low priority");
     MyThread highPriority =
                  new MyThread (7, "high priority");
     lowPriority.start();
     highPriority.start();
     try {
        Thread.sleep(1000);
     } catch ( InterruptedException e) {
        System.out.println("Main thread interrupted.");
     }
     lowPriority.stop();
     highPriority.stop();
     try {
        highPriority.t.join();
        lowPriority.t.join();
     } catch (InterruptedException e) {
          System.out.println(
                  "InterruptedException caught");
     }
  }
}
```

Synchronizing Threads

A major concern when two or more threads share the same resource is that only one of them can access the resource at one time. Programmers address this concern by synchronizing threads, much the same way baseball players take turns being up to bat.

Threads are synchronized in Java through the use of a monitor. Think of a monitor as an object that enables a thread to access a resource. Only one thread can use a monitor at any one time period. Programmers say that the thread *owns* the monitor for that period of time. The monitor is also called a *semaphore*.

A thread can own a monitor only if no other thread owns the monitor. If the monitor is available, a thread can own the monitor and have exclusive access to the resource associated with the monitor. If the monitor is not available, the thread is suspended until the monitor becomes available. Programmers say that the thread is *waiting* for the monitor.

Fortunately, the task of acquiring a monitor for a resource happens behind the scenes in Java. Java handles all the details for you. You do have to synchronize the threads you create in your program if more than one thread will use the same resource.

You have two ways in which you can synchronize threads: You can use the synchronized method or the synchronized statement.

The Synchronized Method

All objects in Java have a monitor. A thread enters a monitor whenever a method modified by the keyword `synchronized` is called. The thread that is first to call the synchronized method is said to be *inside* the method and therefore owns the method and resources used by the method. Another thread that calls the synchronized method is suspended until the first thread relinquishes the synchronized method.

If a synchronized method is an instance method, the synchronized method activates the lock associated with the instance that called the synchronized method, which is the object known as `this` during the execution of the body of the method. If the synchronized method is static, it activates the lock associated with the class object that defines the synchronized method.

Before you learn how to define a synchronized method in your program, let's see what might happen if synchronization is not used in a program. This is the objective of the following example. This program displays two names within parentheses using two threads. This is a three-step process, where the opening parenthesis, the name, and the closing parenthesis are displayed in separate steps.

The example defines three classes: the `Parentheses` class, the `MyThread` class, and the `Demo` class, which is the program class. The `Parentheses` class defines one method called `display()`, which receives a string in its argument list and displays the string in parentheses on the screen. The `MyThread` class defines a thread. In doing so, the constructor of `MyThread` requires two arguments. The first argument is a reference to an instance of the `Parentheses` class. The second ar gument is a string containing the name that will be displayed on the screen. The `run()` method uses the instance of the `Parentheses` class to call its `display()` method, passing the `display()` method the name that is to appear on the screen.

The rest of the action happens in the `main()` method of the `Demo` class. The first statement declares an instance of the `Parentheses` class. The next two classes create two threads. Notice that both threads use the same instance of the `Parentheses` class.

Here's what is displayed when you run this program. It's probably not what you expected to see. Each name should be enclosed within its own parentheses. The problem is that the `display()` method isn't synchronized.

NOTE: If a variable is assigned by one thread and is used or assigned by other threads, all access to the variable should be enclosed in a synchronized method or a synchronized statement.

```
 (Bob(Mary)
)

class Parentheses  {
   void display(String s) {
   System.out.print ("(" + s);
   try {
      Thread.sleep (1000);
   } catch (InterruptedException e) {
        System.out.println ("Interrupted");
   }
   System.out.println(")");
  }
}
class MyThread implements Runnable {
   String s1;
   Parentheses  p1;
   Thread t;
   public MyThread (Parentheses  p2, String s2) {
      p1= p2;
      s1= s2;
      t = new Thread(this);
      t.start();
   }
   public void run() {
     p1.display(s1);
   }
}
class Demo{
   public static void main (String args[]) {
     Parentheses p3 = new Parentheses();
     MyThread name1 = new MyThread(p3, "Bob");
     MyThread name2 = new MyThread(p3, "Mary");
     try {
        name1.t.join();
        name2.t.join();
     } catch (InterruptedException e ) {
          System.out.println( "Interrupted");
     }
   }
}
```

The problem with the previous example is that two threads use the same resource concurrently. The resource is the `display()` method defined in the `Parentheses` class. In order to have one thread take control of the `display()` method, we must synchronize the `display()` method. This is done by using the keyword `synchronized` in the header of the `display()` method, which is illustrated in the next example.

Here's what is displayed when you run the next example. This is what you expected to see in the previous example.

```
(Bob)
(Mary)

class Parentheses  {
   synchronized void display(String s) {
   System.out.print ("(" + s);
   try {
      Thread.sleep (1000);
   } catch (InterruptedException e) {
        System.out.println ("Interrupted");
   }
   System.out.println(")");
  }
}
class MyThread implements Runnable {
   String s1;
   Parentheses  p1;
   Thread t;
   public MyThread (Parentheses  p2, String s2) {
      p1= p2;
      s1= s2;
      t = new Thread(this);
      t.start();
   }
   public void run() {
     p1.display(s1);
   }
}
class Demo{
   public static void main (String args[]) {
     Parentheses p3 = new Parentheses();
     MyThread name1 = new MyThread(p3, "Bob");
     MyThread name2 = new MyThread(p3, "Mary");
     try {
```

```
            name1.t.join();
            name2.t.join();
        } catch (InterruptedException e ) {
            System.out.println( "Interrupted");
        }
    }
}
```

Using the Synchronized Statement

Synchronizing a method is the best way to restrict the use of a method one thread at a time. However, there will be occasions when you won't be able to synchronize a method, such as when you use a class that is provided to you by a third party. In such cases, you don't have access to the definition of the class, which prevents you from using the `synchronized` keyword.

An alternative to using the `synchronized` keyword is to use the synchronized statement. A synchronized statement contains a synchronized block, within which is placed objects and methods that are to be synchronized. Calls to the methods contained in the synchronized block happen only after the thread enters the monitor of the object.

Although you can call methods within a synchronized block, the method declaration must be made outside a synchronized block.

The following example shows how to use a synchronized statement. This is basically the same as the previous example; however, the synchronized statement is used instead of the `synchronized` keyword. The synchronized statement is placed in the `run()` method within the `MyThread` class. The synchronized statement synchronizes the instance of the `Parentheses` class and thus prevents two threads from calling the `display()` method concurrently.

```
class Parentheses  {
   void display(String s) {
   System.out.print ("(" + s);
   try {
      Thread.sleep (1000);
   } catch (InterruptedException e) {
        System.out.println ("Interrupted");
   }
   System.out.println(")");
  }
}
class MyThread implements Runnable {
   String s1;
```

```
    Parentheses  p1;
    Thread t;
    public MyThread (Parentheses  p2, String s2) {
       p1= p2;
       s1= s2;
       t = new Thread(this);
       t.start();
    }
    public void run() {
        synchronized(p1){
           p1.display(s1);
        }
    }
}
class Demo{
    public static void main (String args[]) {
      Parentheses p3 = new Parentheses();
      MyThread name1 = new MyThread(p3, "Bob");
      MyThread name2 = new MyThread(p3, "Mary");
      try {
         name1.t.join();
         name2.t.join();
      } catch (InterruptedException e ) {
           System.out.println( "Interrupted");
      }
    }
}
```

Here, the `display()` method is not modified by `synchronized`. Instead, the synchronized statement is used inside the caller's `run()` method. This causes the same correct output as before, because each thread waits for the prior one to finish before proceeding.

Communicating Between Threads

Threads have opened programmers to a new dimension in programming, where parts of a program can execute asynchronously, each processing independently of the other. However, sometimes threads have to coordinate their processing and therefore need to be able to communicate with each other during processing. Programmers call this *interprocess communication*.

You can have threads communicate with each other in your program by using the wait(), notify(), and notifyAll() methods. These methods are called from within a synchronized method. The wait() method tells a thread to relinquish a monitor and go into suspension. There are two forms of the wait() method. One form doesn't require an argument and causes a thread to wait until it is notified. The other form of the wait() method let's you specify the amount of time to wait. You specify the length of time in milliseconds, which is passed to the wait() method.

The notify() method tells a thread that is suspended by the wait() method to wake up again and regain control of the monitor. The notifyAll() method wakes up all threads that are waiting for control of the monitor. Only the thread with the highest priority is given control over the monitor. The other threads wait in suspension until the monitor becomes available again.

The following example shows you how to use these methods in an application. The objective of the program is to have the Publisher class give a value to the Consumer class through the use of a Queue class. The Publisher class places a value on the queues and then waits until the Consumer class retrieves the value before the Publisher class places another value on the queue.

This example defines four classes: the Queue class, the Publisher class, the Consumer class, and the Demo class. The Queue class defines two instance values: exchangeValue and a flag. The exchangeValue is used to store the value placed on the queue by the publisher. The flag variable is used as a sign indicating whether a value has been placed on the queue. This is set to false by default, which enables the producer to place a value on to the queue. The Queue class also defines a get() method and a put() method. The put() method is used to place a value on to the queue (that is, to assign a value to the exchangeValue variables). The get() method is used to retrieve the value contained on the queue (that is, to return the value of exchangeValue). Once the value is assigned, the put() method changes the value of the flag from false to true, indicating there is a value on the queue. Notice how the value of the flag is used within the get() method and the put() method to have the thread that calls the method wait until either there is a value on the queue or there isn't a value on the queue, depending on which method is being called.

The Publisher class declares an instance of the Queue class and then calls the put() method to place five integers on the queue. Although the put() method is called within a for loop, each integer is placed on the queue and then there is a pause until the integer is retrieved by the Consumer class.

The Consumer class is very similar in design to the Publisher class, except the Consumer class calls the get() method five times from within a for loop. Each call to the get() method is paused until the Publisher class places an integer in the queue.

The `main()` method of the `Demo` class creates instances of the `Queue` class, the `Publisher` class, and the `Consumer` class. Notice that both constructors of the `Publisher` class and the `Consumer` class are passed a reference to the instance of the same `Queue` class. They use the instance of the `Queue` class for interprocess communication.

Here's what you see when you run this program. Notice that the value placed on the queue by the `Publisher` is retrieved by the `Consumer` before the `Publisher` places the next value on the queue.

```
Put: 0
Get: 0
Put: 1
Get: 1
Put: 2
Get: 2
Put: 3
Get: 3
Put: 4
Get: 4

class Queue {
   int exchangeValue;
    boolean busy = false;
    synchronized int get() {
       if (!busy)
          try {
             wait();
          } catch (InterruptedException e) {
               System.out.println(
                   "Get: InterruptedException");
          }
        System.out.println("Get: " + exchangeValue);
         notify();
       return exchangeValue;
    }
    synchronized void put (int exchangeValue) {
       if (busy)
          try {
             wait();
          } catch (InterruptedException e) {
               System.out.println(
                    "Put: InterruptedException");
          }
       this.exchangeValue = exchangeValue;
```

```
        busy = true;
        System.out.println("Put: " + exchangeValue);
        notify();
    }
}
class Publisher implements Runnable {
   Queue  q;
   Publisher(Queue  q) {
      this.q = q;
      new Thread (this, "Publisher").start();
   }
   public void run() {
      for (int i = 0; i < 5; i++){
         q.put(i);
      }
   }
}
class Consumer implements Runnable {
   Queue  q;
   Consumer (Queue  q) {
      this.q = q;
      new Thread (this, "Consumer").start();
   }
   public void run() {
      for (int i = 0; i < 5; i++){
         q.get();
      }
   }
}
class Demo {
  public static void main(String args []) {
     Queue  q = new Queue ();
     new Publisher (q);
     new Consumer (q);
   }
}
```

NOTE: *If your program seems to hang when using two or more threads, you should suspect that a deadlock has occurred. A deadlock occurs when all threads in contention for a resource wait, thinking that another thread is using the resource when actually no thread is using it. Look for code where two threads access two synchronized objects. They could be doing this in an unusual sequence. Redesign your program to avoid this situation. A deadlock can also occur in a rare time-slicing sequence, where the operating system causes a circular dependency of two threads.*

Suspending and Resuming Threads

There might be times when you need to temporarily stop a thread from processing and then resume processing, such as when you want to let another thread use the current resource. You can achieve this objective by defining your own suspend and resume methods, as shown in the following example.

This example defines a `MyThread` class. The `MyThread` class defines three methods: the `run()` method, the `suspendThread()` method, and the `resumeThread()` method. In addition, the `MyThread` class declares the instance variable `suspended`, whose value is used to indicate whether or not the thread is suspended.

The `run()` method contains a `for` loop that displays the value of the counter variable. Each time the counter variable is displayed, the thread pauses briefly. It then enters a synchronized statement to determine whether the value of the `suspended` instance variable is true. If so, the `wait()` method is called, causing the thread to be suspended until the `notify()` method is called.

The `suspendThread()` method simply assigns true to the `suspended` instance variable. The `resumeThread()` method assigns false to the `suspended` instance variable and then calls the `notify()` method. This causes the thread that is suspended to resume processing.

The `main()` method of the `Demo` class declares an instance of `MyThread` and then pauses for about a second before calling the `suspendThread()` method and displaying an appropriate message on the screen. It then pauses for about another second before calling the `resumeThread()` method and again displaying an appropriate message on the screen.

The thread continues to display the value of the counter variable until the thread is suspended. The thread continues to display the value of the counter variable once the thread resumes processing. Here's what is displayed when you run this program:

```
Thread: 0
Thread: 1
Thread: 2
Thread: 3
Thread: 4
Thread: Suspended
Thread: Resume
Thread: 5
Thread: 6
Thread: 7
Thread: 8
Thread: 9
```

```
Thread exiting.

class MyThread implements Runnable {
  String name;
  Thread t;
  boolean suspended;
  MyThread() {
     t = new Thread(this, "Thread");
     suspended = false ;
     t.start();
  }
  public void run() {
     try {
        for (int i = 0; i < 10; i++) {
           System.out.println("Thread: " + i );
           Thread.sleep(200);
           synchronized (this) {
              while (suspended) {
                 wait();
              }
           }
        }
     } catch (InterruptedException e ) {
          System.out.println("Thread: interrupted.");
     }
     System.out.println("Thread exiting.");
  }
  void suspendThread() {
     suspended = true;
  }
  synchronized void resumeThread() {
     suspended = false;
     notify();
  }
}
class Demo {
   public static void main (String args [] ) {
      MyThread t1 = new MyThread();
      try{
         Thread.sleep(1000);
         t1.suspendThread();
         System.out.println("Thread: Suspended");
         Thread.sleep(1000);
         t1.resumeThread();
```

```
            System.out.println("Thread: Resume");
        } catch ( InterruptedException e) {
        }
        try {
           t1.t.join();
        } catch ( InterruptedException e) {
              System.out.println (
                   "Main Thread: interrupted");
        }
    }
}
```

Quiz

1. What is a thread?
2. What is multitasking?
3. What kind of overhead occurs during multitasking?
4. What is a thread priority?
5. What is synchronization?
6. What is the `Runnable` interface?
7. When should you extend the `Thread` class?
8. If you create one thread in your program, how many threads actually run?
9. What method must you override when you create a thread in your program?
10. How do you define the portion of your program that becomes a thread?

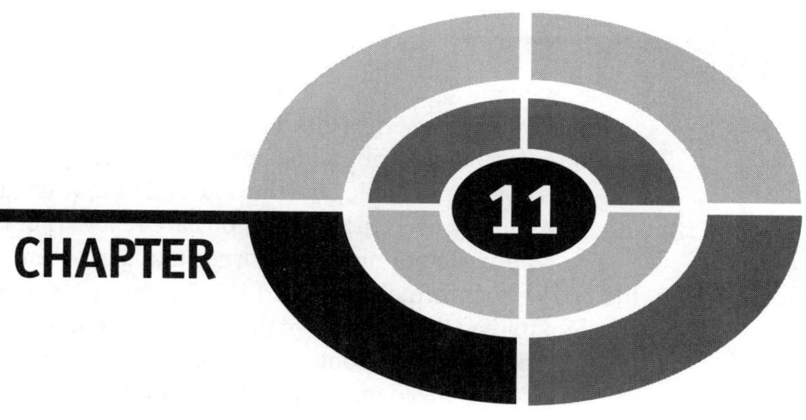

Files and Streams

If memory could last forever, we would never need to store information on a disk. Until that day arrives, you'll need to save information processed by your program to a disk and efficiently retrieve that information from the disk. Java has a variety of file and stream classes designed specifically to handle the storage and flow of information to and from a disk. File classes let your program interact with a computer's file system, and stream classes focus on managing the flow of bytes between your program and the file system. You'll learn how to use both kinds of classes in this chapter.

Files and File Systems

A file is a logical grouping of related bytes stored in secondary storage. Secondary storage is a disk, CD, or tape that is capable of permanently retaining information. A file system is software used to organize and maintain files on a second storage device.

Each file has properties that describe the file. The file system determines the kinds of properties that describe a file; however, typically they include the file's name, permissions to access the file, and the date and time when the file was last updated. The three commonly used file permissions are read/write, read-only, and execute.

The read/write permission signifies that a program can read the contents of the file and write information to the file. The read-only permission gives your program the right to read the contents of the file, but not to write to the file. The execute permission means the file contains a computer program.

Files are organized in a series of directories and subdirectories, sometimes called *folders*. The topmost directory is called the *root* directory. It is from here that the hierarchy of subdirectories begins. Collectively, these directories and subdirectories are referred to as the *directory structure*, which is created by the administrator who is responsible for maintaining the secondary storage device.

The File Class

The `File` class is contained in the `java.io` package and defines the methods you use to interact with the file system and to navigate the directory structure, much the same way you interactively move from one subdirectory to another.

You create an instance of a `File` class by using one of three constructors, as shown here:

```
File file1 = new File(String directory);
File file1 = new File(String directory, String fileName);
File file1 = new File(File directoryObject,
      String fileName);
```

The first constructor requires that you pass it a path to the file. Many times the path is a directory hierarchy that ends with the subdirectory needed by your program. For example, `c:\junk\test` is a directory path that leads to the `test` subdirectory within the `junk` directory of the C drive.

The second constructor requires two parameters. The first parameter is the directory path, and the second parameter is the name of a file contained in the last subdirectory on the path. Let's say the directory path is `c:\junk\test` and the filename is `demo.java`. If we pass these to the second constructor, we are telling Java that the `demo.java` file is located in the `c:\junk\test` subdirectory.

The third constructor is very similar to the second constructor, except the directory path is passed as an instance of the `File` class instead of as a string.

It is important to remember that these constructors do not create a directory or subdirectory, nor do they create a file. Instead, think of these constructors as pointing to either a directory path or a file.

Once your program can point to a directory path or file, you can call methods defined in the `File` class to interact with the directory path or file. Table 11-1 contains a list of commonly used methods. The following program shows you how to use many of these methods. This program points to the `\junk\test` directory path and then inquires about the `test` subdirectory. Here's what is displayed on the screen after this program runs. You can change the directory path to one that you have on your computer. If you do, your results might be slightly different from those shown here:

```
Name: test
Path: \junk\test
Absolute Path: C:\junk\test
Parent: \junk
Exists: true
Write: true
Read: true
Directory: true
File: false
Absolute: false
 Length: 0
```

```
import java.io.*;
class Demo {
   public static void main(String args[]) {
      File file1 = new File ("\\junk\\test");
      System.out.println("Name: " + file1.getName());
      System.out.println("Path: " + file1.getPath());
      System.out.println("Absolute Path: "
            + file1.getAbsolutePath());
      System.out.println("Parent: " + file1.getParent());
      System.out.println("Exists: " + file1.exists());
      System.out.println("Write: " + file1.canWrite());
      System.out.println("Read: " + file1.canRead());
      System.out.println("Directory: "
             + file1.isDirectory());
      System.out.println("File: " + file1.isFile());
      System.out.println("Absolute: "
             + file1.isAbsolute());
      System.out.println("Length: " + file1.length());
   }
}
```

Method	Description
`isFile()`	Returns a Boolean true if the object is a file; otherwise, a false is returned. False is also returned if the instance of the `File` class refers to a directory, subdirectory, a pipe, or a device driver.
`isAbsolute()`	Returns a Boolean true if the file contains an absolute path; otherwise, a Boolean false is returned.
`boolean renameTo(File newName)`	Renames a directory, subdirectory, or file to the name passed to the renameTo() method.
`delete()`	Deletes the disk file.
`void deleteOnExit()`	Removes the file when the Java Virtual Machine terminates.
`boolean isHidden()`	Returns a Boolean true if the directory path or file is hidden; otherwise, this method returns a Boolean false.
`boolean setLastModified( long millisec)`	Sets the timestamp on the file. The timestamp must specify the date and time in milliseconds, beginning with January 1, 1970 and ending with the current date and time.
`boolean setReadOnly()`	Sets the file to read-only.
`compareTo()`	Compares two files.
`length()`	The length of the file in bytes.
`isDirectory()`	Returns a Boolean true if it is a directory; otherwise, a boolean false is returned.
`canRead()`	Returns a Boolean true if the directory path or file has read permission; otherwise, a Boolean false is returned.
`canWrite()`	Returns a Boolean true if the directory path or file has write permission; otherwise, a Boolean false is returned.
`exists()`	Returns a Boolean true if the directory path or file exists; otherwise, a Boolean false is returned.
`getParent()`	Returns the name of the parent directory path that contains the subdirectory.
`getAbsolutePath()`	Returns the absolute path.
`getPath()`	Returns the directory path.
`getName()`	Returns the name of the directory path or file.

Table 11-1 Methods Defined in the `File` Class

NOTE: *Windows uses a backslash as a separator between subdirectories. Unix and Linux use a forward slash for the same purpose. Java converts a forward slash to a backslash if you are running a Windows machine. If you use a backslash, remember that you must use two backslashes instead of one. The first backslash is an escape character, and the second is the backslash. This is illustrated in the previous program.*

Listing Files Contained in a Directory

You can return the contents of a directory by calling the `list()` method. The `list()` method returns an array of strings containing the names of the files stored in the directory. The `list()` method can only be used on a directory; therefore, you should call the `isDirectory()` method prior to calling the `list()` method to determine whether the file is in fact a directory. The `isDirectory()` method returns a Boolean true if the file is a directory; otherwise, a Boolean false is returned.

The following example shows how to use the `isDirectory()` method and the `list()` method to retrieve and display the contents of a directory on the screen. The example begins by referencing the `temp` directory. The name `temp` is assigned to a string, which is then passed to the constructor of the `File` object. Before searching the directory, we determine whether it is indeed a directory by calling the `isDirectory()` method. If it is not a directory, the program displays an appropriate message on the screen; otherwise, the program proceeds to retrieve the contents of the directory.

The `list()` method is called to retrieve the contents of the directory, which is stored in an array of strings called `str`. The program enters a `for` loop in order to step through elements of the string array. Each entry in the array is passed to the constructor of the `File` class. This enables us to call the `isDirectory()` method to determine whether the array element is a subdirectory. If it is, we indicate that it is a subdirectory when the name is displayed on the screen. If it's not, only the name of the entry is displayed.

```
import java.io.File;
class Demo {
   public static void main(String args[] ) {
     String dir = " /temp";
     File file1 = new File(dir);
     if (file1.isDirectory()) {
        System.out.println( "Directory:" + dir);
        String str[] = file1.list();
        for (int i=0; i <str.length; i++) {
```

```
                File file2 = new File (dir + "/" + str[i]);
                if (file2.isDirectory()) {
                   System.out.prinln("Directory: "+ str[i]);
                }
                else {
                   System.out.println(str[i]);
                }
             }
          } else {
             System.out.println("Not a directory ");
          }
       }
    }
```

Streams

No doubt you've heard the term *stream* used to describe water or even electrons flowing across an electrical circuit. A stream in a Java program is very similar to these, except instead of water and electrons, a stream in Java consists of bytes.

Java has several stream classes that are built upon four abstract classes. These are `InputStream`, `OutputStream`, `Reader`, and `Writer`. You indirectly use these classes when you use Java's concrete stream classes to interact with a stream of bytes.

Many subclasses are available in Java to interact with streams. Rather than explore all these subclasses, we'll focus on four commonly used file routines that illustrate some subclasses. You'll learn how to write to a file, read from a file, append to a file, and write and read objects to and from a file.

Typically, a program stores data in one of three ways: as individual pieces of data that are not encapsulated in a class, as data that is encapsulated in a class, or as data stored in a database. The next three sections of this chapter show you how to store and retrieve data that is not encapsulated in a class. The last section of this chapter shows you how to store and retrieve data that *is* encapsulated in a class. Also, in Chapter 13, you'll learn how to store and retrieve data to and from a database.

Writing to a File

In order to write data to a file, you need to first create a file output stream. A file output stream opens the file or creates a new file if the file doesn't exist. Once the file output stream is open, you can write data to the file using a print writer.

You open a file output stream by using the constructor of the `FileOutputStream` class and passing it the name of the file you want to open. You can include the full path as part of the filename if the file isn't in the current directory. The constructor returns a reference to the file output stream.

You create a print writer by calling the constructor of the `PrintWriter` class and passing it a reference to the file output stream. The constructor returns a reference to `PrintWriter`. You use the `PrintWriter` reference to call methods of the `PrintWriter` class to write to the file. After you finish writing to the file, you must call the `close()` method to close the file.

The following example illustrate how to open a file output stream, create a printer writer, and write data to a file. The example begins by declaring and initializing three strings that will be written to the file. Next, the program opens the file output stream and creates a print writer. The file for this example is called `Student.dat` and is stored in the current directory. The example then calls the `print()` method defined in the `PrintWriter` class to write data to the `Student.dat` file. Each time the `print()` method is called, it is passed the data that is to be written to the file. The file is closed after the last data element is written.

Notice that all the statements involved in opening the file output stream and writing to the file are contained within a try block. Should any exceptions occur, such as insufficient disk space, an exception is thrown and caught by the catch block.

```
import java.io.*;
import java.util.*;
public class Demo {
   public  static void main( String args[] )
   {
      String studentFirstName = "Bob ";
      String studentLastName = " Smith ";
      String finalGrade = "A";
      try
{
  PrintWriter out = new PrintWriter(
               new FileOutputStream("Student.dat"));
  out.print(studentFirstName);
  out.print(studentLastName);
  out.println(grade);
}
      catch (IOException e)
{
   System.out.println(e);
}
      finally {
```

```
            out.close();
        }
    }
}
```

Reading from a File

You have several ways to read data from a file. You can read a byte of data at a time. You can read a specific number of bytes at a time. You can also read a line of bytes at one time. A line consists of a series of bytes that end with a byte that corresponds to a newline character. This is similar to pressing the ENTER key at the end of a sentence. The ENTER key typically causes the program to insert a newline character. Once the line is read, you have the program divide the line into meaningful segments, such as a student's first name and last name, by using functions defined in the `String` class. Alternatively, your program can simply display the entire line on the screen. Another common approach to reading from a file is to read data as strings. That is, a string is read from a file rather than bytes. You'll see how this is done later in this section.

In order to read a file, you'll need to open the file. There are a number of ways to do this in Java. A common way is to create a file reader by using the constructor of the `FileReader` class and passing it the name of the file you want opened. The filename should include the full path name if the file isn't in the current directory.

It takes time to read bytes from a disk drive. Programmers refer to this as *necessary overhead*, the cost of reading a file. In order to reduce this overhead, programmers read a chunk of bytes at one time and store them in memory called a *buffer*. The program then reads bytes from the buffer instead of the disk drive.

You can use this same technique in your program by creating a *buffer reader*, which creates the buffer for storing data from the disk drive. You create a buffer reader by using the `BufferedReader` constructor and passing it a reference to the `FileReader` used to open the file. The `BufferedReader` class defines the methods you use to read data from the buffer. This approach also applies to writing data, and in the previous example, using `BufferedWriter` would have made the program more efficient.

The following example shows how to create a file reader and buffer reader. It then uses them to read from the file created in the previous example. This example opens the `Student.dat` file, which contains data about one student. This data is copied from the file and into the buffer. The `readLine()` method is then called to read one line at a time from the buffer, which is assigned to a string variable.

Notice that all this takes place in the conditional expression of the `while` loop. We do this in order to determine when we've reached the end of the file. The `readLine()` method returns a null when the end of the file is reached. The program enters the `while` loop to print the line on the screen as long as the line isn't null (that is, as long as we haven't reached the end of the file). Once the end of file is reached, the program breaks out of the `while` loop and calls the `close()` method, which closes the file.

```
import java.io.*;
import java.util.*;
 public class Demo {
    public  static void main( String args[] )
    {
       String line;
       try
       {
          BufferedReader in = new BufferedReader(
               new FileReader("Student.dat"));
          while (( line = in.readLine()) != null)
          {
             System.out.println(line);
          }

       }
       catch (IOException e)
       {
           System.out.println(e);
       }
       finally {
          in.close();
       }
   }
}
```

Appending to a File

Think of a file as a long strip of tape, where the first byte written to the file is at the beginning of the tape, and subsequent bytes fall into place behind the first byte. When you wrote data to a file previously in this chapter, the data was always written at the beginning of the file. This is fine if you don't want to retain the data already stored in the file, because the new data will overwrite the existing data in the file.

However, programmers usually want to add data to a file rather than replace existing data. To do this, new data must be written after the last byte in the file rather than being written at the beginning of the file. Programmers call this *appending data to a file.*

You append data to a file by setting the second parameter of the `FileOutputStream` constructor to true. As you'll recall from the "Writing to a File" section of this chapter, the `FileOutputStream` constructor is used to open a file for writing. The version of the constructor used in the "Writing to a File" section consisted of one argument, which is the filename. Bytes are written at the beginning of the file by default.

Another version of the `FileOutputStream` constructor uses two arguments. The first argument is again the filename, and the second argument is the Boolean value true. This causes bytes to be written at the end of the file. The file is created if it doesn't exist.

The following example illustrates how to append data to a file. This example is nearly the same program as the example shown in the "Writing to a File" section, except we use the second version of the `FileOutputStream` constructor and pass it a Boolean true as the second argument, causing data to be written at the end of the file.

```
import java.io.*;
import java.util.*;
public class Demo {
   public  static void main( String args[] )
   {
      String studentFirstName = "Mary";
      String studentLastName = " Jones ";
      String grade = "A";
      try
      {
         PrintWriter out = new PrintWriter(
                new FileOutputStream("Student.dat", true));
         out.print(studentFirstName);
         out.print(studentLastName);
         out.println(grade);

     }
     catch (IOException e)
     {
        System.out.println(e);
     }
     finally {
        out.close();
     }
   }
}
```

Reading and Writing an Object to a File

Previously in this chapter, you learned how to write data to a file and read data from a file that is not encapsulated in the class definition. That is, the student name and grade used in previous examples were not associated with each other in a class.

In the real world, many data elements you want stored in a file will be data members of a class. As you'll recall, a class is a cookie cutter that describes attributes and behaviors of an object, such as a student. Attributes are basically data, and behaviors are methods. When you press the cookie cutter into the dough, you make a real cookie. When you declare an instance of a class, you create a real object of the class (in this case, a real student).

Many attributes of a class are held in instance variables. An instance variable represents a memory location used to store data for an instance of the object. Suppose two instance variables are defined in a class definition, and you created five objects of that class. Java sets aside five sets of instance variables, each independent of the other. However, each of these five objects share the same set of methods associated with the class.

When a programmer needs to retain an instance of a class, the programmer saves the instance to the file. In doing so, only the instance variables are stored in the file. Methods are not saved in the file. This is a different technique than we used previously in this chapter, where we saved individual data elements.

We retrieve this data from a file by reading an object from the file rather than reading individual data elements. That is, we read the entire set of instance variables from the file, which are stored in memory and accessed by using a reference to the class.

Here are the steps you must follow in order to be able to write and read an object to and from a file. The initial step is to implement the `Serializable` interface in the class whose objects you are going to write to a file. The `Serializable` interface enables instances of the class to be converted to a byte stream that can be written to disk or transmitted over a network. Programmers call this *serialization*. The byte stream is then deserialized when the object is read and reconstituted back to the instance of the class.

Next, you create an instance of the class and assign values to instance variables. With the data in place, you're ready to open the file. You open a file by using the `new` operator to call the constructor of the `FileOutputStream` class and pass it the name of the file, which you learned how to do previously in this chapter. The `new` operator returns a reference to `FileOutputStream`. This reference is passed to the constructor of the `ObjectOutputStream` class, which defines the methods used to write an object to a file.

Once you create an instance of the ObjectOutputStream, you are ready to write an object to the file. In order to do this, you need to call the writeObject() method and pass it a reference to the instance of the object you want written to the file. Instance variables of the object are saved to the file. Static variables of the object are not saved. You then call the close() method to close the file.

Reading an object from a file is just as easy as writing an object to a file. However, you use the FileInputStream instead of the FileOutputStream, and you use the ObjectInputStream class rather than the ObjectOutputStream class. You read an object from the file by calling readObject(), which is defined in the ObjectInputStream class. The readObject() method returns an instance of the Object class. You'll need to cast this to the specific class of the object. For instance, in the next example we save instances of the Student class. When we read an instance from the file, we cast it as Student. The object returned by the readObject() method is then assigned to a reference to that object and used as you would any object in your program.

Let's take a look at how this works in real life by examining the following example. The example defines a Student class consisting of three instance variables. These are the student's first and last name and grade. Notice that the class implements the Serializable interface, so we can convert the instance to a byte stream. Three instances of the class are declared, each passing data to the constructor of the class. This data is assigned to instance variables. Notice that we used an array of objects for this purpose so that a for loop can be used to write each object to the file. This reduces the number of lines of code that needs to be written.

We then open the Student.dat file by calling the FileOutputStream constructor and passing it two arguments. The first argument is the filename, and the second argument is a Boolean true signifying that we want to append to the file.

The writeObject() method is then called within the first for loop and passed a reference to each instance of the Student class that is declared in this program. After the last instance is written to the file, the file is closed.

Next, we open the file again. This time the file is opened so we can read objects from the file. The readObject() method is called within the second for loop to retrieve each object from the file. Notice that we cast the return value of the readObject() method to Student. We do this because the readObject() method returns a reference to the Object class, which is too general to be used in this program. The Object class is the superclass of all objects. The readStudentInfo array is used to store each object after it is read from the file.

After the last object is read from the file, the file is closed and each instance variable of each object read from the file is displayed on the screen.

```
import java.io.*;
import java.util.*;
```

```
public class Demo {
   public  static void main( String args[] )
    {
      Student[] writeStudentInfo = new Student[3];
      Student[] readStudentInfo = new Student[3];
      writeStudentInfo [0] = new Student (
                "Bob", "Smith", "B");
      writeStudentInfo [1] = new Student (
                 "Mary", "Jones", "A");
      writeStudentInfo [2] = new Student (
                 "Tom", "Jones", "B+");
      try
       {
         ObjectOutputStream out = new ObjectOutputStream(
                  new FileOutputStream("Student.dat",true));
         for (int y = 0; y < 3; y ++){
            out.writeObject(writeStudentInfo[y]);
         }
         out.close();
         ObjectInputStream in = new ObjectInputStream(
                 new FileInputStream("Student.dat"));
          for (int x = 0; x < 3; x++) {
            readStudentInfo[x] =
                   (Student) in.readObject();
         }
         in.close();
         for (int i = 0; i < 3; i++){
            System.out.println(
                 readStudentInfo [i].studentFirstName);
            System.out.println(
                 readStudentInfo [i].studentLastName);
            System.out.println(
                readStudentInfo [i].studentGrade);
         }
       }
      catch (Exception e)
      {
        System.out.println(e);
      }
    }
}
class Student implements Serializable
{
```

```
  String studentFirstName, studentLastName,studentGrade;
  public Student () { };
  public Student (String fn, String ln, String grade)
  {
    studentFirstName = fn;
    studentLastName = ln;
    studentGrade = grade;
  }
}
```

Quiz

1. Why do you need to serialize a class in order to save its objects to a file?
2. What is a stream?
3. What is the benefit of using the `File` class?
4. What is the difference between saving data elements to a file and saving an object to a file?
5. What is the purpose of a filename filter?
6. Can the `PrintWriter` class open a file?
7. How would you specify the path when opening a file?
8. What is the purpose of using the `BufferedReader` class?
9. How would you append data to the end of a file?
10. How can you determine the parent directory path that contains a subdirectory?

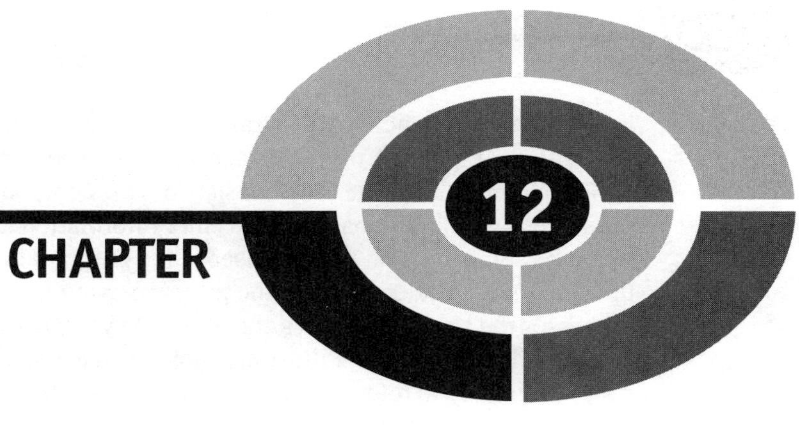

Graphical User Interface

If someone mentioned to you the word *Excel*, you probably conjure the image of an Excel spreadsheet that consists of columns, rows, menus, buttons, and assorted components. You might say that this image is the *face* of the Excel program because it is the portion of the program that you see. Programmers call that image a *graphical user interface (GUI)* because, collectively, those components are used to interact with the program. In this chapter, you'll learn how to use in your own program the push buttons, radio buttons, text boxes, and other components found in commercial programs.

What Is a User Interface?

An *interface* is a way to interact with something. For example, your television remote control is an interface to your television. Throughout this book, you learned how to use the Application Program(ming) Interface (API) to write code that interacts with a computer. A user interface is the way someone interacts with a program.

The simplest user interface consists of two components: a prompt displayed on the screen and the keyboard used to enter information into the program. The prompt might be some text that tells the user of the program to enter a student ID. The user then enters the student ID into the program using the keyboard. The program then processes the student ID when the ENTER key is pressed.

The following example illustrates how to create this simple user interface. `System.in` is used to reference the standard input to the computer, which by default is the keyboard. The person running your program could redirect the standard input to another input device, such as a file.

This example uses an `InputStreamReader` object and a `BufferedReader` object to improve reading information from the keyboard. Information entered by the user into the keyboard is stored as a series of bytes. However, our example needs a sequence of characters. The `InputStreamReader` converts the bytes into characters. We want to read information from the keyboard quickly. To do so, we want to read characters from memory (called a *buffer)* rather than directly from the keyboard. However, the `InputStreamReader` doesn't use a buffer. Therefore, we need to use the `BufferedReader`, which reads characters from the `InputStreamReader` and saves them to a buffer. We then called the `readLine()` method defined in the `BufferedReader` class to read one full line of text from the buffer.

This example illustrates a very simple user interface. It displays a prompt on the screen and then calls the `readLine()` method. The `readLine()` method returns all the characters that were entered into the keyboard, which are then collectively assigned to the String `studentID` and displayed on the screen.

```
import java.io.*;
public class Demo {
  public static void main(String args[]) {
     BufferedReader stdin = new BufferedReader(
           new InputStreamReader(System.in));
     try {
        System.out.print("Enter your student ID: ");
        String studentID = stdin.readLine();
        System.out.println( "Student ID: " + studentID);
     } catch (IOException e) {
        System.out.println( "Exception:" + e );
   }
  }
}
```

What Is a GUI?

No doubt you've heard the term *GUI* used whenever anyone talks about a user interface for a program. GUI is an acronym for *graphical user interface*. Practically every program used today uses graphics as a way for a user to interact with the program because a GUI is an intuitive and efficient way to collect information from a user and to display information for a user to read.

Researchers at Xerox's Palo Alto Research Center (PARC) are credited with developing the GUI, which was later enhanced by Apple Computer and then by Microsoft. At the heart of a GUI are the standard graphical elements that collectively form the user interface. These elements are commonly recognized as windows, menus, push buttons, labels, text boxes, radio buttons, and other similar GUI objects that you see used in nearly all commercial programs today.

Besides making a program look pretty, the standard GUI dramatically reduces the time necessary for someone to learn how to use a new program. Arguably, 75 percent of every program is the same. That is, it uses the same two-dozen or so graphical elements. Each of those graphical elements operates identically across programs. For example, nearly everyone who has used a computer program knows to select the down arrow to the right of a text box in order to see a list of values that can be entered into the text box. The values are likely to change from program to program, but the process used to select those values is the same in all programs.

You have two ways in which you can create a GUI for your program. First is the simple approach of using a message dialog box and an input dialog box. A dialog box is a small window. You've seen a dialog box when you select File | Open from the menu bar—the Open dialog box is displayed.

A message dialog box is a dialog box that displays a message and an OK push button, which is what you see whenever a warning message is displayed on the screen. An input dialog box is similar to a message dialog box, except you can enter information into an input dialog box.

Both the message dialog box and the input dialog box are displayed by calling one method, which you'll learn how to do in the next section. This is a quick-and-dirty way to create a GUI for your program. However, these are very limiting because you won't be able to use all the GUI elements in these dialog boxes.

The second way to create a GUI for your program is to use radio buttons, push buttons, and other GUI objects that you see in most programs. Most of this chapter shows you how to create a GUI object for your program.

A Simple GUI

The easiest way to create a GUI for your program is to use a message dialog box and an input dialog box. A message dialog box is used to display a message on the screen, and an input dialog box prompts the user to enter information that is returned to your program for processing.

Let's take a look at how to create a message dialog box. You create a message dialog box by calling the `showMessageDialog()` method, which is defined in the `JOptionPane` class contained in the `javax.swing` package. This means you'll need to import the `javax.swing` package at the top of your program in order to call the `showMessageDialog()` method.

The `showMessageDialog()` method requires four arguments. The first argument is a reference to the parent that calls the `showMessageDialog()` method. Many programmers simply use null as the value for this argument because there isn't a parent for this dialog box.

The second argument is the message you want displayed on the screen. The third argument is the caption that appears in the title bar of the dialog box, and the last argument is a constant that states the kind of message dialog box you want displayed. Table 12-1 contains a list of the most commonly used message constants. Each one displays an icon within the message dialog box that corresponds to the kind of message being displayed.

Constants	Description
`JOptionPane.PLAIN_MESSAGE`	Used to display a general-purpose message
`JOptionPane.ERROR_MESSAGE`	Used to display an error message
`JOptionPane.INFORMATION_MESSAGE`	Used to display a general-purpose message
`JOptionPane.WARNING_MESSAGE`	Used to display a warning message
`JOptionPane.QUESTION_MESSAGE`	Used to question the user regarding a user response to your program

Table 12-1 Constants Used to Determine the Kind of Message Dialog Box to Display

The `showMessageDialog()` method also displays an OK push button that the user selects to acknowledge the message. The push button closes the dialog box when selected.

Here is how you call the `showMessageDialog()` method:

```
JOptionPane.showMessageDialog(null, "Message", "Window Caption",
JOptionPane.PLAIN_MESSAGE);
```

Figure 12-1 shows the dialog box created by this method call.

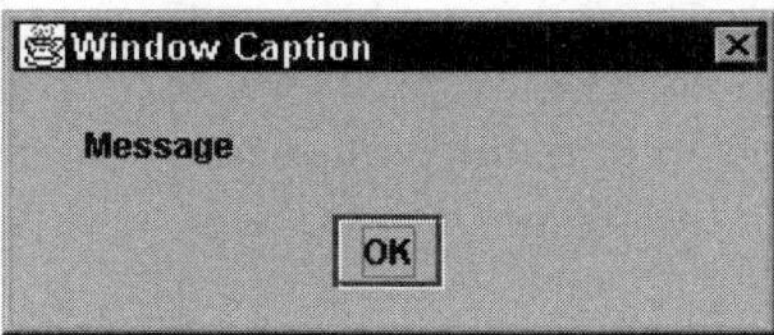

Figure 12-1 Here is a "plain" message dialog box. It is useful for displaying any kind of message on the screen.

An input dialog box is created by calling the `showInputDialog()` method, which is also defined in the `JOptionPane` class. The `showInputDialog()` method requires one argument, which is a message prompting the user to enter information into the dialog box.

The `showInputDialog()` method displays the message and a text box, which is where the user enters information. In addition, the OK and Cancel push button are displayed. Selecting OK causes the `showInputDialog()` method to return the information that the user entered into the text box. Selecting either push button closes the dialog box.

Information that the user enters into the text box is returned by the `showInputDialog()` method as a string, which is usually assigned to a String variable and then processed by the program. Here is how to call the `showInputDialog()`:

```
String  str = JOptionPane.showInputDialog("Enter Student ID: ");
```

Figure 12-2 shows the input dialog that is displayed when this method is called.

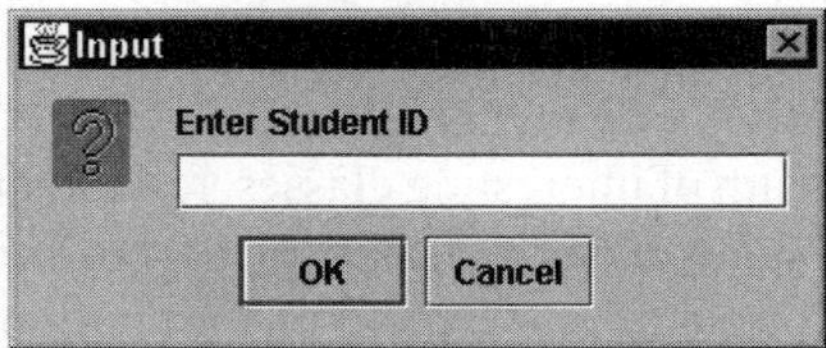

Figure 12-2 The **`showInputDialog()`** method displays an input dialog box that is used to gather information from the user of your program.

The following example illustrates how to call both the `showMessageDialog()` method and the `showInputDialog()` method from within a program. This example begins by importing all the swing classes, which is necessary to call either dialog box method. Next, a string is declared and is later used to store information returned by the showInputDialog() method. The showMessageDialog() method is called first to display the message dialog box. Once the user acknowledges the message by selecting the OK push button, the message dialog box closes and the showInputDialog() method is called to display the input dialog box. The information returned by the showInputDialog() method is then assigned to the string.

```
import javax.swing.*;
public class Demo {
   public static void main(String[] args) {
      String str;
      JOptionPane.showMessageDialog(null,
           "Message", "Window Caption", JOptionPane.
PLAIN_MESSAGE);
      str = JOptionPane.showInputDialog (
            "Enter Student ID ");
      System.exit(0);
   }
}
```

swing

In the previous section, you learned how to use the JOptionPane class that's contained in the javax.swing package. The javax.swing package contains a large collection of GUI classes that have become known as the *Java Foundation Classes (JFC)*. The javax.swing package contains a richer collection of graphic classes than the Abstract Windows Toolkit (AWT) packages of classes. AWT and JFC are complementary. Programmers use both libraries to create a graphical interface to their programs.

The JFC contains a wealth of interesting classes you can incorporate into your program. In fact, the JFC contains so many classes, there aren't enough pages in this book to explain each of them. Therefore, we'll focus on the common classes used to create a GUI for a typical program. You can learn about the entire JFC at java.sun.com.

Let's begin by covering the basics of a GUI. All GUIs require a window that can be minimized, maximized, and resized by the person using the computer. A window needs a content container that is used to contain push buttons, text boxes, and other

GUI elements that comprise the GUI for your program. The content container appears inside the window.

Typically, programmers define their own window class that contains the definition for all the elements of their window, including the content container and GUI elements. An instance of the window class is then declared any time the programmer needs a window. Any changes to the window occur in one place—the window class.

The window class extends the `JFrame` class. The `JFrame` class is a JFC that defines all the methods necessary to manage the window, such as the methods for resizing it. This means that your window class has all the features found in the `JFrame` class.

Three commonly used methods are defined in the `JFrame` class. These are the `setSize()` method, the `setDefaultCloseOperation()` method, and the `setVisible()` method. The `setSize()` method requires two arguments: the integers that define the width and height of the window, measured in pixels. For example, the following method defines the size of the window to be 400 pixels wide and 100 pixels high:

```
setSize(400,100);
```

The `setDefaultCloseOperation()` method defines how the window behaves when the user closes the window (for example, by clicking the "X" in the window's upper-right corner). The `setDefaultCloseOperation()` method requires one argument: a constant that defines the behavior. Many programmers use the `EXIT_ON_CLOSE` constant (which causes the window to exit when the user selects Close), as shown here:

```
setDefaultCloseOperation(JFrame.EXIT_ON_CLOSE);
```

The window you create is not shown until you call the `setVisible()` method. The `setVisible()` method requires one argument: a Boolean true or false. A Boolean true causes the window to be displayed. A Boolean false causes the window to be hidden from view. Here's the `setVisible()` method.

```
setVisible(true);
```

Typically, each window has a caption on the title bar that describes the purpose of the window. You create the window caption by calling the constructor of the `JFrame` class and passing it the caption. Because your window class extends the `JFrame` class, you can call the constructor by using `super`, as shown here:

```
super ("Window Title");
```

The follow example illustrates how to define your own window class and display the window on the screen. Figure 12-3 shows the window it displays.

Figure 12-3 You create a window by defining your own window class that extends the **JFrame** class.

```
import javax.swing.*;
   public class Demo {
      public static void main(String[] args) {
         Window win = new Window();
      }
}
class Window extends JFrame {
   public Window () {
       super ("Window Title");
       setSize(400,100);
       setDefaultCloseOperation(JFrame.EXIT_ON_CLOSE);
       setVisible(true);
 }
}
```

Content Container

Before you can insert GUI elements into the window, you need to create a container for them. Think of a container as a box into which you place the GUI elements. The container is then placed inside the window.

A container is defined in the `Container` class found in the Abstract Windowing Toolkit. You can access the `Container` class by importing the `java.awt` package. You declare an instance of the `Container` class by calling the `getContentPane()` method of the `JFrame` class within the window class you defined for your program. The `getContentPane()` method returns a reference to the content container, which is assigned to a `Container` object reference. This is illustrated in the following statement:

```
Container ca = getContentPane();
```

The `Container` class defines many methods, but the method that is most commonly used is the `setBackground()` method. The `setBackground()` method colors the content container, giving your window a background color. The `setBackground()` method requires one argument: the constant defined in the

Color class that refers to the color you want for the background. Table 12-2 lists the most commonly used color constants.

Constant	Color
Color.white	White
Color.lightGray	Light Gray
Color.gray	Gray
Color.black	Black
Color.blue	Blue
Color.green	Green
Color.cyan	Cyan
Color.magenta	Magenta
Color.orange	Orange
Color.pink	Pink
Color.yellow	Yellow

Table 12-2 Color Constants Used to Paint the Content Container of a Window

The follow example shows how to declare an instance of a container and display the container within the window. You'll notice that this example builds upon the previous example. This example colors the background of the container light gray:

```
Import java.awt.*;
import javax.swing.*;
   public class Demo {
      public static void main(String[] rgs) {
         Window win = new Window();
      }
}
class Window extends JFrame {
   public Window () {
       super ("Window Title");
       setSize(400,100);
       setDefaultCloseOperation(JFrame.EXIT_ON_CLOSE);
       setVisible(true);
       Container ca = getContentPane();
       ca.setBackground(Color.lightgray);
 }
}
```

Java Layout Managers

In some programming languages you specify the pixel coordinates where the GUI element should appear within the window. Programmers call this specifying the exact position of the GUI element. Positing GUI elements within the container is a little tricky because you specify relative positions rather than exact positions. That is, you specify generally where you want the GUI element to be positioned on the screen, and the Java virtual engine determines the exact location.

At first, this technique of locating GUI elements within the container appears archaic. However, there is a very logical reason Java uses this technique. Remember that a Java program is machine independent. This means that the program that runs on your computer must also be able to run on any kind of computer that has a Java Virtual Machine running. And those other computers are likely to have a different screen than the screen you used to design your program.

To compensate for these differences, Java requires the Java Virtual Machine to determine the exact screen location for GUI elements. You simply provide a general location on the screen for where you want the GUI element.

Your first step is to decide on a layout manager for the container. Think of a layout manager as a way that Java organizes the container. There are four commonly used layout managers: the Flow Layout Manager, the Border Layout Manager, the Grid Layout Manager, and the Gridbag Layout Manager.

Flow Layout Manager

The Flow Layout Manager is used to place GUI elements in the container the way words are placed on a page—that is, from left to right then at the beginning of the next line. GUI elements are automatically repositioned in the center of the container whenever the window is resized.

You use the Flow Layout Manager by declaring an instance of the `FlowLayout` class, as shown here:

```
FlowLayout flm = new FlowLayout();
```

As you'll soon discover when you begin placing GUI elements in a container, you have little control over the placement of the elements. For example, the `FlowLayout` class enables you to specify if you want GUI elements to be centered, flush left, or flush right by passing the constructor an appropriate constant. The default behavior is to center elements, so you don't need to pass the constructor a constant to center the elements. You can specify left or right by passing the constructor the `FlowLayout.LEFT` or `FlowLayout.RIGHT` constant. You can also specify the horizontal and vertical gap between GUI elements by passing the constructor integers for both these values. The integer represents the number of pixels that will separate elements.

Many of the examples in this chapter use the Flow Layout Manager.

Border Layout Manager

The Border Layout Manager divides the container into five regions. These are north, south, east, west, and center. You use the Border Layout Manager by declaring an instance of the `BorderLayout` class, which is shown in the next example.

The `add()` method of the container class is used to place a GUI element in the container. A version of the `add()` method requires two arguments. The first argument is a reference to the GUI element. The second argument is the layout manager reference used to position the element.

You use one of the `BorderLayout` class's constants to specify the position. The `BorderLayout` class's constants are listed here:

```
BorderLayout.NORTH

BorderLayout.SOUTH

BorderLayout.EAST

BorderLayout.WEST

BorderLayout.CENTER
```

The following example illustrates how to use the Border Layout Manager. This example displays a window that contains two push buttons. You'll learn more about push buttons in the "Push Buttons" section. One button is placed in the west area of the container, and the other button is displayed in the east area of the container (Figure 12-4).

Figure 12-4 The Border Layout Manager divides the container into five areas, known as north, south, east, west, and center.

```
import java.awt.*;
import javax.swing.*;
   public class Demo {
      public static void main(String[] args) {
         Window win = new Window();
      }
}
class Window extends JFrame {
   public Window () {
      super ("Window Title");
      setSize(400,100);
      setDefaultCloseOperation(JFrame.EXIT_ON_CLOSE);
      setVisible(true);
      Container ca = getContentPane();
      ca.setBackground(Color.lightGray);
      BorderLayout blm = new BorderLayout();
      ca.setLayout(blm);
      JButton bt1 = new JButton("Start Test 1");
      ca.add(bt1,blm.WEST);
      JButton bt2 = new JButton("Start Test 2");
      ca.add(bt2,blm.EAST);
      setContentPane(ca);
   }
}
```

Grid Layout Manager and the Gridbag Layout Manager

The Grid Layout Manager divides the container into rows and columns. You create the Grid Layout Manager by declaring an instance of the `GridLayout` class, which is shown here:

```
GridLayout glm = new GridLayout();
```

You specify the number of rows and columns that form the grid when you declare the instance of the `GridLayout` class. You do so by passing the constructor two arguments. Both arguments are integers. The first argument specifies the number of rows, and the second argument specifies the number of columns. Each cell is of equal size regardless of the size of the GUI element assigned to that cell.

A drawback of using the Grid Layout Manager is that you cannot specify the cell to place a GUI element. Elements are placed in cells from left to right in the order in which they are added to the container.

It is for this reason that some programmers prefer to use the Gridbag Layout Manager. The Gridbag Layout Manager enables you to place a GUI element into a specific

cell. You create a Gridbag Layout Manager by declaring an instance of the `GridbagLayout` class, which is shown in the next example.

You'll also need to declare an instance of the `GridBagConstraints` class. The `GridBagConstraints` class is used to specify where to position the GUI element in the grid. You assign a row and column number to the `gridx` and `gridy` attributes, respectively, and then pass a reference to the instance of the `GridBagConstraints` class to the container's `add()` method when adding a new GUI element to the container.

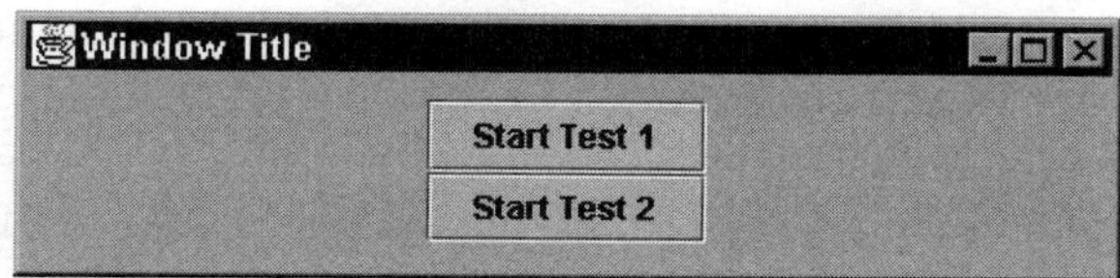

Figure 12-5 You can create a grid and specify the location of GUI elements on the grid by using the Gridbag Layout Manager.

The following example shows how to create a grid and then position two buttons within the grid. Figure 12-5 displays the grid created by this example.

```
import java.awt.*;
import javax.swing.*;
   public class Demo {
      public static void main(String[] args) {
         Window win = new Window();
      }
}
class Window extends JFrame {
   public Window () {
      super ("Window Title");
      setSize(400,100);
      setDefaultCloseOperation(JFrame.EXIT_ON_CLOSE);
      setVisible(true);
      Container ca = getContentPane();
      ca.setBackground(Color.lightGray);
      GridBagLayout gblm = new GridBagLayout();
      GridBagConstraints gbc = new GridBagConstraints();
      ca.setLayout(gblm);
      JButton bt1 = new JButton("Start Test 1");
      gbc.gridx = 1;
      gbc.gridy = 0;
      ca.add(bt1,gbc);
      JButton bt2 = new JButton("Start Test 2");
```

```
        gbc.gridx = 1;
        gbc.gridy = 1;
        ca.add(bt2,gbc);
        setContentPane(ca);
    }
}
```

Push Buttons

Now that you've learned how to create a window and a container and then specify a layout manager, we can turn our attention to adding GUI elements to the container. Let's begin by creating a push button.

You must follow three steps to add a push button to the container. First, you'll need to create the push button. This is done by declaring an instance of the `JButton` class. With few exceptions, most buttons you'll create will have a label on them. Passing text to the constructor creates the label. Here's how you'd create a "Start" button:

```
JButton start = new JButton("Start");
```

The second step is to pass a reference to the instance of `JButton` to the `add()` method of the container. Depending on the layout manager you choose, you may also want to specify the location of the button as the second argument to the `add()` method (see "Java Layout Managers").

The third step is to pass a reference to the content pane of the container to the `setContentPane()` method. Think of the content pane as a pane of glass that fits into the container. GUI elements are on this pane of glass. The `setContentPane()` method places the pane of glass into the window (container). You create a content pane by calling the `getContentPane()` method, as shown in the following example.

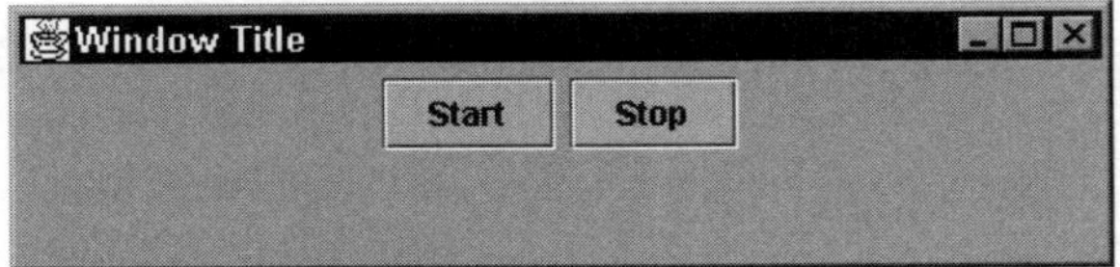

Figure 12-6 Adding two push buttons to the window

Figure 12-6 shows the window displayed when you run the example.

```
import java.awt.*;
import javax.swing.*;
    public class Demo {
```

```
      public static void main(String[] args) {
         Window win = new Window();
      }
}
class Window extends JFrame {
   public Window () {
        super ("Window Title");
        setSize(400,100);
        setDefaultCloseOperation(JFrame.EXIT_ON_CLOSE);
        setVisible(true);
        Container ca = getContentPane();
        ca.setBackground(Color.lightGray);
        FlowLayout flm = new FlowLayout();
        ca.setLayout(flm);
        JButton start = new JButton("Start");
        ca.add(start);
        JButton stop = new JButton("Stop");
        ca.add(stop);
        setContentPane(ca);
 }
}
```

Labels and Text Fields

Two of the most commonly used GUI elements are the label and the text field. The label element is used to place text in the container, and the text field element enables the person who uses your program to enter text.

You create a label by declaring an instance of the `JLabel` class and passing its constructor the text that will appear as the label, as shown here, where "Student Information" is the text of the label:

```
JLabel lab1 = JLabel("Student Information");
```

You create a text field by declaring an instance of the `JTextField` class and passing the constructor of this class two arguments. The first argument is the text that will appear in the text field. The second argument is the number of characters that can be entered into the text field. Some programmers simply leave out the first argument because they'll use the label GUI element to label the text field instead of placing default text within the text field.

The following example shows how to add a label and text field to a container. Notice that that `add()` method is called for each GUI element. Once all the elements have been added to the content pane, the `setContentPane()` method is called to

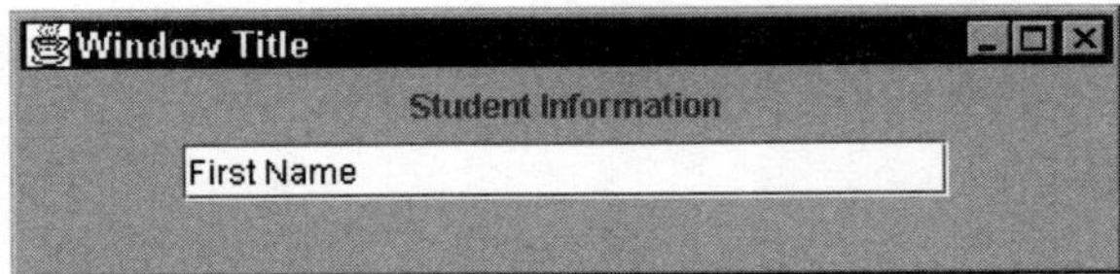

Figure 12-7 The **JLabel** class is used create a label, and the **JTextField** class is used to create a text field.

place the content pane in the container. Figure 12-7 shows the window that is displayed when this example runs.

```
import java.awt.*;
import javax.swing.*;
   public class Demo {
      public static void main(String[] args) {
         Window win = new Window();
      }
}
class Window extends JFrame {
   public Window () {
        super ("Window Title");
        setSize(400,100);
        setDefaultCloseOperation(JFrame.EXIT_ON_CLOSE);
        setVisible(true);
        Container ca = getContentPane();
        ca.setBackground(Color.lightGray);
        FlowLayout flm = new FlowLayout();
        ca.setLayout(flm);
        JLabel lab1 = new JLabel("Student Information");
        ca.add(lab1);
        JTextField text = new JTextField("First Name",25);
        ca.add(text);
        setContentPane(ca);
 }
}
```

Radio Buttons and Check Boxes

Radio buttons and check boxes enable the user of your program to choose a selection rather than having to enter the selection into a text field. Radio buttons are usually displayed in a group. Only one radio button within the group can be selected. All other radio buttons become deselected automatically when the user selects one radio button within the group. Typically, one radio button within the group must be se-

lected. In contrast, check boxes are not grouped together, enabling a user to select none, all, or a combination of check boxes.

You create a radio button by declaring an instance of the `JRadioButton` class. Each radio button is uniquely identified within the group by a label. You create the label by passing text to the `JRadioButton` constructor, as shown here:

```
JRadioButton rb1 = new JRadioButton("Pass");
```

You must also create a radio button group. You do this by declaring an instance of the `ButtonGroup` class, as shown here:

```
ButtonGroup passFail = new ButtonGroup();
```

You add a radio button to the button group by calling the `add()` method of the instance of the `ButtonGroup` class. This is shown in the following statement, where the radio button rb1 is added to the button group passFail:

```
passFail.add(rb1);
```

You then add the button group to the content pane by calling the `add()` method, as shown in previous examples.

You create a check box by declaring an instance of the `JCheckBox` class and passing its constructor the text that will be used as the label for the check box. This is shown here:

```
JCheckBox cb1 = new JCheckBox("Completed");
```

A reference to the check box is passed to the `add()` method of the content pane in order for the check box to appear in the content pane. This is basically the same step used to pass a reference to the button group to the `add()` method of the content pane.

Once all the GUI elements are added to the content pane, the `setContentPane()` method is called and is passed a reference to the content pane.

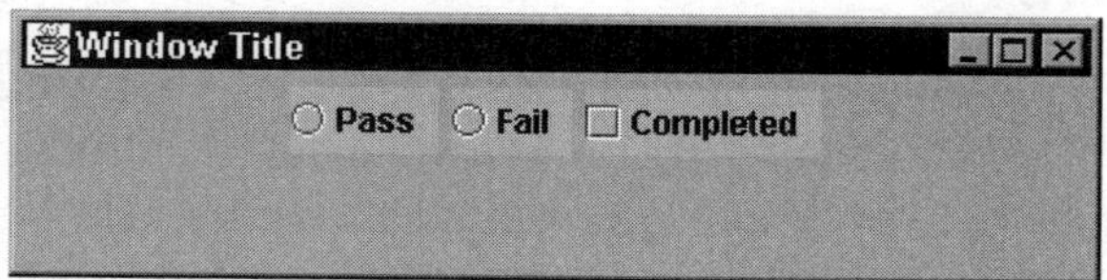

Figure 12-8 Radio buttons must appear in a button group. Check boxes do not have to appear in a button group.

The following example shows how to display radio buttons and a check box in the content pane of a window. Figure 12-8 shows the window that is displayed when you run the following example:

```
import java.awt.*;
import javax.swing.*;
```

```
public class Demo {
   public static void main(String[] args) {
      Window win = new Window();
   }
}
class Window extends JFrame {
   public Window () {
         super ("Window Title");
         setSize(400,100);
         setDefaultCloseOperation(JFrame.EXIT_ON_CLOSE);
         setVisible(true);
         Container ca = getContentPane();
         ca.setBackground(Color.lightGray);
         FlowLayout flm = new FlowLayout();
         ca.setLayout(flm);
         JCheckBox cb1 = new JCheckBox("Completed");
         ButtonGroup passFail = new ButtonGroup();
         JRadioButton rb1 = new JRadioButton("Pass");
         JRadioButton rb2 = new JRadioButton("Fail");
         passFail.add(rb1);
         passFail.add(rb2);
         ca.add(cb1);
         ca.add(rb1);
         ca.add(rb2);
         setContentPane(ca);
   }
}
```

Combo Boxes

A combo box is a GUI element that enables the user of your program to select an item from a list of items contained in a drop-down menu. You create a combo box by declaring an instance of the `JComboBox` class, as shown here:

```
JComboBox combo1 = new JComboBox();
```

Once the instance is declared, you insert items into the drop-down list by calling the `addItem()` method defined in `JComboBox`. The `addItem()` method requires one argument: the text of the item you want added to the combo box. The following statement inserts the text "One" into the instance of the `JComboBox` called combo1.

```
combo1.addItem("One");
```

Two additional steps are necessary to place the combo box in the container of the window. First, you'll need to place the combo box in the content pane by calling the `add()` method of the content pane. Second, you'll place the content pane in the container by calling the `setContentPane()` method.

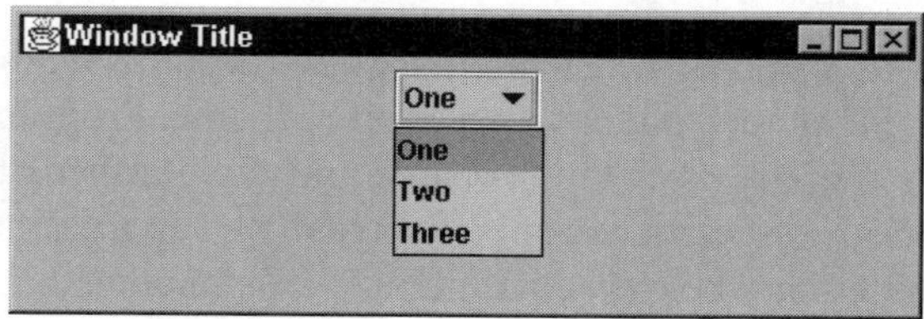

Figure 12-9 A combo box GUI element contains a drop-down list from which the user of your program selects an item.

The following example shows how to create a combo box in a Java program. Figure 12-9 shows the window displayed when you run this example.

```
import java.awt.*;
import javax.swing.*;
   public class Demo {
      public static void main(String[] args) {
         Window win = new Window();
      }
}
class Window extends JFrame {
   public Window () {
      super ("Window Title");
      setSize(400,100);
      setDefaultCloseOperation(JFrame.EXIT_ON_CLOSE);
      setVisible(true);
      Container ca = getContentPane();
      FlowLayout flm = new FlowLayout();
      ca.setLayout(flm);
      ca.setBackground(Color.lightGray);
      JComboBox combo1 = new JComboBox();
      combo1.addItem("One");
      combo1.addItem("Two");
      combo1.addItem("Three");
      ca.add(combo1);
      setContentPane(ca);
   }
}
```

Text Area

The text area GUI element is used to place a block of text in the window. You create a text area by declaring an instance of the JTextArea class, as shown here:

```
JTextArea ta = new JTextArea("Default text",5, 30);
```

The constructor of the JTextArea requires two arguments: the number of lines and the number of characters that can appear on each line. Programmers refer to the number of lines as the *height* of the text area and the number of characters as its *width*. The number of characters you specify is really an approximation made by the Java Virtual Machine because the actual number of characters that fit on a line depends on the font used to display the text.

Another version of the JTextArea() constructor uses three arguments, the first of which is the text that appears in the text area. This is illustrated in the statement at the beginning of this section. The other two arguments are the number of lines and the number of characters, which define the height and width of the text area.

You can place text within the text area by calling the setText() method and passing it the text you want displayed in the text area. This is illustrated in the next statement, where the instance of the JTextArea is called ta:

```
ta.setText("Default text");
```

A text area can be used to display text, but you can also use it to have the user of your program enter text or edit text that already appears in the text area. You determine whether the user can edit the text area by calling the setEditable() method and passing it either a Boolean true (to make the text area editable) or a Boolean false (to make the text read-only). This is shown here:

```
ta.setEditable(true);
```

Figure 12-10 The text area GUI element is used to display a block of text or to receive a block of text from the user of your program.

The following example shows how to create a text area in a window. This example shows a text area that is five lines high and approximately 30 characters wide. It contains default text. Figure 12-10 shows the window displayed by this example:

```
import java.awt.*;
import javax.swing.*;
```

```
    public class Demo {
       public static void main(String[] args) {
          Window win = new Window();
       }
}
class Window extends JFrame {
   public Window () {
      super ("Window Title");
      setSize(400,100);
      setDefaultCloseOperation(JFrame.EXIT_ON_CLOSE);
      setVisible(true);
      Container ca = getContentPane();
      FlowLayout flm = new FlowLayout();
      ca.setLayout(flm);
      ca.setBackground(Color.lightGray);
      JTextArea ta = new JTextArea("Default text",5, 30);
      ca.add(ta);

      setContentPane(ca);
   }
}
```

Scroll Pane

Sometimes the entire contents of a GUI element won't fit in the space allocated for the element. This is the case when text exceeds the height of a text area. In order to enable the user to see additional contents, you can use a scroll pane. A scroll pane is a GUI element that enables the user to scroll another GUI component both horizontally and vertically by using a scroll bar.

You create a scroll pane by declaring an instance of the `JScrollPane` class, as shown here:

```
JScrollPane sp = new JScrollPane(
           ta, JScrollPane.VERTICAL_SCROLLBAR_ALWAYS,
JScrollPane.HORIZONTAL_SCROLLBAR_ALWAYS);
```

The constructor of the `JScrollPane` class accepts three arguments. The first argument is a reference to the GUI element that will use the scroll bars. In the preceding statement, ta is a reference to a text area GUI element. The second and third arguments are constants of the `JScrollPane` class that specify the behavior of the vertical and horizontal scroll bars. The preceding statement causes both the vertical and horizontal scroll bars to always appear, even if all the content of the GUI element appears on the screen. Table 12-3 contains the list of constants you can use to set the behavior of the scroll bars.

Constant	Description
`JScrollPane.VERTICAL_SCROLLBAR_AS_NEEDED`	Displays a vertical scroll bar only when the contents extend beyond the area of the GUI element
`JScrollPane.VERTICAL_SCROLLBAR_NEVER`	Indicates to never use a vertical scroll bar, even if the contents extend beyond the area of the GUI element
`JScrollPane.VERTICAL_SCROLLBAR_ALWAYS`	Indicates to always show a vertical scroll bar, even if the contents do not extend beyond the area of the GUI element
`JScrollPane.HORIZONTAL_SCROLLBAR_AS_NEEDED`	Displays a horizontal scroll bar only when the contents extend beyond the area of the GUI element
`JScrollPane.HORIZONTAL_SCROLLBAR_NEVER`	Indicates to never use a horizontal scroll bar, even if the contents extend beyond the area of the GUI element

Table 12-3 Constants for Use with the Scroll Pane

The follow example illustrates how to use a scroll pane in your program. This example displays both a vertical and horizontal scroll bar around a text area. Figure 12-11 shows the window displayed by this example.

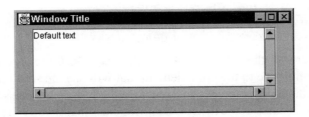

Figure 12-11 A vertical and a horizontal scroll bar can be added to the text area by using the scroll pane GUI element.

```
import java.awt.*;
import javax.swing.*;
public class Demo {
   public static void main(String[] args) {
      Window win = new Window();
   }
}
class Window extends JFrame {
   public Window () {
      super ("Window Title");
      setSize(400,100);
      setDefaultCloseOperation(JFrame.EXIT_ON_CLOSE);
      setVisible(true);
      Container ca = getContentPane();
      FlowLayout flm = new FlowLayout();
      ca.setLayout(flm);
      ca.setBackground(Color.lightGray);
      JTextArea ta = new JTextArea("Default text",5, 30);
      JScrollPane sp = new JScrollPane(
           ta, JScrollPane.VERTICAL_SCROLLBAR_ALWAYS,
      JScrollPane.HORIZONTAL_SCROLLBAR_ALWAYS);
     ca.add(sp);
     setContentPane(ca);
   }
}
```

Getting Data from GUI Components

The purpose of using GUI elements is to make it easy for the user to enter information into your program. So far in this chapter, you learned how to create a window and display GUI elements in the window. Now we'll turn our attention to gathering information from those GUI elements.

Each time a person interacts with a GUI element, they cause an event to occur. Your program must have two features in order to react to an event: an event listener and a handler method, also called an *event-handling method.*

Think of an event listener as a part of your program that monitors the GUI looking for a particular event to occur, such as when the user clicks a push button. When the event happens, the listener detects the event and then calls an event handler. An event handler is a method that reacts to a specific event, such as the selection of a particular push button.

Suppose that you have two text areas and a push button on the window. A person can select all or a portion of the text appearing in the first text area and then click the push button to copy the text to the second text area. You'll see how this works a little later in this chapter. For now, we'll simply explain how this is done.

The program uses a listener to monitor events that happen with the push button. When the user clicks the push button, the listener recognizes the event and then calls the event handler that is associated with the push button. The event handler is a method that contains statements that read the selected text in the first text area and then places a copy of the text into the second text area.

An event listener is an interface that your program must implement. Actually, there are many event listeners, each designed to listen for particular GUI events. Table 12-4 contains commonly used event listeners.

Event Listener	GUI Element
`ActionListener`	Buttons
`ItemListener`	Check boxes, radio buttons, and combo boxes
`KeyListener`	Keyboard input
`MouseListener`	Mouse actions
`MouseMotionListener`	Mouse movements

Table 12-4 Commonly Used Event Listeners

You need to perform two steps in order to use an event listener. First, you'll need to implement the appropriate event listener interface. You'll see how this is done in examples throughout the rest of this chapter.

Second, you need to associate the listener with a GUI element. Let's say you created a push button using the following statement:

```
JButton bt = new JButton("Copy");
```

A push button GUI element requires an `ActionListener` interface, so you'll need to implement that `ActionListener` interface in the class that creates the push button. You associate the push button to the `ActionListener` interface by calling the `addActionListener()` method that is defined by the `JButton` class. The `addActionListener()` method requires that you pass it the `this` keyword to reference the action event. This is illustrated in the following statement:

```
bt.addActionListener(this);
```

The `ActionListener` detects when the push button is selected by the user and then calls the `actionPerformed()` method. The `actionPerformed()` method is a method you define in your program that reacts to the event. The

`actionPerformed()` method requires one argument—a reference to the event, as shown here:

```
actionPerformed(actionEvent event)
```

Statements within the method can use the event to determine the proper course of action to take.

Reading a Push Button

As mentioned in the previous section, you'll need to implement the `ActionListener` in order for your program to respond to the push button GUI element. The following example shows how to react to the selection of a push button. This example displays two text areas and one push button called Copy.

The `addActionListener()` method is called for the push button to associate the push button with the action listener. If you fail to call the `addActionListener()` method, your program won't be able to react to the selection of a push button.

The push button and the text areas are then added to the content pane through a call to the `add()` method; then the content pane is placed in the container through a call to the `setContentPane()` method.

The `actionPerformed()` method is defined next. Statements within this method are executed when the user clicks the push button. This example causes the highlighted text in the first text area to be copied to the second text area when the user clicks the push button. Figure 12-12 shows the window when this example is run.

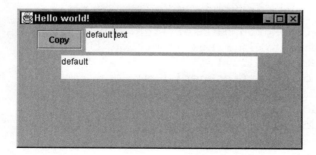

Figure 12-12 The second text area contains selected text copied from the first text area when the Copy push button is clicked.

The `actionPerformed()` method is called whenever any push button is clicked. Although this example shows one push button, typically you'll have multiple push buttons in the window of your application. You determine which push button was clicked by calling the `event.getSource()` method. The event.getSource() method returns the reference of the push button that was selected by the user. You can compare this reference using an if statement to reference each push button on the screen to determine which push button was clicked.

You can also determine the kind of action that was performed by calling the event.getActionCommand() method. Try displaying the action that is returned by the event.getActionCommand() method and see the kinds of actions that occur for the push button.

```
import javax.swing.*;
import java.awt.*;
import java.awt.event.*;
public class Demo {
     public static void main(String[] args)
      {
          Window win = new Window();
      }
}
class Window extends JFrame implements ActionListener {
   JTextArea ta1 = new JTextArea("default text", 2, 25);
   JTextArea ta2 = new JTextArea(2, 25);
   JButton bt1 = new JButton("Copy");
   public Window ()
   {
      super ("Hello world!");
      setSize(400,200);
      setDefaultCloseOperation(JFrame.EXIT_ON_CLOSE);
      setVisible(true);
      Container ca = getContentPane();
      ca.setBackground(Color.lightGray);
      FlowLayout flm = new FlowLayout();
      ca.setLayout(flm);
      bt1.addActionListener(this);
      ca.add(bt1);
      ca.add(ta1);
      ca.add(ta2);
      setContentPane(ca);
   }
   public void actionPerformed(ActionEvent event) {
      ta2.setText(ta1.getSelectedText());
   }
}
```

Reading Radio Buttons and Check Boxes

Radio buttons and check boxes are read using the `ItemListener`, which you'll need to implement in the class that reacts to these GUI elements. An `ItemListener` is very similar to an `ActionListener` in that a radio button and a check box button have an `addItemListener()` method that is called to associate the button with the `ItemListener`. Also, as with the `addActionListener()` method, you must pass the `ItemListener()` method the `this` keyword.

The `ItemListener` calls the `itemStateChanged()` method each time the status of the radio button or check box changes. Therefore, you need to define an `itemStateChanged()` method into your program in order to react to these changes. The `itemStateChanged()` method must have one argument—an `ItemEvent` object.

The following example shows how to react to a check box, which is the same technique used to react to a radio button, only a reference is made to the radio button inside of the check box. You change a check box by either selecting the check box or deselecting the check box. This is referred to as a *state change.* You can determine what changed by calling the `getStateChange()` method. The `getStateChange()` method returns an integer that is compared to two `ItemEvent` constants. These are `ItemEvent.SELECTED` and `ItemEvent.DESELECTED`.

Let's take a look inside the `itemStateChanged()` method to see how the `getStateChange()` method is used. The first statement calls the `getStateChange()` method and assigns the return value to the state integer. The value of the state integer is compared to both `ItemEvent` constants using an `if` statement. Each `if` statement has a nested `if` that is used to determine which check box generated the event. The `getItem()` method is called to retrieve a reference to the check box, which is then compared to references of check boxes that we created in the program. When there is a match, an appropriate message is displayed in the text area through a call to the `setText()` method. Figure 12-13 shows the window created by this example.

```
import javax.swing.*;
import java.awt.*;
import java.awt.event.*;
public class Demo {
    public static void main(String[] args)
     {
         Window win = new Window();
     }
```

```
}
class Window extends JFrame implements ItemListener {
   JTextArea ta = new JTextArea(2, 25);
   JCheckBox cb1 = new JCheckBox("Test 1");
   JCheckBox cb2 = new JCheckBox("Test 2");
   public Window ()
   {
       super ("Hello world!");
       setSize(400,200);
       setDefaultCloseOperation(JFrame.EXIT_ON_CLOSE);
       setVisible(true);
         Container ca = getContentPane();
         ca.setBackground(Color.lightGray);
         FlowLayout flm = new FlowLayout();
         ca.setLayout(flm);
         cb1.addItemListener(this);
         cb2.addItemListener(this);
         ca.add(cb1);
         ca.add(cb2);
         ca.add(ta);
         setContentPane(ca);
   }
   public void itemStateChanged(ItemEvent event) {
          int state = event.getStateChange();
          if (state == ItemEvent.SELECTED) {
            if(event.getItem() == cb1)
             ta.setText("Test 1 Selected");
              if(event.getItem() == cb2)
                   ta.setText("Test 2 Selected");
        }
        if (state == ItemEvent.DESELECTED) {
           if(event.getItem() == cb1)
          ta.setText("Test 1 Deselected");
      if(event.getItem() == cb2)
     ta.setText("Test 2 Deselected");
   }
   }
}
```

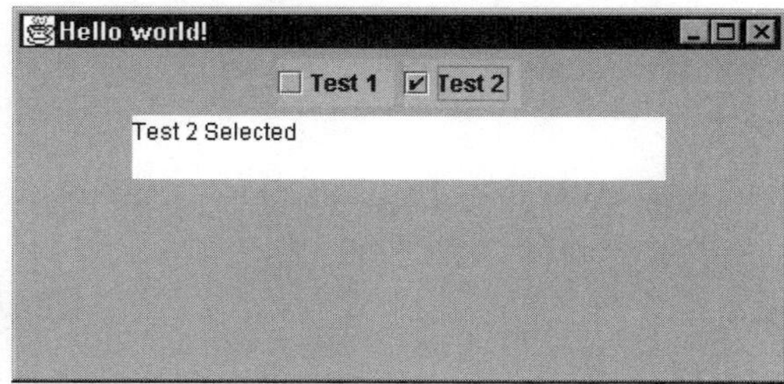

Figure 12-13 The status of the check box is read through a call to the **`getStateChange()`** method, which is then used to determine the appropriate message to display in the text area.

Reading a Combo Box

A combo box also uses the `ItemListener`; therefore, you use the same technique for associating a combo box with the `ItemListener` as you use to associate a check box with the `ItemListener`.

You'll also need to define an `itemStateChanged()` method. Within the `itemStateChanged()` method, you need to call the `getItem()` method in order to retrieve the text displayed in the combo box. You'll need to convert the return value to a string by using the following statement (note that the `getItem()` method is prefaced by a reference to the `ItemEvent`):

```
String pick = event.getItem().toString();
```

The following example shows how to read the contents of a combo box. This example displays a combo box and a text area. Whenever someone selects a different item from the drop-down list, the `ItemListener` calls the `itemStateChanged()` method, where the text appearing in the combo box is retrieved through a call to the `getItem()` method and then displayed in the text area. Figure 12-14 shows what you'll see when you run this example.

```
import javax.swing.*;
import java.awt.*;
import java.awt.event.*;

public class Demo {
     public static void main(String[] args)
```

```
        {
            Window win = new Window();
        }
  }
  class Window extends JFrame implements ItemListener {
     JTextArea ta = new JTextArea(2, 25);
         JComboBox combo1 = new JComboBox();
     public Window ()
     {
         super ("Hello world!");
         setSize(400,200);
         setDefaultCloseOperation(JFrame.EXIT_ON_CLOSE);
         setVisible(true);
         Container ca = getContentPane();
         ca.setBackground(Color.lightGray);
         FlowLayout flm = new FlowLayout();
         ca.setLayout(flm);
         combo1.addItemListener(this);
         combo1.addItem("Test 1");
           combo1.addItem("Test 2");
         ca.add(combo1);
         ca.add(ta);
         setContentPane(ca);
     }
     public void itemStateChanged(ItemEvent event) {
         String pick = event.getItem().toString();
         ta.setText(pick);
     }
  }
```

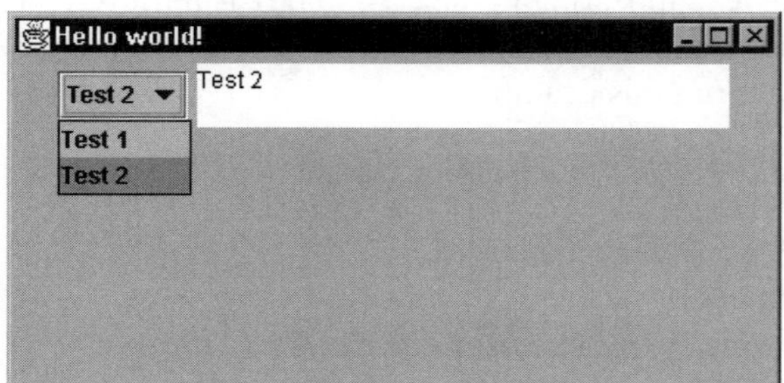

Figure 12-14 Each time text in the combo box changes, the event triggers the program to copy the text into the text area.

Disabling and Enabling GUI Elements

You've probably noticed when using a GUI application that some GUI elements are grayed out and inaccessible to you. Programmers call these *disabled* GUI elements. GUI elements are disabled whenever they shouldn't be used or do not apply to the current process.

For example, you'll recall in a previous section that we used a push button to copy text from one text area to another text area. We could disable the push button until the user enters text into the first text area because we cannot copy something that isn't there. Once text is entered into the first text area, we would then enable the push button.

You can enable and disable a GUI element by calling the `setEnabled()` method and passing it a Boolean true to enable the element or a Boolean false to disable the element. Here's a statement that enables button 1 (bt1 is a reference to a button):

```
bt1.setEnabled(true);
```

Quiz

1. What is the purpose of an event listener?
2. What is an event handler?
3. Can you display GUI elements in a window?
4. What is the purpose of a content pane?
5. Why would you want to disable a GUI element?
6. Can a window be created but not shown?
7. How do you place a content pane in a container?
8. What is the purpose of a layout manager?
9. Can you explicitly specify the location of a GUI element in a window?
10. What is a major difference between creating a GUI in Java as opposed to creating a GUI in another programming language such as C++?

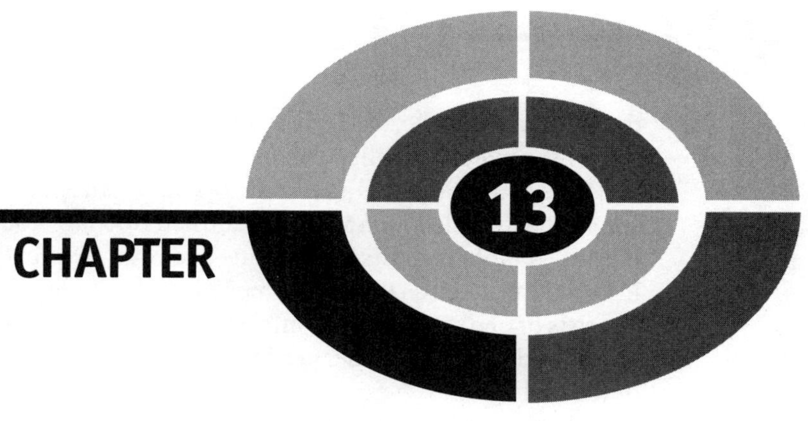

JDBC and Java Data Objects

Whenever you go through the checkout counter at your local supermarket, information about your purchase is stored in a computer database. When you use your credit card, the date, time, place, and information about your purchase is recorded in the credit card company's database. Your school records and medical records are stored in a database. In fact, there is practically nothing you do that isn't stored in some database. Information is collected, stored, updated, retrieved, and deleted by a computer program. In this chapter, you'll learn how to create a Java program that performs these interactions with a database.

Database 101

Let's take a moment to review basic database concepts before you learn how to write your own program that talks to a database. Skip this section if you are familiar with databases; otherwise, read on because you'll need this information to understand the rest of the material in this chapter.

Think of a database as an Excel workbook. An excel workbook consists of several spreadsheets called *tables*, each identified by a tab. You display a table by selecting the tab. A table consists of columns and rows. Typically, each column has similar information, such as the first names of all the students in your class. A row usually consists of one set of relation information. You might find a student's first name, last name, student ID, and other pertinent information about a particular student in a row of the table.

A database is nearly the same organization of information as an Excel workbook. A database is a collection of tables. A table is a collection of rows. A row is a collection of columns. Data is stored where a row and column intersect. You know this as a *cell* in Excel.

Database management software (DBMS) is a type of application that enables you to organize data into a database. It also manages the data for you. You simply tell the DBMS to do something, and it does it. For example, you might say, "Store this student registration in the database," and information about the registration is placed in the proper rows and tables in the database. Likewise, you might say, "Show me all courses Bob Smith is taking this term," and the DBMS searches the database and gives you a copy of the information that you requested.

Many commercially available DBMS products are on the market. These include familiar names such as Microsoft Access, IBM's DB2, Oracle, Sybase, and MySQL, to mention a few. All these products organize and manage data for you and are capable of following your instructions.

Those instructions, called *queries*, are written using Structured Query Language (SQL). SQL is beyond the scope of this book; however, later in this chapter, you'll learn how to incorporate SQL queries into your program and have your program send those queries to the DBMS for processing.

There is a lot more to learn about databases, but I'll leave you to explore that in another book. For now, we'll turn our attention to learning how your program connects to a DBMS, sends a query, and retrieves the data returned by the DBMS.

The Concept of JDBC

Sun Microsystems faced a challenge in the late 1990s. They had to find a way for Java developers to write high-level Java code to access popular DBMS products.

The problem was a language barrier. Each DBMS required that its own low-level language be used whenever a program needed to interact with it. As a result, low-level code written to interact with Oracle needed to be rewritten to interact with DB2.

Sun Microsystems created specifications for a JDBC driver and the JDBC Application Programming Interface (API) to meet this challenge. The JDBC driver specifications described detail functionality of how the JDBC driver should work. It was up to the DBMS manufacturers to build the drivers.

The JDBC driver is a translator that converts low-level proprietary DBMS messages to messages that are understood by the Java run-time environment. The driver also converts Java code written using the JDBC API to low-level proprietary DBMS messages through the Java run-time environment.

This two-way street enables Java developers to write instructions in Java that can talk to any DBMS so long as a JDBC driver is available for the DBMS. JDBC drivers are available for nearly every commercial DBMS from the Sun Microsystems website (www.sun.com) or from the DBMS manufacturer's website.

JDBC Driver Types

JDBC drivers fall into four groups, which are called the *JDBC driver types*. The JDBC driver types are as follows:

- **Type 1 JDBC to ODBC driver** This driver type converts the Java JDBC API to Microsoft's Open Database Connection (ODBC) driver, which in turn talks to the DBMS. The ODBC driver is also called the *JDBC/ODBC bridge*. Avoid using the JDBC/ODBC bridge in a mission-critical application because the extra translation might negatively impact performance.
- **Type 2 Java/Native Code driver** The Java/Native Code driver is specific to each DBMS. The disadvantage of using a Java/Native Code driver is the loss of code portability.
- **Type 3 JDBC driver** The Type 3 JDBC driver is referred to as the *Java Protocol* and is the most commonly used JDBC driver.
- **Type 4 JDBC driver** Type 4 JDBC driver is known as the *Type 4 Database Protocol* and is similar to the Type 3 JDBC driver, except SQL queries are translated into the format required by the DBMS. This is the fastest way to communicate SQL queries to the DBMS.

JDBC API Packages

You don't have to be concerned about JDBC drivers except to make sure that the proper JDBC driver for your DBMS is installed. Instead, you'll focus on using the JDBC API to have your program communicate with the DBMS.

The JDBC API consists of a bunch of classes that are contained in two packages. The first package is called `java.sql` and contains core Java data objects of the JDBC API. The second package is called `javax.sql` and extends the `java.sql` package.

As you'll see throughout this chapter, you'll need to import both the `javax.sql` and the `java.sql` package into your program in order to use the JDBC API to connect to and interact with the DBMS.

The JDBC Process

Your program needs to perform five routines to connect the DBMS before you begin interacting with it. Collectively, these five routines are called the *JDBC process* and are as follows:

1. Load the JDBC driver.
2. Connect to the DBMS.
3. Create and execute an SQL query.
4. Process the response from the DBMS.
5. Disconnect the DBMS.

Load the JDBC Driver

The first routine is to load the JDBC driver. This tells the Java run-time environment which JDBC driver to use with your program. You load the JDBC driver by calling the `Class.forName()` class and passing it the name of the driver as an argument to the method. We'll be using the JDBC/ODBC bridge as the driver in the examples throughout this chapter because this is the driver you use to connect your program to Microsoft Access, which is the DBMS most likely to be available on your computer.

The JDBC/ODBC bridge is called `sun.jdbc.odbc.JdbcOdbcDriver`. You load this driver by placing the following statement in your program:

```
Class.forName( "sun.jdbc.odbc.JdbcOdbcDriver");
```

Associating the JDBC/ODBC Bridge with the Database

Before you can load the JDBC/ODBC bridge, you must associate the database with the driver. Use the ODBC Data Source Administrator to associate the database with the JDBC/ODBC bridge by following these steps:

1. Select Start| Settings and then select the Control Panel.
2. Select ODBC 32 to display the ODBC Data Source Administrator.
3. Add a new user by selecting the Add button.
4. Select the driver, then select Finish. Use the Microsoft Access driver if you are using Microsoft Access; otherwise, select the driver for the DBMS you are using. If you don't find the driver for your DBMS on the list, you'll need to install the driver. Contact the manufacturer of the DBMS for more information on how to obtain the driver.
5. Enter the name of the database as the data source name in the ODBC Microsoft Access Setup dialog box. This is the name that will be used within your Java database program to connect to the DBMS.
6. Enter a description for the data source. This is optional. It will be a reminder of the kind of data stored in the database.
7. Click the Select button. You'll be prompted to browse the directory of each hard drive connected to your computer in order to define the direct path to the database. Click OK once you locate the database, and the directory path and the name of the database will be displayed in the ODBC Microsoft Access Setup dialog box.
8. Because this is your database, you can determine whether a login name and password are required to access the database. If this is the case, click the Advanced button to display the Set Advanced Options dialog box. This dialog box is used to assign a login name, also referred to as a *user* ID, and a password to the database. Select OK. Otherwise, skip this step.
9. When the ODBC Microsoft Access Setup dialog box appears, select OK.
10. Select OK to close the ODBC Data Source Administrator dialog box.

Connect to the DBMS

Once you load the driver, you must connect to the DBMS by calling the `DriverManager.getConnection()` method that is defined in the `DriverManager` class, which is responsible for managing driver information.

You must pass the `DriverManager.getConnection()` method the URL of the database along with the user ID and password, if required by the DBMS.

The `DriverManager.getConnection()` method returns a `Connection` interface that is used throughout the process to reference the database. The `java.sql.Connection` interface manages communication between the driver and your program.

The following example shows routines that load the driver and connect to the database. The database is called CustomerInformation. The actual location of the CustomerInformation database is specified when you associate the ODBC driver with the DBMS by using Windows. The user ID is "jim" and the password is "keogh". You create the user ID and password using the DBMS application.

This example begins by declaring the `url`, `userID`, and `password` strings. The program then declares a reference to an instance of the `Connection` class call `dB`. The program enters a try block where the `forName()` method is called to load the driver. The `getConnection()` method is called in the next statement and is passed the `url`, `userID`, and `password` strings. This connects to the database and logs on to the DBMS. Both `userID` and `password` are optional arguments if the DBMS doesn't require a logon. The `getConnection()` method returns an instance of the `Connection` class, which is assigned to the `Connection` reference declared earlier in the program. At this point, the program is connected, logged onto the DBMS, and ready to send the DBMS a query.

NOTE: This example is a partial program that is expanded throughout the chapter.

```
String url = "jdbc:odbc:CustomerInformation";
String userID = "jim";
String password = "keogh";
private Connection dB;
 Class.forName( "sun.jdbc.odbc.JdbcOdbcDriver");
   dB = DriverManager.getConnection(url,userID,password);
```

Create and Execute an SQL Query

Once the connection is made and you log onto the DBMS, your program is ready to create an SQL query and send it to the DBMS for processing. An SQL query consists of one or more SQL commands that are contained in an SQL statement.

Your program needs to perform several steps in order to send the SQL query to the DBMS. For the first step, you need an instance of the `Statement` class because the `Statement` class defines the `executeQuery()` method used to send and execute the SQL query to the DBMS. You create an instance of the `Statement` class by calling the `createStatement()` method defined in the `Connection` class. The `createStatement()` class returns an instance of the `Statement` class.

Next, you must send the SQL query to the DBMS. You do this by calling the `executeQuery()` method and passing it the SQL query. The `executeQuery()` method returns an instance of the `ResultSet` class, which contains the response from the DBMS. You then use the methods defined in the `ResultSet` class to access the DBMS responses. Once your program receives a response, you'll need to terminate the statement by calling the `close()` method.

Let's see how this is done. The following example enhances the previous example by creating an SQL query and sending it to the DBMS. Like the previous example, this example isn't a complete program. You'll see the completed version of this program later in the chapter after you learn how all five routines work.

The first portion of this example is nearly identical to the previous example, except for two statements. One statement declares a reference to an instance of the `Statement` class, and the other declares a reference to a `ResultSet` class.

Let's jump inside the second try block. The first statement creates an SQL query, which is used to initialize the String object called `query`. This is the query that will be sent by the program to the DBMS.

The query tells the DBMS to return all the columns from the Registration table where the studentID column equals 1234. The `SELECT` keyword is used to identify the name of column(s) you want the DBMS to return. This example uses an asterisk in place of column names. The asterisk is a wildcard character that tells the DBMS to return all columns. The `FROM` keyword is used to specify the name of the table that contains the columns. The `WHERE` keyword, called a `WHERE` *clause*, sets the selection criteria the DBMS uses to choose rows to return to the program.

Beneath the query is the call to the `createStatement()` method. This returns an instance of the `Statement` class, which is assigned to the `Statement` reference called `DataRequest`. Next, the query is passed to the `executeQuery()` method. The `executeQuery()` method sends the query to the DBMS. The DBMS response is then assigned the reference to the `ResultSet` class called `result`. You use this to reference data returned by the DBMS in response to your query. You'll see how this is done in the next section.

```
String url = "jdbc:odbc:CustomerInformation";
String userID = "jim";
String password = "keogh";
Statement dataRequest;
ResultSet results;
private Connection dB;
try {
```

```
   Class.forName( "sun.jdbc.odbc.JdbcOdbcDriver");
   dB = DriverManager.getConnection(url,userID,password);
}

      String query =
          "SELECT * FROM Registration WHERE studentID = '1234'";
      dataRequest = dB.createStatement();
     results = dataRequest.executeQuery (query);
```

Process Data Returned by the DBMS

The `ResultSet` class defines methods used to interact with the data returned by the DBMS. Later in this chapter, you'll learn how to use these methods. However, the following abbreviated example gives you a preview of a commonly used routine for extracting data returned by the DBMS. Error-catching code is purposely removed from this example in order to minimize code clutter. You'll find the completed version of this routine later in this chapter.

This example picks up where the previous example leaves off. At this point in the program, the response from the DBMS is already assigned the reference to the `ResultSet` called `result`. Before we can do anything with the data, we need places in our program to store the data. Therefore, the first three statements in this example declare three strings. The first two strings will be assigned data returned by the DBMS. The `printRow` string is used to combine the values of `firstName` and `lastName` into one string, which is then displayed on the screen.

Now that we have space reserved in memory to store data returned from the DBMS, the next thing we need to do is determine whether any data was returned by the DBMS. You can never assume that the DBMS found data to match your query. We determine whether at least one row of data was returned by calling `next()`. The next method returns a Boolean value indicating whether there is a next row.

The return value of the `next()` method is evaluated by the `if` statement. If the return value is false, there isn't a next row and therefore an appropriate message is displayed on the screen and the program exits this routine.

If the return value of the `next()` method is true, the program proceeds to retrieve the data. The data is stored in a row set. Think of a row set as one row of a table. You access each column of the row by calling a version of the `get()` method that is appropriate to the data type of the column.

We call the `getString()` method in this example because both columns of the row set contain strings. The `getString()` method as well as the `get()` methods for other data types require one argument, which is a reference to the column whose value you want to retrieve. The reference can be the name of the column or the column number. We use the column name in this example.

The `getString()` method returns the value of the specified column. We assign this value to the appropriate string variable declared previously in this program. You can then use the variable as you use any other variable within your program. In this example, the `firstName` and `lastName` variables are concatenated and assigned to the `printRow` variable, which is displayed on the screen.

Notice that we call the `getString()` method and display the `printRow` variable within a `do...while` loop. After data from the first row set is copied to variables and displayed, the `next()` method is called once again to determine whether the response from the DBMS contains another row of data. If it does, the statements within the `do...while` loop are executed again to retrieve data from the next row in the row set. Otherwise, the program exits the `do...while` loop.

```
String firstName;
String lastName;
String printrow;
boolean records = results.next();
if (!records ) {
   System.out.println( "No data returned");
   return;
}
else
{
   do {
        firstName = results.getString ('FirstName') ;
        lastName = results.getString ('LastName') ;
        printRow = firstName + " " + lastName;
        System.out.println(printrow);
   } while ( results.next() );
}
```

Terminate the Connection to the DBMS

The fifth routine of the process is to close the instance of `ResultSet` and the connection to the DBMS. You do this by calling the `close()` method, as shown here:

```
result.close();
bD.close();
```

The instance of `ResultSet` is automatically closed when you close the connection to the DBMS; however, many programmers prefer to explicitly close the instance of `ResultSet`.

Trapping Exceptions

Previous examples in this chapter did not address the likelihood that there could be exceptions when connecting to and interacting with a DBMS. We purposely did this to keep the examples simple. Now that you've learned how to use the basic JDBC API, we'll turn our attention to handling exceptions.

Let's begin with loading the driver. First, `Class.forName()` throws a `ClassNotFoundException` if anything unusual happens when the driver is being loaded. You trap this exception by using a catch block, as shown in the following example.

When the catch block catches the `ClassNotFoundException`, the `getMessage()` method is called to retrieve the description of the exception, which is then displayed on the screen. The `exit()` method is then called to terminate the program. Notice that the `exit()` method is passed the integer 1. This value is returned to the operating system by the program when the program terminates, indicating that the program terminated abnormally because it couldn't load the driver.

```
try {
   Class.forName( "sun.jdbc.odbc.JdbcOdbcDriver");
}
catch (ClassNotFoundException e) {
   System.err.println(
         "Unable to load the JDBC/ODBC bridge." + e.getMessage());
   System.exit(1);
}
```

The next chance of an exception occurring is when the program tries to connect to the DBMS. A number of things can go wrong, such as inaccurate URL for the database or an inaccurate user ID and/or password. If the `getConnection()` method encounters something unusual, it throws an `SQLException`.

The following example builds on the previous example to illustrate how to catch the `SQLException` in your program. This exception is caught in the second catch block. Notice that the `exit()` method is called within the catch block to terminate the program. The `exit()` method is passed the integer 2, which is returned when the program terminates, indicating that the program terminated abnormally because of a problem encountered when connecting to the database.

```
String url = "jdbc:odbc:Registration";
String userID = "jim";
String password = "keogh";
Connection dB;
try {
   Class.forName( "sun.jdbc.odbc.JdbcOdbcDriver");
```

```
   dB = DriverManager.getConnection(url,userID,password);
}
catch (ClassNotFoundException e) {
   System.err.println(
        "Unable to load the JDBC/ODBC bridge." + e);
   System.exit(1);
}
catch (SQLException e) {
     System.err.println(
          "Cannot connect to the database." + e);
     System.exit(2);
}
finally {
      dB.close();
}
```

Avoid Timing Out

In the real world, the DBMS may not be available at the time your program needs to connect to it. This is typically caused by a high demand for the DBMS at the moment your program tries to connect to it.

It is not too unusual for a program to end up on a seemingly never-ending line waiting for a turn to connect to the DBMS. Rather than wait forever, you can set a timeout period after which the `DriverManager` ceases its attempt to connect to the DBMS.

You set the timeout period by calling the `DriverManager.setLoginTimeout()` method. This method requires that you pass the number of seconds for it to wait before timing out.

You can find out the current timeout period by calling the `DriverManager.getLoginTimeout()` method. This method returns an integer that represents the number of seconds the `DriverManager` waits before timing out.

More on Statement Objects

Previously in this chapter, you learned that after you open a connection to the DBMS, you call the `createStatement()` method, which returns an instance of the `Statement` class. The instance of the `Statement` class is used to call the `executeQuery()` method, which sends your SQL query to the DBMS.

Three types of statement objects can be used to execute the query: `Statement`, `PreparedStatement`, and `CallableStatement`. The `Statement` statement object executes a query immediately when the query is executed. The query is compiled before it is executed by the DBMS. The `PreparedStatement` statement object is used to execute a compiled query. A compiled query is one in which the statements in the query are already translated into code understood by the DBMS.

The `CallableStatement` statement object is used to execute a stored procedure. A stored procedure is a query written by a programmer that is stored in the DBMS. You execute a stored procedure by sending an SQL query to the DBMS that tells the DBMS to run a specific stored procedure. This is faster to execute than a regular SQL query. When a regular SQL query executes, your program must send the query to the DBMS, where it is compiled and then executed. When a stored procedure is executed, you don't send the full query because it already resides in the DBMS. Instead, you send the command to run the stored procedure followed by the name of the stored procedure.

The *Statement* Object

Use the `Statement` object when you need to execute a query immediately. You execute a query that uses the `Statement` object by calling the `executeQuery()` method, which you've seen previously in this chapter.

If the query is inserting a new row or updating or deleting a row, you use the `executeUpdate()` method instead of the `executeQuery()` method. The `executeUpdate()` method returns an integer that indicates the number of rows updated by the query.

The following example illustrates how to use the `Statement` object. This example returns all columns in the Registration table. Nothing is displayed when this program runs. In order to display data retrieved from the DBMS, you need to replace the comment in the second try block with statements that read data from the resultsets, which you saw how to do earlier in this chapter.

```
String url = "jdbc:odbc:Registration";
String userID = "jim";
String password = "keogh";
Statement dataRequest;
ResultSet results;
Connection dB;
try {
   Class.forName( "sun.jdbc.odbc.JdbcOdbcDriver");
   dB = DriverManager.getConnection(url,userID,password);
```

```
 }
catch (ClassNotFoundException e) {
      System.err.println(
            "Unable to load the JDBC/ODBC bridge." + e);
      System.exit(1);
}
catch (SQLException e) {
      System.err.println(
            "Cannot connect to the database." + e);
      System.exit(2);
}
 try {
      String query = "SELECT * FROM Registration";
      dataRequest = dB.createStatement();
      results = dataRequest.executeQuery (query);
      //Place code here to interact with the ResultSet
 }
catch ( SQLException e ){
      System.err.println("SQL error." + e);
      System.exit(3);
}
finally {
      dataRequest.close();
      dB.close();
}
```

The next example shows how to used the `executeUpdate()` method. This program is nearly the same as the previous example, except for two statements. The SQL query changes the value of a column in a particular row of a table.

Here's what the query is telling the DBMS to do: Update the Registration table. Find the row where the value of the StudentID column is 123. When you find that row, change the value of the Enrolled column of that row to Y.

The other statement that is changed calls the `executeUpdate()` method, which is passed the SQL query that changes the value of the Enrolled column in the Registration table. We must use the `executeUpdate()` method because the query changes the table rather than simply requesting data from the table.

```
String url = "jdbc:odbc:Registration";
String userID = "jim";
String password = "keogh";
Statement dataRequest;
Connection dB;
int rowsUpdated;
try {
```

```
   Class.forName( "sun.jdbc.odbc.JdbcOdbcDriver");
   dB = DriverManager.getConnection(url,userID,password);
 }
catch (ClassNotFoundException e) {
     System.err.println(
          "Unable to load the JDBC/ODBC bridge." + e);
     System.exit(1);
}
catch (SQLException e) {
     System.err.println("Cannot connect to the database." + e);
     System.exit(2);
}try {
     String query =
          "UPDATE Registration SET Enrolled='Y' WHERE StudentID = '123';
     dataRequest = dB.createStatement();
     rowsUpdated = dataRequest.executeUpdate (query);
     dataRequest.close();
 }
catch ( SQLException e ){
     System.err.println("SQL error." + e);
     System.exit(3);
}
finally {
      dataRequest.close();
       dB.close();
}
```

The *PreparedStatement* Object

An SQL query must be compiled before the DBMS processes it. Compiling occurs after an execution method is called. Programmers precompile an SQL query before execution whenever the SQL query is going to be executed multiple times. This reduces the time necessary to execute the SQL query because it only needs to be compiled once, not each time it executes. An SQL query can be precompiled and executed by using the `PreparedStatement` object.

Rarely in the real world is the same SQL query executed multiple times because usually the search criterion changes with each execution. Suppose you want to find out whether a student is registered for a course. You'd use nearly the same SQL query each time, but you'd probably change the student ID for each execution of the SQL query.

In situations like this, you still can use the PreparedStatement object if you write the SQL query a certain way. You'll need to use a question mark as a placeholder for data that changes with each execution of the SQL query. For example, you'd use a question mark instead of the student ID.

Executing a PreparedStatement object is a three-step process. The first step is to declare a PreparedStatement object and assign it to a PreparedStatement reference, as shown here. Remember that dB is a reference to the connection to the DBMS. You pass the query to prepared Statement.

```
PreparedStatement pstatement = dB.prepareStatement(query);
```

The second step is to replace the question mark with the value that will be used for the SQL query. You do this by calling one of the setXXX() methods, where XXX represents the data type of the value.

The setXXX() method requires two arguments. The first argument is an integer that represents the position of the question mark in the SQL query. You can use as many question marks as you need in the SQL query as along as you identify the position of the question mark that the value will replace. The second argument is the value. In the following statement, we're replacing the first question mark in the SQL query with the string "123":

```
pstatement.setString(1, "123");
```

The third step is called the executeQuery() method, as shown here. Notice that you don't pass the executeQuery() method the SQL query like you did previously when you called this method. You don't need to because the SQL query was already passed when the instance of the PreparedStatement object was declared.

```
Results = pstatement.executeQuery ();
```

The following example shows how to use the PreparedStatement object in your program. This program lets you change student ID numbers each time the SQL query executes.

```
String url = "jdbc:odbc:Registration";
String userID = "jim";
String password = "keogh";
ResultSet results;
Connection dB;
try {
   Class.forName( "sun.jdbc.odbc.JdbcOdbcDriver");
   dB = DriverManager.getConnection(url,userID,password);
```

```
 }
catch (ClassNotFoundException e) {
     System.err.println(
         "Unable to load the JDBC/ODBC bridge." + e);
     System.exit(1);
}
catch (SQLException e) {
     System.err.println(
          "Cannot connect to the database." + e);
     System.exit(2);
}try {
     String query = "
           SELECT * FROM Registration WHERE studentID = ?";
     PreparedStatement pstatement =
           dB.preparedStatement(query);
     pstatement.setString(1, "123");
     results = pstatement.executeQuery ();
     //Place code here to interact with the ResultSet
 }
catch ( SQLException e ){
     System.err.println("SQL error." + e);
     System.exit(3);
}
finally {
pstatement.close();
   dB.close();
}
```

The *CallableStatement* Object

Programmers use the `CallableStatement` object to call a stored procedure. A stored procedure is a block of code that is identified by a unique name and is stored in the DBMS. The nature of the block of code is dependent on the DBMS. Typically, the code is written in PS/SQL, TransactSQL, C, or another programming language.

You execute a stored procedure by sending the DBMS the name of the stored procedure and then telling the DBMS to run it. Programmers call this *invoking the name* of the stored procedure. Stored procedures are frequently used in applications where a block of code is executed multiple times in order to minimize the time necessary to transport the block of code across the network and have it compiled. A stored procedure is transported and compiled once, and you execute it subsequent times by invoking its name.

Three parameters are used when calling a stored procedure with the CallableStatement object. These are IN, OUT, and INOUT. The IN parameter contains the data needed for the stored procedure to execute, which is similar to a parameter of a method. You set the value of the IN parameter by calling the setXXX() method, which was described in the previous section.

The OUT parameter contains the value returned after the stored procedure finishes executing. The out parameter must be registered using the registerOutParameter() method and then is later retrieved by using the getXXX() method. The getXXX() method is very similar to the setXXX() method except the getXXX() method retrieves a value instead of setting a value. The XXX is replaced with the appropriate data type of the value identical to the setXXX() method.

The INOUT parameter is used to pass information to the stored procedure and to retrieve information from a stored procedure using the techniques described in the previous two paragraphs.

The following example illustrates how to call a stored procedure and retrieve a value returned by the stored procedure. This example is similar to other listings used in this chapter, but it has been modified slightly to call a stored procedure.

```
String url = "jdbc:odbc:Registration";
String userID = "jim";
String password = "keogh";
String lastOrderNumber;
Connection dB;
try {
   Class.forName( "sun.jdbc.odbc.JdbcOdbcDriver");
   dB = DriverManager.getConnection(url,userID,password);
 }
catch (ClassNotFoundException e) {
     System.err.println(
            "Unable to load the JDBC/ODBC bridge." + e);
     System.exit(1);
}
catch (SQLException e) {
     System.err.println(
             "Cannot connect to the database." + e);
     System.exit(2);
}try {
     String query = "{ CALL LastOrderNumber}";
     CallableStatement cstatement = dB.prepareCall(query);
     cstatement.registerOutParameter(1, Types. VARCHAR);
     cstatement.execute();
```

```
        lastOrderNumber = cstatement.getString(1);
 }
catch ( SQLException e ){
     System.err.println("SQL error." + e);
     System.exit(3);
}
finally {
     cstatement.close();
     dB.close();
}
```

You'll notice that the first statement in the second `try { }` block creates the SQL query that calls the stored procedure `LastOrderNumber`, which retrieves the most recently used order number.

Next, the `prepareCall()` method of the `Connection` object is called and is passed the SQL query, which returns a `CallableStatement` object called `cstatement`. The `OUT` parameter must be registered using the `registerOutParameter()` method of the `CallableStatement` object.

The `registerOutParameter()` method requires two parameters. The first parameter is an integer that represents the number of the parameter, which is 1. This means that the parameter is the first parameter of the stored procedure. The second parameter of `registerOutParameter()` is the data type of the value returned by the stored procedure, which is Types.VARCHAR.

Next, the `execute()` method of the `CallableStatement` object is called to execute the SQL query. Notice that the `execute()` method doesn't require the name of the query. This is because the query is already identified when the `CallableStatement` object is returned by the `prepareCall()` SQL query method.

The `getString()` method is called once the stored procedure executes to retrieve the return value of the stored procedure, which is the last order number.

The `ResultSet` Object

The `executeQuery()` method sends the SQL query to the DBMS for processing and returns a `ResultSet` object that contains data returned by the DBMS. You use the methods defined in the `ResultSet` object to copy data returned by the DBMS to a Java collection or variable(s) for further processing.

Data returned by the DBMS is stored in a *resultset*. Think of a resultset as a virtual table that consists of rows and columns similar to a spreadsheet. The resultset also contains *metadata*, which is information that describes data, such as the name of a column and its size and data type.

You move through the resultset by using a virtual pointer to point to each row in the table. You move the virtual pointer by using methods defined in the `ResultSet` object. Once you point to a row, you can then use other methods of the `ResultSet` object to retrieve values stored in each column of that row.

The virtual cursor is positioned above the first row when the DBMS returns the resultset. This means that you must move the virtual cursor to the first row in order to access data returned by the DBMS. The `next()` method is used to move the virtual cursor down a row. If there is a next row, the `next()` method returns true; otherwise, a false is returned, indicating that you have reached the end of the resultset.

Use the `getXXX()` method to copy data from a column of the current row to an element of a Java collection or a variable. Previously in this chapter, you learned about the `getXXX()` method. The `XXX` is a placeholder for the data type of the column. For example, the `getString()` method copies value of a String column from the resultset to a Java collection or a variable. You must make sure that the data type used in the `getXXX()` method corresponds to the data of the column.

The `getXXX()` method requires one parameter—an integer that represents the number of the column within the resultset whose value you want to copy to your program. Columns appear in the order in which they are entered into the SQL query's `SELECT` statement.

Suppose your SQL query requested StudentFirstName and StudentLastName as the first two columns in the `SELECT` statement. These would become the first and second columns of the resultset. Therefore, to copy the value of the StudentFirstName column, you'd type `getString(1)`, and the `getString()` method would return the value of the StudentFirstName column of the current row. The student's last name is copied by using `getString(2)` because the student's last name is in the second column returned by the DBMS.

Reading the Resultset

The following example illustrates how to read values from the resultset into variables that can be further processed by your program. You'll notice that many of the statements used in this example were used in previous examples, so you probably know what to tell Java to do. Feel free to return to previous sections of this chapter to review any statements that seem unfamiliar to you.

```
String url = "jdbc:odbc:Registration";
String userID = "jim";
String password = "keogh";
```

```
String printRow;
String firstName;
String lastName;
Statement dataRequest;
ResultSet results;
Connection dB;
try {
   Class.forName( "sun.jdbc.odbc.JdbcOdbcDriver");
   dB = DriverManager.getConnection(url,userID,password);
 }
catch (ClassNotFoundException e) {
     System.err.println(
           "Unable to load the JDBC/ODBC bridge." + e);
     System.exit(1);
}
catch (SQLException e) {
     System.err.println(
          "Cannot connect to the database." + e);
     System.exit(2);
}
try {
     String query = "SELECT FirstName,LastName FROM Students";
     dataRequest = dB.createStatement();
     results = dataRequest.executeQuery (query);
}
catch ( SQLException e ){
     System.err.println("SQL error." + e);
     System.exit(3);
}
boolean records = results.next();
if (!records ) {
   System.out.println("No data returned");
   System.exit(4);
}
try {
  do {
      firstName = results.getString ( 1 ) ;
     lastName = results.getString ( 2 ) ;
     printRow = firstName + " " + lastName;
     System.out.println(printRow);
  } while (results.next() );
  dataRequest.close();
 }
```

```
catch (SQLException e ) {
   System.err.println("Data display error." + e);
   System.exit(5);
}
finally {
     dB.close();
}
```

Here's what is happening in this example. After a connection is made to the database, a query is defined in the second try block that retrieves the students' first name and last name from the Students table of the Registration database.

The students' names are returned in the resultset. Before the program can copy these names, the virtual pointer must be moved from the row above the first row of the resultset to the first row. This is done by calling the `next()` method.

We can't assume that any data was returned by the DBMS because maybe no data matches the data requested by the SQL query. Therefore, we must test the results returned by the `next()` method. If a false is returned, no row exists. Therefore, the "No data returned" message is displayed and the program terminates.

However, if a true value is returned, the `do...while` loop is entered. The `do...while` loop is where the `getString()` method is called to copy values from the first and second columns of the resultset to the variables `firstName` and `lastName`. The values of these variables are then concatenated and assigned to the `printRow` variable, which is then displayed on the screen.

The `next()` method is called again to move the virtual cursor to the next row in the resultset. The value returned by the `next()` method is evaluated by the conditional statement in the `do...while` loop. If a true is returned, the program executes the statements within the `do...while` loop again; otherwise, the program exits the `do...while` loop and calls the `close()` method, which closes the `Statement` object. You learned how the `close()` method works previously in this chapter.

Positioning the Virtual Cursor

Six methods are defined by the `ResultSet` object: `first()`, `last()`, `previous()`, `absolute()`, `relative()`, and `getRow()`. These methods are used to move the virtual cursor in the resultset.

The `first()` method moves the virtual cursor to the first row in the resultset, and the `last()` method positions the virtual cursor at the last row. The `previous()` method moves the virtual cursor to the previous row. The `absolute()` method enables you to specify the number of the row where you want the virtual cursor positioned. You specify the row number as an integer that you pass to the absolute() method.

The relative() method moves the virtual cursor a specified number of rows from the current row. You pass the relative() method an integer that represents the number of rows to move. You use a positive (optional) or negative sign to indicate the direction in which to move the virtual cursor. For example, a value of -6 moves the virtual cursor back six rows from the current row, whereas a value of 3 moves the virtual cursor forward three rows.

You can always determine the number of the current row by calling the getRow() method. The getRow() method returns an integer, which is the number of the current row.

In order to position the virtual cursor in the resultset, you must create a scrollable resultset. You do this by passing the createStatement() method one of three constants: TYPE_FORWARD_ONLY, TYPE_SCROLL_INSENSITIVE, or TYPE_SCROLL_SENSITIVE.

The TYPE_FORWARD_ONLY constant restricts the virtual cursor to downward movement, which is the default setting. This means you won't be able to move the virtual cursor to previous rows.

The TYPE_SCROLL_INSENSITIVE and TYPE_SCROLL_SENSITIVE constants enable the virtual cursor to move in both directions. The TYPE_SCROLL_INSENSITIVE constant makes the resultset insensitive to changes made by another program to data in the table whose rows are reflected in the resultset. The TYPE_SCROLL_SENSITIVE constant makes the resultset sensitive to those changes.

Suppose that another program updates, deletes, or changes data in the Students table while your program is copying the student names from the resultset to variables in your program. If you created the resultset as insensitive, it will not automatically be updated to reflect those changes. However, if you create the resultset as sensitive, those changes will be reflected in the resultset.

A word of caution: The values of variables that have already been copied from columns in the resultset are not updated automatically. Let's say that you've copied names from the first row to variables and then moved the virtual cursor to the next row. Then, while you're on the next row, the names in the first row are updated in the Students table. The resultset will be updated with those changes if you created a sensitive resultset; however, your variables will not be updated because you already copied those values from the row.

The following example shows how to reposition the virtual cursor in the resultset. This example creates an insensitive resultset and then uses various methods to move the virtual cursor up and down within the resultset.

```
String url = "jdbc:odbc:Registration";
String userID = "jim";
String password = "keogh";
String printRow;
String firstName;
String lastName;
Statement dataRequest;
ResultSet results;
Connection dB;
try {
   Class.forName( "sun.jdbc.odbc.JdbcOdbcDriver");
   Db = DriverManager.getConnection(url,userID,password);
 }
catch (ClassNotFoundException e) {
     System.err.println(
          "Unable to load the JDBC/ODBC bridge." + e);
     System.exit(1);
}
catch (SQLException e) {
     System.err.println(
          "Cannot connect to the database." + e);
     System.exit(2);
}
try {
     String query = "SELECT FirstName,LastName FROM Students";
     dataRequest = dB.createStatement(
           TYPE_SCROLL_INSENSITIVE);
     results = dataRequest.executeQuery (query);
}
catch ( SQLException e ){
     System.err.println("SQL error." + e);
     System.exit(3);
}
boolean records = results.next();
if (!records ) {
   System.out.println("No data returned");
   System.exit(4);
}
try {
  do {
     results.first();
     results.last();
     results.previous();
```

```
        results.absolute(10);
        results.relative(-2);
        results.relative(2);
        firstName = results.getString ( 1 ) ;
        lastName = results.getString ( 2 ) ;
        printRow = firstName + " " + lastName;
        System.out.println(printRow);
    } while (results.next() );
    dataRequest.close();
}
catch (SQLException e ) {
    System.err.println("Data display error." + e);
    System.exit(5);
}
finally {
    dB.close();
}
```

How to Test Whether the JDBC Driver Is Scrollable

Some JDBC drivers may not support some or all of the scrollable features mentioned in this section. The following example shows how you can test whether the JDBC driver your program uses supports the scrollable features.

```
boolean forward, insensitive, sensitive;
DataBaseMetaData meta = dB.getMetaData();
forward = meta.supportsResultsSetType(
            ResultSet.TYPE_FORWARD_ONLY);
insensitive = meta.supportsResultsSetType(
            ResultSet. TYPE_SCROLL_INSENSITIVE);
sensitive = meta.supportsResultsSetType(
            ResultSet. TYPE_SCROLL_SENSITIVE);
System.out.println("forward: " + forward);
System.out.println("insensitive: " + insensitive);
System.out.println("sensitive: " + sensitive);
```

Fetching Rows

Whenever you request rows from a DBMS, the JDBC driver fetches the number of rows defined by the fetch size and discards the previously fetched set of rows. It is important to understand that there is a difference between the number of rows fetched from the DBMS and the number of rows that appear in a resultset.

For example, the JDBC driver might fetch 500 rows from the DBMS, but include only 100 of those rows in the resultset based on the resultset's maximum row setting. In this case, the resultset silently drops 400 rows, although all 500 rows are transferred over the network from the DBMS to your program.

You can increase the efficiency of fetching rows by using the `setFetchSize()` method to set the number of rows that the JDBC fetches from the DBMS. In the real world, the DBMS administrator will tell you the preferred fetch size setting to use because this is dependent on the performance specification of the DBMS in use. Some DBMS may not implement the fetch size control. If fetch size isn't supported, the methods will compile and execute, but have no effect.

The following example shows you how to set the fetch size from within your program by calling the `setFetchSize()` method defined in the `Statement` object. Here, we've set the fetch size to 500 rows. This means no more than 500 rows will be fetched at a time.

```
String url = "jdbc:odbc:CustomerInformation";
String userID = "jim";
String password = "keogh";
String printRow;
String firstName;
String lastName;
Statement dataRequest;
ResultSet results;
Connection dB;
try {
   Class.forName( "sun.jdbc.odbc.JdbcOdbcDriver");
   dB = DriverManager.getConnection(url,userID,password);
 }
catch (ClassNotFoundException e) {
     System.err.println(
            "Unable to load the JDBC/ODBC bridge." + e);
     System.exit(1);
}
catch (SQLException e) {
     System.err.println(
            "Cannot connect to the database." + e);
     System.exit(2);
}
try {
     String query = "SELECT FirstName,LastName FROM
Students";
     dataRequest = dB.createStatement(
             TYPE_SCROLL_INSENSITIVE);
```

```
        dataRequest.setFetchSize(500);
       results = dataRequest.executeQuery (query);
}
catch ( SQLException e ){
       System.err.println("SQL error." + e);
       System.exit(3);
}
finally {
    db.close();
}
```

Updatable Resultset

Previously in this chapter, you learned that a resultset is a virtual table of rows and columns that contain data copied from one or more tables of a database. Throughout this chapter, you've seen examples of how to select a subset of rows and columns from tables in the database and copy them into the resultset. You then copy data from the resultset into your program for further processing.

You can also update data in the resultset. For example, you might want to change the value of a column before further processing the data. You can do this by passing the `Connection` object's `createStatement()` method the constant `CONCUR_UPDATABLE`. Once you do this, you can then change the values of a row, delete a row, or insert a new row.

Note: Use the constant `CONCUR_READ_ONLY` to prevent the resultset from being updated.

Changing the Value of a Resultset

You can change the value of a column in the current row of the resultset by calling the `updateXXX()` method, where `XXX` is replaced with the data type of the column you're updating.

The `updateXXX()` method requires two parameters. The first parameter indicates the column of the current row whose value is being changed. You indicate the column in one of two ways. You can use the number of the column or the column name. Some programmers prefer to use the column name rather than the column number because they don't have to be concerned with the column sequence. The second parameter of the `updateXXX()` method is the new value that will override the current value of the column in the current row.

Sometimes you'll want to simply leave the column empty. You do this by calling the `updateNull()` method. A null value, as you'll recall, is another way of saying that the column is empty. The `updateNull()` method requires one parameter, which is the column number whose contents will become null. The `updateNull()` method doesn't accept the name of the column as a parameter.

Once the `updateXXX()` method is called, you'll need to call the `updateRow()` method. The `updateRow()` method changes the values in the columns of the current row of the resultset based on the values of the `updateXXX()` methods.

The following example shows how to update a resultset. In this example, Mary Jones was recently married and changed her last name to Smith. The `updateString()` method is used to change the value of the last name column of the resultset to 'Jones'. The change takes effect once the `updateRow()` method is called.

```
String url = "jdbc:odbc:Registration";
String userID = "jim";
String password = "keogh";
Statement dataRequest;
ResultSet results;
Connection dB;
try {
   Class.forName( "sun.jdbc.odbc.JdbcOdbcDriver");
   dB = DriverManager.getConnection(url,userID,password);
 }
catch (ClassNotFoundException e) {
     System.err.println(
            "Unable to load the JDBC/ODBC bridge." + e);
     System.exit(1);
}
catch (SQLException e) {
     System.err.println("Cannot connect to the database." + e);
     System.exit(2);
}
try {
     String query =
           "SELECT FirstName,LastName FROM Students
            WHERE FirstName = 'Mary' and LastName = 'Jones'";
     dataRequest = dB.createStatement(
            ResultSet.CONCUR_UPDATABLE);
     results = dataRequest.executeQuery (query);
}
catch ( SQLException e ){
```

```
      System.err.println("SQL error." + e);
      System.exit(3);
}
boolean records = results.next();
if (!records ) {
   System.out.println("No data returned");
   System.exit(4);
}
try {
      results.updateString ("LastName", "Jones");
      results.updateRow();
      dataRequest.close();
}
catch (SQLException e ) {
   System.err.println("Data display error." + e);
   System.exit(5);
}
```

Deleting a Row in the Resultset

You can remove a row from the resultset by calling the `deleteRow()` method. Programmers frequently use this method to pare down the number of rows that must be processed by their program. Those rows that shouldn't be processed are eliminated from the resultset rather than you having to refine the SQL query selection criteria and rerun the SQL query.

The `deleteRow()` method requires one parameter—an integer that indicates the row number of the row being deleted. Typically, a programmer moves the virtual cursor to the row in the resultset that is to be deleted. Before deleting the row, however, the programmer usually examines the values in relative columns in order to be sure that the row should be deleted.

Once you're sure the current row is the row you want deleted, you call the `deleteRow()` method, as shown here:

```
Results.deleteRow();
```

Inserting a Row in the Resultset

You might have a need to incorporate a row of your own data into the resultset supplied by the DBMS. You can do this by inserting a new row in the resultset. Keep in mind that you still need to write and execute an SQL query to insert a new row into the underlying table in the database if you want or need data to be contained in the table.

Inserting a row into the resultset is a three-step process. First, position the cursor at the row by calling the `moveToInsertRow()` method.

Second, place values into the columns of the new row. You do this by calling the `updateXXX()` method, as described previously in this chapter. The `updateXXX()` method must be passed the column name or number as the first parameter and the value that will be placed in the column as the second parameter. Remember that `XXX` must be replaced with the data type of the column.

Third, you call the `insertRow()` method after calling the `updateXXX()` method. The `insertRow()` method opens a new row in the resultset and places values specified in the `updateXXX()` method into each column. The following example illustrates how to insert a new row in a resultset:

```
String url = "jdbc:odbc:Registration";
String userID = "jim";
String password = "keogh";
Statement dataRequest;
ResultSet results;
Connection dB;
try {
   Class.forName( "sun.jdbc.odbc.JdbcOdbcDriver");
   dB = DriverManager.getConnection(url,userID,password);
 }
catch (ClassNotFoundException e) {
     System.err.println(
           "Unable to load the JDBC/ODBC bridge." + e);
     System.exit(1);
}
catch (SQLException e) {
     System.err.println(
          "Cannot connect to the database." + e);
     System.exit(2);
}
try {
     String query = "SELECT FirstName,LastName FROM Students";
     DataRequest = dB.createStatement(CONCUR_UPDATABLE);
     results = dataRequest.executeQuery (query);
}
catch ( SQLException e ){
     System.err.println("SQL error." + e);
     System.exit(3);
}
boolean records = results.next();
if (!records ) {
```

```
      System.out.println("No data returned");
     System.exit(4);
}
try {
        results.moveToInsertRow ();
        results.updateString (1, "Tom");
        results.updateString (2, "Smith");
        results.insertRow();
        results.moveToCurrentRow();
        dataRequest.close();
}
catch (SQLException e ) {
     System.err.println("Data display error." + e);
     System.exit(5);
}
finally {
       dB.close();
}
```

Metadata

As you previously learned in this chapter, metadata is data about data, such as the name of a column, the data type of a column, and the size of the column. Metadata is returned by the DBMS as part of the resultset. You can access metadata by using the `DatabaseMetaData` interface.

In order to access metadata, you must call the `getMetaData()` method, which is defined in the `Connection` class. The `getMetaData()` method returns a `DatabaseMetaData` object that contains metadata. An assortment of metadata is available to your program. You retrieve specific metadata by calling the appropriate method. Here are some of the more commonly used methods (notice that the name of the method implies the nature of the metadata it returns):

- **`getDatabaseProductName()`** Returns the product name of the database
- **`getUserName()`** Returns the user's name
- **`getURL()`** Returns the URL of the database

- **getSchemas()** Returns all the schema names available in this database
- **getPrimaryKeys()** Returns primary keys
- **getProcedures()** Returns stored procedure names
- **getTables()** Returns the names of tables in the database

Two types of metadata can be retrieved from the DBMS. The first type contains metadata that describes the database in the DBMS, which is accessible by calling the appropriate method in the preceding table.

The other type of metadata describes the resultset. In order to access metadata of the resultset, you need to call the `getMetaData()` method defined by the `ResultSet` object, as shown here:

```
ResultSetMetaData rm = result.getMetaData();
```

The `getMetaData()` method returns a `ResultSet`MetaData object that contains the metadata for the resultset. Here are the commonly called methods used to retrieve specific metadata from the resultset:

- **getColumnCount()** Returns the number of columns contained in the resultset
- **getColumnName(int** number) Returns the name of the column specified by column number
- **getColumnType(int** number) Returns the data type of the column specified by the column number

We don't have room in this chapter to fit in all the methods used to retrieve metadata. You can find information about those methods by visiting Sun Microsystems' website at java.sun.com.

Data Types

Throughout this chapter, we refer to the `setXXX()` and `getXXX()` methods used to store a value in a column of a resultset and to retrieve a value from a column of a resultset.. The `XXX` refers to the data type of the column. Table 13-1 contains a list of data types and their Java equivalents. You can use this list to determine the proper data name to use when replacing the `XXX` in the `setXXX()` and `getXXX()` methods.

SQL Type	Java Type
CHAR	String
VARCHAR	String
LONGVARCHAR	String
NUMERIC	java.math.BigDecimal
DECIMAL	java.math.BigDecimal
BIT	Boolean
TINYINT	Byte
SMALLINT	Short
INTEGER	Integer
BIGINT	Long
REAL	Float
FLOAT	Float
DOUBLE	Double
BINARY	Byte[]
VARBINARY	Byte[]
LONGVARBINARY	Byte[]
BLOB	java.sql.Blob
CLOB	java.sql.Clob
ARRAY	java.sql.Array
STRUCT	java.sql.Struct
REF	java.sql.Ref
DATALINK	java.sql.Types
DATE	java.sql.Date
TIME	java.sql.Time
TIMESTAMP	java.sql.Timestamp

Table 13-1 A List of Data Types for Use with the `setXXX()` and `getXXX()` Methods

Exceptions

JDBC methods throw three kinds of exceptions: `SQLExceptions`, `SQLWarnings`, and `DataTruncation`. `SQLExceptions` commonly reflects an SQL syntax error in the query and is thrown by many of the methods contained in the `java.sql` package. Hopefully, the syntax errors in your code get resolved quickly. In production, connectivity issues with the database most commonly cause this exception. It can also be caused by subtle coding errors, such as trying to access an object that has been closed. For example, you try to roll back a transaction in a `catch` clause and don't check first whether the database connection is still valid. The `getNextException()` method of the `SQLExceptions` object is used to return details about the SQL error or a null value if the last exception was retrieved. The `getErrorCode()` method of the `SQLException` object is used to retrieve vendor-specific error codes.

The `SQLWarnings` exception throws warnings received by the `Connection` object from the DBMS. The `getWarnings()` method of the `Connection` object retrieves the warning, and the `getNextWarning()` method of the `Connection` object retrieves subsequent warnings.

Finally, whenever data is lost due to truncation of the data value, a `DataTruncation` exception is thrown.

Quiz

1. How is storing data in a DBMS different from storing data in a file?
2. What is a resultset?
3. How can you retrieve data stored in a resultset?
4. How do you move the virtual cursor throughout the resultset?
5. How can you update a value in a resultset?
6. How can you update a value in a table?
7. What is metadata?
8. How do you update metadata?
9. How do you select a column in a resultset?
10. Why would you retrieve metadata?

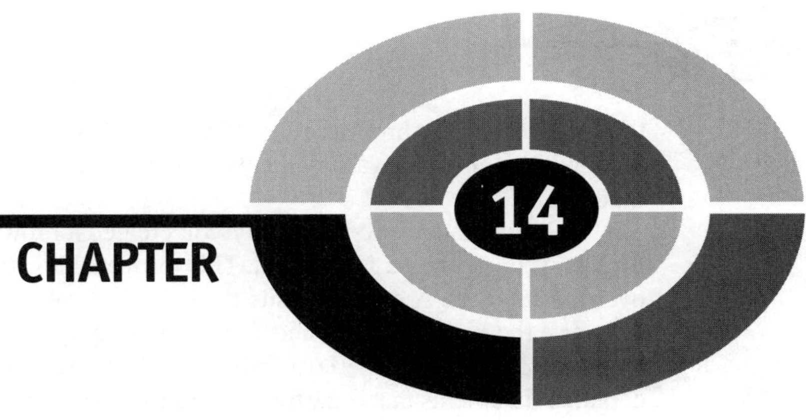

Java Applets

A Java *applet* is a small Java application used to enhance the capabilities of a web page because a Java applet can do things that the web page can't do directly itself, such as calculations. A web page is a document that is written in Hypertext Markup Language (HTML). HTML instructions function similarly to how keywords and statements in Java instruct the Java environment to do something. However, HTML lacks the keywords that are common to Java. For example, HTML cannot tell a web browser to make decisions or repeat instructions. This is where a Java applet comes in—a Java applet embellishes the capabilities of HTML. You'll learn how to create your own Java applets in this chapter.

Java Applet Basics

A Java applet is a program you write using Java, in much the same way as the other Java applications you created throughout this book. However, a Java applet does not have a `main()` method. Instead, a Java applet has 200 or so methods inherited from the `JApplet` class. These methods are called by the browser in response to events that occur when the browser runs. Your job is to override these methods, providing them with your own Java statements that are executed when the browser calls these methods.

Here's how this works: Let's say you created a browser-based registration form for your school using a Java applet. This form enables students to register for classes over the Internet. A student visits the school's website and clicks the registration link, and the browser loads and runs your Java applet. One of the first things the browser does is to call the Java applet's `paint()` method. The `paint()` method contains statements that draw the registration form of your Java applet on the screen. Your job is to place statements in the `paint()` method that draw the form.

Now suppose the student drags the browser window to a different location on the desktop. This becomes a browser *event*—something that happens that might require the browser to react. In this example, the browser needs to redraw the form in the new location on the desktop. The browser reacts to this event by calling the Java applet's `paint()` method.

You're probably puzzled at why there isn't a `main()` method in the Java applet. To answer this question, we need to return to the concepts you learned at the beginning of this book. The `main()` method is the entry point into a Java application. Whenever a Java application executes, the Java environment calls the `main()` method and executes each statement within the `main()` method sequentially, until the last statement executes or until a statement tells the Java environment to terminate the program.

A Java applet is really an extension of the browser program, and they both work as a team. The entry point is the browser, not the Java applet. The Java applet simply defines methods that supplement the browser program.

A program that runs a Java applet is called an *applet container*. Therefore, a browser is an applet container. The Java 2 Software Development Kit has a program called the appletviewer that's used to test Java applets. This, too, is an applet container, and you'll learn how to use it later in this chapter. We'll use the term *browser* throughout this book to refer to an applet container because most of your Java applets will be running in a browser.

A browser doesn't understand Java. Therefore, the browser gets help from the Java class loader whenever the browser encounters a Java applet. The Java class loader is a program that loads a Java applet into memory and creates an object of the Java applet class that contains methods that can be called upon when the browser needs certain tasks to be performed.

Writing a Java Applet

Let's begin by easing your mind. Although there are more than 200 methods in a Java applet, you only have to overwrite a few of them because the `JApplet` class's definitions of the other methods are adequate to handle most browser request. In fact, many of these methods are empty, and others contain a minimum number of statements to respond to calls from the browser.

Your job is to overwrite selected methods in order to control how these methods react to requests made by the browser. The five methods that most programmers overwrite in their Java applets are `init()`, `start()`, `paint()`, `stop()`, and `destroy()`. You must overwrite the `init()`, `start()` and `paint()` methods.

The `init()` method is called when the browser begins the Java applet for the first time. Typically, you'll place statements in this method that declare objects and initialize variables used in the Java applet.

The `start()` method is called whenever the browser restarts the Java applet after temporarily stopping it by calling the `stop()` method. Let's say that a student is using your Java applet to register for a course, but temporarily opens an e-mail. The browser calls the `stop()` method to stop the Java applet and then calls the `start()` method when the student again selects the open browser window on the desktop.

The `paint()` method is called whenever the browser needs to draw the screen. The browser draws the screen the first time the Java applet runs and while the Java applet is running, if the screen needs to be refreshed (such as when the student moves the browser window on the desktop).

The `destroy()` method is called immediately before the termination of the Java applet.

Structure of a Java Applet

A Java applet looks very similar to a Java application because both have an application class. However, a Java applet must extend the `JApplet` class, which is not the case with a Java application. The `JApplet` class is contained in the `javax.swing` package.

The following example is a Java applet. You might think that something is missing because the body of the class is empty. Although it is true that the class is empty, the `JApplet` class contains the definitions of the 200+ methods that might be called by the browser.

```
import javax.swing.JApplet;
public class Demo extends JApplet {
}
```

Now let's customize this Java applet by overwriting the `JApplet` class's `paint()` method to display "Hello word!" onscreen. The `paint()` method requires one argument, which is a reference to a Graphics object. The Graphics object is used to call methods of the `Graphics` class that enable you to, among other things, display text and lines on the screen. The method receives reference to a Graphics object when the browser calls the `paint()` method.

We'll place one statement within the `paint()` method, which is called the `drawString()` method. The `drawString()` method displays a string of characters on the screen. You'll need to pass the `drawString()` method three arguments. The first augment is the string that is to be displayed on the screen. The other two arguments are screen coordinates that specify where the string is to be placed on the screen. The second argument is called the *x* coordinate and the third argument is called the *y* coordinate.

The screen is referred to as the *Java applet window* and is divided into columns and rows. Where a column and row meet is called a *picture element* (or *pixel)*. An x, y coordinate identifies each pixel. The x coordinate (x-axis) represents the column number, and the y coordinate (y-axis) represents the row number. This is similar in concept to a cell of a spreadsheet.

The pixel in the upper-leftmost corner of the Java applet window has the coordinate 0,0. The maximum coordinate depends on the size of the Java applet window and the resolution of the computer monitor used to display the Java applet. Many com puters have a resolution that is 800 pixels wide (columns) and 600 pixels high (rows).

The following example illustrates how to write a Hello word! Java applet. Notice that we place the text at coordinate 15, 15.

```
import javax.swing.JApplet;
public class Demo extends JApplet {
    public void paint(Graphics g){
       g.drawString("Hello world!", 15,15);
    }
}
```

You compile a Java applet the same way you compile a Java application. First, you write the Java applet source code using an editor and save it in a file that has an extension of `.java`. Next, you compile the source code using the Java compile, such as `javac Demo.java`. This produces the Java class (in this case, `Demo.class`) that is made available to the HTML document that calls the Java applet.

Calling a Java Applet

You cannot directly run a Java applet from the Java environment as you do a Java application. Java applets must be called from a document written in HTML. HTML is called a *markup language* because it consists of standard tags that describe how text and images are to be displayed on the screen. A browser interprets tags in an HTML document and displays text and images on the screen appropriately.

Many HTML tags consist of an opening tag and a closing tag. The opening and closing tags tell the browser how to display everything that appears between these tags in the HTML document. The name of a tag is contained within angle brackets, such as `<applet>`, which is the HTML tag used to tell the browser to load and run an applet. The closing tag is identical except a forward slash is placed in front of the name, as in `</applet>`.

An HTML document must begin with the `<html>` tag and end with the `</html>` tag. All other tags are placed within these two tags. In order to run a Java applet, you must place the opening `<applet>` tag and the closing `</applet>` tag within the `<html>` and `</html>` tags.

The `<applet>` tag requires three attributes. Think of an *attribute* as an argument to a method. Each attribute must use the corresponding HTML attribute name followed by the assignment operator (=), and then a value. Attributes are placed within the angle brackets following the name of the applet in the opening tag.

The first attribute is called `code`, and its value is the name of the Java applet enclosed within double quotations. The second attribute is called `width`. It defines the width of the window within which the Java applet appears on the screen. Width is measured as an integer that represents the number of pixels that fit across the window. The third attribute is called `height`, and it's an integer that identifies the number of pixels that fit between the top and bottom of the Java applet window.

The following example shows you an HTML document that loads and runs a Java applet. The Java applet is called `Demo.class` and runs in a window 300 pixels wide by 45 pixels high. The Java applet window should not be larger than 800 pixels wide and 600 pixels high; otherwise, it may not fit on most computer screens. An HTML document must be saved in a file that has the extension of either `.html` or `.htm`. For example, you might save the following program in a file called `demo.html`:

```
<html>
  <applet code="Demo.class" width="300" height="45">
  </applet>
</html>
```

Running a Java Applet

In order to run the Java applet, you need to display the HTML document that contains the call to the Java applet. Typically, the HTML document and the Java applet both reside on a web server that is connected to the Internet or to an intranet, which is commonly used on local networks in corporations. The browser is usually located on a PC that is connected to the Internet or intranet.

You probably have experience displaying web pages. A web page is an HTML document. Therefore, you display the HTML document that calls your Java applet the same way in which you display a web page.

In the real world, programmers don't use a web server in the early stages of testing a Java applet. Instead, they display the HTML document that calls the Java applet from an appletviewer, such as the appletviewer that comes with the Java 2 Platform Standard Edition. In this way, programmers don't have to waste time copying the HTML document file and Java applet file to the web server each time they want to test a change. Instead, they display the HTML document from their computer using the appletviewer. Here's what you type to run the appletviewer. Notice that you call the HTML document and not the Java applet. This is because the HTML document calls the Java applet.

```
Appletviewer Demo.htm.
```

Other Attributes

The three attributes of the `<applet>` tag are just the minimum attributes for a Java applet. Other attributes are available that provide additional information to the browser or appletviewer on how to call the Java applet. These are shown in Table 14-1.

Attribute	Description
codebase	Assigns the base URL of the applet. The *base URL* is the directory on the remote computer that contains the applet class. The default directory is the same directory where the HTML document that contains the applet tag is stored.
code	The name of the applet. This is a required attribute.
alt	Text that is displayed if the web browser is unable to run the Java applet for any reason, such as the Java applet cannot be found on the remote computer.
name	Specifies the name for the instance of the Java applet. The `name` attribute is then used by other Java applets called by the same HTML document to communicate with the instance of the Java applet.
width, height	Used to tell the web browser the number of pixels that define the width and height of the Java applet window.
vspace, hspace	Used to specify the space above and below the Java applet (`vspace`) and on both sides of the applet (`hspace`).
param, name, value	Used to define a parameter that is available to the Java applet once it is loaded and executed. `param` is a tag. `name` is an attribute of the `param` tag that is assigned the name of the parameter. `value` is also an attribute of the `param` tag and is assigned the value of the parameter.

Table 14-1 Attributes for the Applet Tag

Adding Graphics to the Applet Window

A Java applet can perform nearly everything that a Java application can perform. For example, you can enhance the previous example by including graphical elements such as a line and rectangle.

You draw a line on the screen by calling the `drawLine()` method defined in the `Graphics` class. Beginning and ending coordinates define the line. These coordinates are integers that correspond to pixels on the applet window. Each coordinate consists of two integers. The first integer represents the column and the second integer represents the row position of the pixel in the applet window. For example, coordinate 10,5 means ten pixels from the left of the applet window (ten columns) and five pixels from the top of the applet window (five rows).

In order to draw a line, you must pass the `drawLine()` method four arguments. The first two arguments are coordinates for the beginning point of the line, and the last two arguments are coordinates for the endpoint of the line.

For example, the following statement tells Java to draw a line beginning at coordinate 10, 5 (column 10, row 5) and ending at coordinate 375, 5 (column 375, row 5):

```
g.drawLine(10, 5, 375,5);
```

All coordinates must be specified as an integer. Coordinates that exceed the size of the applet window will have no effect. That is, you won't see a line beyond pixels that falls within the applet window.

The next example illustrates how to draw a line in an applet window. This example forms a box and then displays a person's name on the screen. Previously, you learned how to use the `drawString()` method to position text at a location specified by coordinates passed in the last two arguments to the `drawString()` method. It is important to remember that the coordinates passed to the `drawString()` method relate to the applet window and are not related to the lines the applet draws on the screen. You can run this example by using the HTML document that appears after this Java applet.

```
import java.awt.Graphics;
import javax.swing.JApplet;
public class Demo extends JApplet {
   public void paint (Graphics g)
   {
      g.drawLine(10, 5, 375,5);
      g.drawLine(10, 5,2,25);
      g.drawLine(375, 5,375,100);
      g.drawLine(2, 25,2,100);
      g.drawString("Mary Jones", 15,15);
   }
}
```

```
<html>
  <applet code="Demo.class" width="400" height="45">
  </applet>
</html>
```

You can also dress up an applet window by drawing a rectangle around the text using the `drawRect()` method. The `drawRect()` method also requires two coordinates to be passed as arguments. The first coordinate (first two arguments) specifies the upper-left corner of the rectangle, and the second coordinate (last two arguments) specifies the lower-right corner of the rectangle.

The following example illustrates how to call the `drawRect()` method to draw a rectangle around a name. You can use the previous HTML document to run this applet.

```
import java.awt.Graphics;
import javax.swing.JApplet;
```

```
public class Demo extends JApplet {
  public void paint (Graphics g)
   {
     g.drawRect(10, 5, 375,75);
     g.drawString("Mary Jones", 20,20);
   }
}
```

Passing Parameters

Many times your applet requires information from the HTML document in order to process information. Let's say that the applet displays a personal greeting on the screen; however, the name of the person being greeted isn't included in the applet. Instead, the name is provided by the HTML document when the applet is called.

You can pass information to an applet from an HTML document by using the `<param>` HTML tag. The `<param>` tag consists of two attributes: `name` and `value`. The `name` attribute is used to identify the name used in the applet to represent the parameter. Think of this as the name of an argument for a Java method. The `value` attribute is used to identify the value being passed to the applet. Think of this as the value that is passed to an argument for a Java method.

The `<param>` tag must be placed within the opening and closing `<applet>` tags in the HTML document. This is shown in the next example, where the parameter `FirstName` is assigned the value "Bob" and then passed to the applet. Although this example shows one parameter, you can use as many parameters as necessary by inserting additional `<param>` tags in the HTML document.

```
<html>
   <applet code="Demo.class" width="400" height="45">
      <param name="FirstName" value="Bob">
    </applet>
</html>
```

Next, you need to modify the applet so it reads the parameter passed from the HTML document. To do this, you need to do two things to your applet. First, you need to reserve memory so you can store the parameter. You do this by declaring a String variable. Second, you call the `getParameter()` method. The `getParameter()` method requires one parameter—the name of the `name` parameter specified in the corresponding attribute of the `<param>` tag. The `getParameter()` method returns the corresponding value.

Programmers commonly place the `getParameter()` method call in the `init()` method that the applet overwrites because an applet reads a parameter once when it begins. This is shown in the next example, where a person's name is passed as a parameter and placed in a welcome message. Notice that the variable used to store the parameter is combined with strings to create the greeting. These are joined by using the concatenation operator (**+**).

```
import javax.swing.JApplet;
import java.awt.Graphics;
public class Demo extends JApplet {
     private String firstName;
     public void init()
        {
           firstName = getParameter("FirstName");
        }
     public void paint( Graphics g)
        {
            g.drawString( "Hello, "+ firstName +"!", 30, 30 );
        }
}
```

Restrictions

A Java application can do certain things that an applet cannot. For example, an application can delete files on the local computer, but an applet cannot because an applet is considered untrustworthy.

An applet runs in a sandbox. It can display and receive information, but it cannot access the local file system unless the person using the Java applet gives it the necessary privilege to access the local file system. This privilege is granted via a web browser setting.

The web browser examines an applet using a bytecode verifier before the Java applet runs to make sure that the applet complies with the Java security policy. The Java security policy restricts what a Java applet can and cannot do on the local computer. These restrictions may vary based on the web browser and whether the Java applet is loaded from the local computer or from a remote computer.

Anticipate that an applet won't be able to initiate a print job or read and write local files. In addition, an applet usually cannot access the following items:

- The clipboard
- A local computer's event queue
- The local computer's operating system properties
- The local computer's operating security properties

Using Dialog Boxes with an Applet

Practically all the techniques you learned to use when writing a Java application can also be used to write an applet. One of those features is a professional-looking user interface for your applet that includes dialog boxes, push buttons, text boxes, and all the other niceties that we've come to expect from a computer program.

You learned how to create a graphical user interface (GUI) for your program in the previous chapter. You can use many of those techniques to create a user interface for your applet. The quickest way to incorporate a GUI in an applet is to use a message dialog box and an input dialog box.

As you'll recall from the previous chapter, a message dialog box is a GUI display that presents the user with a message and an OK button. An input dialog box presents the user with a message, a text box used to enter information, and an OK button. Information entered into the input dialog box becomes available for use by your applet.

You create both of these dialog boxes by using a method defined in the `JOptionPane` class, which is contained in the `javax.swing` package. A number of very useful methods are defined in the `JOptionPane` class; however, we're interested in only two of them: `showMessageDialog()` and `showInputDialog()`.

The `showMessageDialog()` method displays a message dialog box. This method requires four arguments. The first argument is a reference to its parent dialog box. Typically, there isn't a parent, so you'll pass it a null. The second argument is a string that contains the message that will be displayed in the dialog box. The third argument is also a string. It's used as the caption for the dialog box. The last argument is a static variable indicating the kind of message dialog box you want displayed. We'll use `PLAIN_MESSAGE` for our purposes. The other kinds of message dialog boxes are mentioned in the previous chapter. Here is the way you call the `showMessageDialog()` method:

```
JOptionPane.showMessageDialog(null, "Message" , "Caption",
JOptionPane.PLAIN_MESSAGE);
```

The `showInputDialog()` method is used to display an input dialog box and requires one argument—a string containing the message that tells the user to enter information into the dialog box. After the user selects OK, the `showInputDialog()` method returns the information entered by the user as a string. You can then process the string within your applet. Here's how you call the `showInputDialog()` method. In this case, `value` is a string variable that was previously declared somewhere in the program that executes this statement.

```
value  = JOptionPane.showInputDialog ("Message");
```

The following example shows how both dialog boxes are used in an applet. This example calculates a grade. First, the user is asked to enter the total number of questions on the test (see Figure 14-1). Next, the user is asked to enter the number of correct answers (see Figure 14-2). The applet then calculates the grade and displays the grade in a message box (see Figure 14-3). The HTML document used to run this applet is shown at the end of the example.

```
import java.awt.Graphics;
import javax.swing.*;
public class Demo extends JApplet {
    double doubleGrade;
    public void init()
    {
       String totalNumberQuestions;
       String totalCorrectAnswers;
       double doubleNumberQuestions;
       double doubleCorrectAnswers;
       totalNumberQuestions = JOptionPane.showInputDialog (
          "Enter the total number of
test questions.");
       totalCorrectAnswers = JOptionPane.showInputDialog (
           "Enter the total number of
correct answers.");
       doubleNumberQuestions = Double.parseDouble(
           totalNumberQuestions);
       doubleCorrectAnswers = Double.parseDouble(
           totalCorrectAnswers);
       doubleGrade = (
           doubleCorrectAnswers/doubleNumberQuestions) *
100;
    }
    public void paint (Graphics g)
    {
        JOptionPane.showMessageDialog(null,
            "Your grade is " + doubleGrade + "%",
             "Grade", JOptionPane.PLAIN_MESSAGE);
    }
}

<html>
<applet code="Demo.class" width="400" height="75">
</applet>
</html>
```

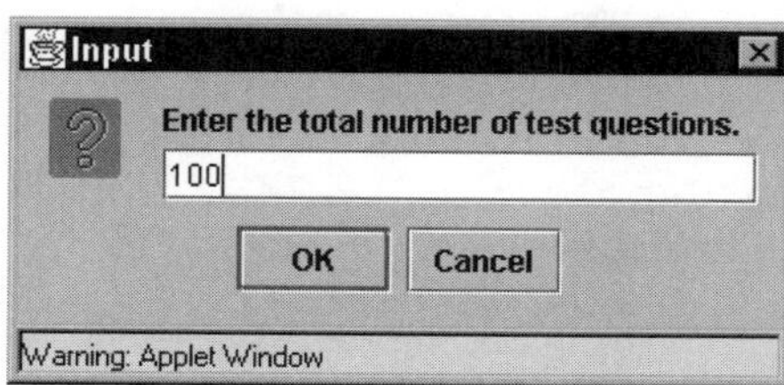

Figure 14-1 Prompts the user to enter the total number of questions that appear on the test

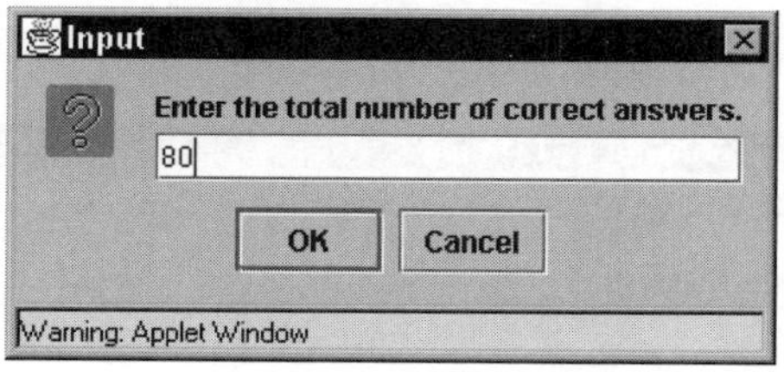

Figure 14-2 Prompts the user to enter the total number of correctly answered questions

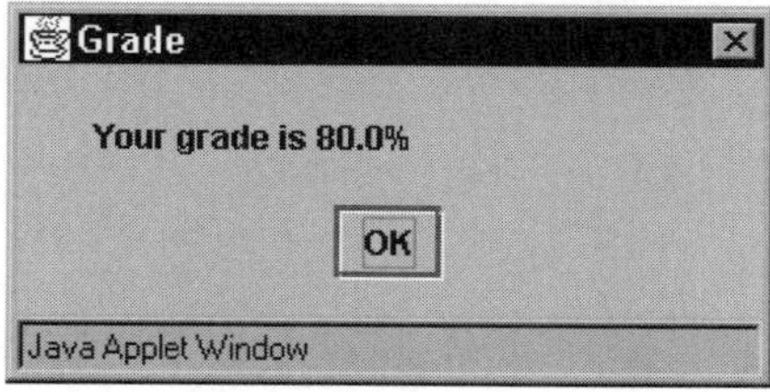

Figure 14-3 Displays the grade for the test

The Status Window

It is always good programming practice to give the user of your applet a status while your applet is running. In this way, if your applet is busy processing, the user will see a frequently changing message telling the user that the applet is working fine or that the applet experienced an error.

The status line, located at the bottom of the applet window, is used to display the current status of your applet. You write to the status line by calling the `showStatus()` method. The `showStatus()` method requires one argument—the message you want displayed on the status line.

The following example illustrates how to display the status of your applet on the status line of the applet window. You can use the HTML document shown in the previous example to run this applet. Figure 14-4 shows what happens when you run this applet.

```
import javax.swing.JApplet;
import java.awt.Graphics;
public class Demo extends JApplet {
    public void paint(Graphics g)
    {
      g.drawString( "Hello world!", 30, 30 );
      showStatus("The Hello world applet is running.");
    }
}
```

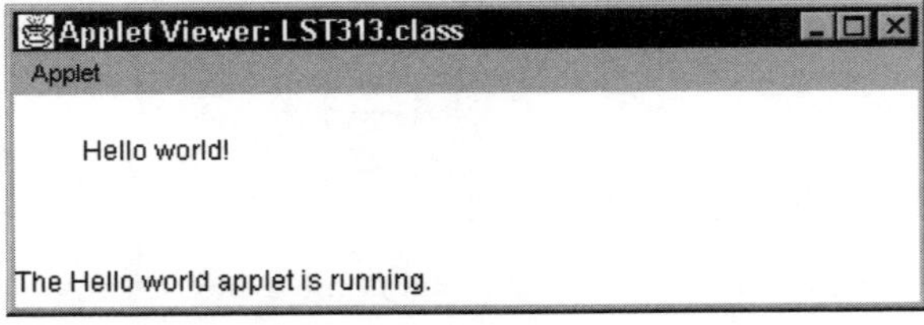

Figure 14-4 Displays a message on the status line of the applet window

Quiz

1. What is an applet?
2. What restrictions are imposed on an applet?
3. How do you execute an applet?
4. Why doesn't an applet have a `main()` method?
5. Why don't you have to overwrite all the methods of the `JApplet` class?
6. Why can't an applet be run from the command line?
7. What is the purpose of the `init()` method?
8. Why would you use an applet?
9. What is the purpose of a status line?
10. How is a parameter passed to an applet?

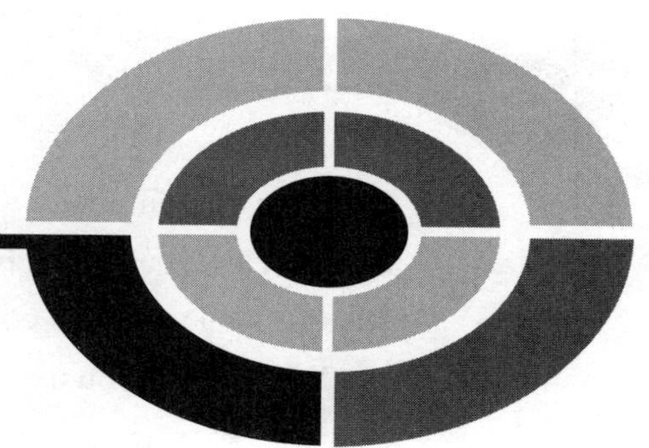

Final Exam

1. What is the difference between an applet and a Java application?
2. Can statements in an applet write a file to the local computer?
3. Can an applet be executed from the command line?
4. What is the entry point into an applet?
5. What are the three methods that should be overwritten in every applet?
6. What method is called once the applet is loaded?
7. What is the purpose of the `start()` method?
8. Can an applet use GUI elements?
9. How do you run an applet?
10. Can a parameter be passed to an applet from the command line?
11. What method do you call to display a GUI window?
12. For which GUI elements do you use the `ItemListener`?
13. Is the following the correct order in which you assemble a GUI window?
    Window, container, content pane, GUI elements
14. What is the relationship between the content pane and GUI elements?
15. True or false? All GUI elements should always be enabled.

16. How do you obtain a content pane?
17. How do you set the background color of the container?
18. Can you use pixel coordinates to position GUI elements in a window?
19. Why would you use the Gridbag Layout Manager over the Grid Layout Manager?
20. What is a major difference between creating a GUI in Java as opposed to creating a GUI in another programming language such as C++?
21. What is the purpose of an access specifier?
22. What is an interface?
23. True or false? Each instance of a class has its own instance variable.
24. How can one class inherit another class?
25. What is an abstract class?
26. What is overloading?
27. What is a method signature?
28. What does encapsulation refer to in Java?
29. What is the entry point to a Java application?
30. What is the Java Virtual Machine?
31. How can a Java application run on practically any computer?
32. What is a resultset?
33. What is an embedded query?
34. What is a DBMS?
35. What is the difference between a `while` loop and a `do...while` loop?
36. What is the difference between an int and a float?
37. What is *System* in `System.out.println()`?
38. What does the `new` operator do?
39. Assuming that x equals 10, evaluate this expression: `!x==10`
40. Why would you create an endless loop?
41. What is the difference between an array and the `Arrays` class?
42. What kind of code is generated by the Java compiler?
43. How do you temporarily change from one data type to another?
44. What does a variable identifier represent?

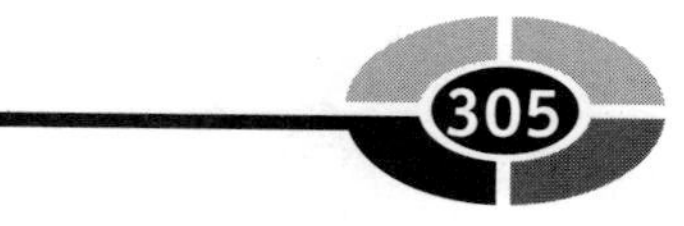

45. What determines the accuracy of a value?
46. Can variables of the same data type be declared in the same statement?
47. When does a variable go out of scope?
48. How is a value assigned to a character variable represented in memory?
49. How precise is a single-precision value?
50. What kind of operator requires one operand?
51. What rules does Java follow to evaluate an expression?
52. What is the importance of the position of the incremental operator?
53. In a `switch...case` statement, can all the `case` statements be evaluated?
54. How would you make sure that a `switch...case` statement responds to a `switch` value if the value isn't included in a `case` statement?
55. How do you describe placing one `if` statement within another `if` statement?
56. In a loop, how do you tell Java to skip the remaining statements in the loop and go to the top of the loop?
57. How do you identify an array element?
58. How do you group together and distribute classes that you've defined and want to use in other programs?
59. What term is used to describe Java's capability to have a method take on a different form depending on the context in which the method is called within a program?
60. What kind of member method can be called without first declaring an instance of its class?
61. What is the purpose of a constructor?
62. What is like a cookie cutter and describes a new data type consisting of member variables and member methods?
63. When is a constructor called?
64. What method is automatically called immediately before Java garbage collection releases memory used by an instance of a class?
65. What is the purpose of an argument list?
66. How would you determine whether a subclass should inherit a superclass?
67. How do you prevent a subclass from overwriting a method of a superclass?
68. What class is automatically inherited by all other classes in Java?
69. How can you explicitly call a superclass method in a subclass?

70. How do you design a program to handle exceptions?
71. What kind of exceptions should you trap in your program?
72. How are exceptions handled if you don't trap exceptions within your program?
73. Are all exceptions generated by Java?
74. Is there a way to make sure statements are executed regardless of whether an exception is or is not thrown?
75. What is the term used to describe executing two processes simultaneously?
76. How does thread priority work?
77. How do you prevent two threads from trying to access the same resource at the same time?
78. What interface would you implement to create threads within your program?
79. Do you have any threads running in a program in which you don't create a thread?
80. What method must be overwritten if you implement the `Runnable` interface?
81. How do you create a thread?
82. How do you convert instance variables into a byte stream?
83. What is a flow of bytes called?
84. What is the purpose of using the `File` class?
85. How does a `BufferedReader` work?
86. What does the `getParent()` method of the `File` class return?
87. You use the `getXXX()` method to retrieve data from a resultset. What does the `XXX` stand for?
88. Can all resultsets be updated?
89. What is the term used to describe the column name in a resultset?
90. True or false? The only way you can refer to a column in a resultset is by using the name of the column.
91. What does the `last()` method do in relationship to a resultset?
92. When you declare an instance of the `FileOutputStream` class, you pass its constructor two arguments. The first argument is the filename. What is the second argument?
93. If you require 15 significant digits to the right of the decimal, what kind of precision do you require?
94. What computer language does a computer understand?

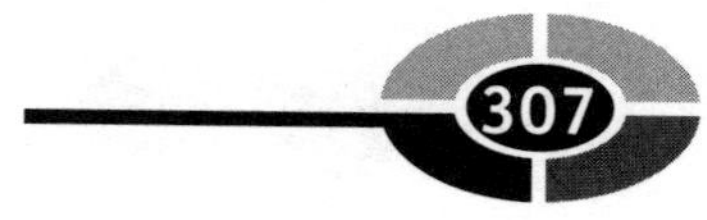

95. What uniquely identifies each block of computer memory?
96. What operator returns the remainder after dividing two numbers?
97. What value is returned by a relational operator?
98. How would you change the value of a bit?
99. In the expression `a == 10 || b == 20`, what condition(s) must be met for this expression to be true?
100. What is the normal flow of a Java application?

Final Exam

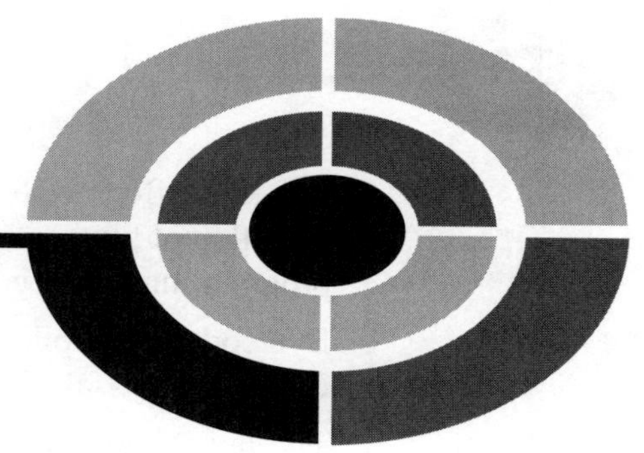

Answers to Quizzes and Final Exam

Chapter 1

1. A compiler is a program that translates a program written in a high-level programming language into bytecode or object code, depending on the language used to write the program.
2. A high-level programming language contains English-like words used by programmers to instruct a computer to perform specific functionality.
3. Machine language is the only language a computer understands. Instructions written in machine language are written as a series of zeros and ones.
4. The key difference between C and Java is that Java enables a programmer to define classes. Classes cannot be defined in C.

5. The key difference between C++ and Java is that a Java program can run on different kinds of computers without having to be recompiled. A C++ program must be recompiled to run on different kinds of computers.
6. Bytecode is compiled Java code that can be executed on any computer that is running the Java Virtual Machine.
7. The Java Virtual Machine is a program that interprets Java bytecode.
8. The `main()` method in a Java application is the entry point into the application.
9. No. You can define a Java class without declaring an attribute as a member of the class.
10. A Java application terminates after the last statement in the `main()` method executes.

Chapter 2

1. A data type is a keyword a programmer uses to tell Java the kind of data that needs to be stored in memory.
2. No. Only variables of the same data type can be declared in the same statement.
3. Casting is a way to temporarily convert a value from one data type to another in order to make it compatible with an operation.
4. The best way to determine the proper data type for a variable is to decide the minimum and maximum values that need to be stored in memory and then find the data type whose range complements these values.
5. A variable identifier is a name that you give a variable. You use this name throughout your program to refer to the memory location that Java associates with the variable identifier.
6. A memory address is a unique number that identifies a location in memory. A variable identifier is a name the programmer uses to refer the corresponding memory location.
7. The scope of a variable is defined by the code block within which the variable is declared. A variable goes out of scope when the program leaves the code block within which the variable is declared.
8. Precision is the number of digits that are accurate to the right of the decimal point.

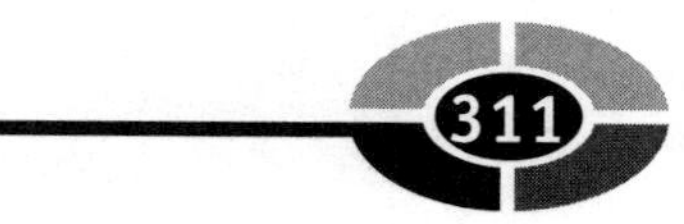

9. The integer assigned to the character in Unicode is stored in memory when a character is assigned to a char variable.
10. No. A float is single precision (seven significant digits to the right of the decimal), whereas double is double precision (15 significant digits to the right of the decimal).

Chapter 3

1. A compound expression is an expression that is composed of two or more subexpressions.
2. A unary operator is an operator that requires one operand.
3. An operator tells Java to perform an operation using one or more values that are referred to as *operands*.
4. Parentheses are placed around subexpressions that are to be evaluated before other subexpressions.
5. Precedence defines the order in which Java performs operations in an expression.
6. The modulus operator returns the remainder after dividing two numbers.
7. If the increment or decrement operator is used in a compound expression, such as `a = ++b`, the position of the increment or decrement operator tells Java to increment/decrement a value either before the assignment operation or after the assignment. If the increment/decrement operator is positioned before the variable, the value is incremented/decremented *before* the assignment. If the increment/decrement operator is positioned after the variable (for example, `a++`), the value is incremented/decrement *after* the assignment.
8. A relational operator compares two values and returns a Boolean value.
9. A bitwise operator changes the value of a bit.
10. The OR logical operator (||) compares the results of two expressions. If either expression is true, then the OR logical operator returns a true value; otherwise, a false value is returned.

Chapter 4

1. The normal flow of a program begins with the first statement in the `main()` method. Then statements are executed sequentially until the last statement in the `main()` method executes.

2. An endless loop is a loop where the conditional expression is always true.
3. A conditional expression is a relational expression that determines whether Java should or should not execute one or more statements.
4. No. A `switch` statement cannot use a Boolean value as the `switch` variable.
5. A constant is a value associated with a `case` statement that is compared to a `switch` variable within a `switch` statement.
6. Statements within the body of a `while` loop execute only if the condition statement is true. Statements within the body of a `do while` loop execute at least once, even if the condition statement is false.
7. The purpose of a default statement in a `switch` statement is to specify statements that are to be executed if none of the `case` constants match the `switch` value.
8. The term *nested* means that one control statement is placed within another control statement.
9. The `break` statement tells Java to exit a block such as a `for` loop or a `switch` statement.
10. The `continue` statement tells Java to go to the top of the loop without executing statements that appear below the `continue` statement in the loop.

Chapter 5

1. An index is an integer used to identify an array element.
2. A reference to an array points to the memory address of the first element of the array.
3. The `new` operator dynamically allocates memory for an array and returns the memory address of the first array element.
4. The index of the first element of an array is always zero.
5. You pass an array to a method by passing the array name.
6. You return an array from a method by returning the array name.
7. You determine the number of array elements of an array by using the `length` data member of the array.
8. The third parameter of the `fill()` tells the `fill()` method to stop filling when it reaches the array element that has the index passed as the third parameter.

9. The `binarySearch()` method returns a negative number when the search criteria isn't found in the array.
10. A package is a group of predefined classes that is imported into your program whenever you want to use one of the predefined classes in your program.

Chapter 6

1. A method header consists of three elements: the method name, the method argument, and the data type of the value returned by the method.
2. The components of a method signature are the method name and the method argument list.
3. A return statement in used in a method to return a value to the statement that calls the method.
4. The two components of an argument are the data type and the name of the argument.
5. A command-line argument is an argument passed to a program while the program is being run from the command line.
6. In order to pass a quotation mark as a command-line argument, you must precede the quotation mark with a backslash.
7. Polymorphism is a term used by programmers to describe Java's capability to have a method take on different meanings (forms), depending on the context in which the method is called within a program.
8. Overloading a method is the technique of defining two or more methods with the same method name but with different argument lists.
9. A method is the part of a Java program that contains the logic to perform a task.
10. The two kinds of methods in Java are nonstatic methods and static methods.

Chapter 7

1. An instance variable is a nonstatic variable declared as a member of a class.
2. An instance and an object both refer to a declaration of a class. Programmers use these terms interchangeably.
3. A class is like a cookie cutter that describes a new data type that consists of instance variables and method members.

4. A constructor is a method member of a class that is automatically called when an instance of the class is declared.
5. Both are method members of a class. However, a destructor is called automatically when an instance of a class goes out of scope. The `finalize()` method member is called automatically, immediately before Java garbage collection releases the memory used by the instance of the class.
6. Overloading a method member means that two or more method members of a class have the same method name but have different argument lists.
7. You declare an instance of a class by using the `new` operator, as shown here:

   ```
   new myClass()
   ```
8. An access specifier is used to limit access to the members of a class.
9. Yes. A constructor can have an argument list.
10. A constructor is overloaded for many reasons, the most common of which is to give the programmer the opportunity to provide an initial value for instance variables.

Chapter 8

1. An abstract method member of a class is a member method that must be overridden by a subclass that inherits the class that defines the abstract method member. An abstract method member does not have a method body because an abstract method member cannot be called. Only method members that override an abstract method member can be called.
2. The "is a" rule of inheritance defines the relationship between a superclass and a subclass. This rule requires that a subclass "is a" superclass. For example, a student class (subclass) should be a person in order to inherit the person class.
3. The keyword `extends` is used by a subclass to specify a superclass to inherit.
4. The keyword `final` prohibits a method member that is designated as final from being overridden by a method member of a subclass.
5. A superclass is a class that is being inherited by a subclass.
6. An abstract class is a class that contains at least one abstract method member. You cannot declare an instance of an abstract class.

7. The Object class is a class defined by Java that is automatically inherited by all other classes defined in Java, including the classes you define in your program.
8. You can prevent a class from being inherited by designating the class with the keyword final.
9. The keyword super is used in a subclass to explicitly reference method members of the superclass.
10. Multilevel inheritance occurs when a subclass is inherited by another subclass.

Chapter 9

1. An exception is something that doesn't normally occur. In programming, two kinds of exceptions might occur with a program. These are commonly referred to as *compile errors* and *run-time errors*. Exception classes in Java handle run-time errors.
2. A try block contains statements that are monitored for exceptions.
3. A catch block immediately follows a try block and handles exceptions thrown by statements within the try block.
4. If an exception is thrown and you didn't catch it within your program, Java's default handlers will respond to the exception.
5. The Throwable class is the parent of the Exception class.
6. You create your own exception class by inheriting Java's Exception class or any subclass of Exception, such as the RuntimeException class.
7. If you define a method that might throw a checked exception but you don't catch the exception within the method definition, you must use the keyword throws in the method header and list the exceptions that can be thrown by the method.
8. One exception class can be caught by a catch block. You can use multiple catch blocks to catch multiple exceptions.
9. The finally block contains statements that are executed regardless of whether an exception is thrown or not thrown.
10. Yes, you can override methods inherited by your exception class from the Throwable class.

Chapter 10

1. A thread is a portion of a program that runs concurrently with other portions of a program.
2. Multitasking is doing two or more tasks concurrently.
3. CPU processing time is needed to switch among concurrent threads. This is called *overhead* because this processing is not directly related to processing the program.
4. A thread priority is an integer, 1 through 10, that specifies whether or not a thread should be preempted by a higher-priority thread. The lowest priority is 1. The default normal priority is 5. The highest priority is 10.
5. Synchronization is the technique of requiring only one thread to have access to a resource at one time. Other threads that need the resource must wait until the resource is available.
6. A `Runnable` interface is an interface used to create threads within your program because you only need to define the `run()` method.
7. You should extend the `Thread` class rather than implementing the `Runnable` interface in your program if you need to override more than the `run()` method of the `Thread` class.
8. You have two threads—the main thread and the child thread you created.
9. You must override the `run()` method.
10. You define the portion of your program that becomes a thread by overriding the `run()` method. Statements within the `run()` method become the thread.

Chapter 11

1. Synchronizing a class converts its instance variables into a byte stream.
2. A stream is a flow of bytes.
3. The `File` class is used to interact with the file system of a computer.
4. Data saved with an object is encapsulated within the object and is usually treated as a single unit by your program. That is, you save and read an instance of a class and not instance variables of the class. Saving data elements using the `PrintWriter` class saves data individually.

5. A filename filter is used to filter a file directory so that only filenames that contain a specified pattern of characters are returned to your program.
6. The `PrintWriter` class cannot open a file. It uses a reference to another class, such as the `FileOutputStream` class, that opens the file.
7. You specify the path when opening a file by including the full path with the filename.
8. The `BufferedReader` class is used to read data from a file into a memory buffer and then to read data from the memory buffer into your program.
9. You append data to the end of a file by using the version of the FileOpenStream construct that accepts two arguments. The first argument is the filename, and the second argument is a Boolean true, which causes all data to be written to the end of the file.
10. You can determine the parent directory path that contains a subdirectory by calling the `getParent()` method defined in the `File` class.

Chapter 12

1. An event listener monitors changes that occur to a GUI element.
2. An event handler is a method you define that is called when an event occurs to a GUI element.
3. You cannot display GUI elements in a window. You must place GUI elements in a content pane and then place the content pane in the container of the window.
4. The purpose of a content pane is to group together GUI elements that are placed within the container of a window.
5. You would you want to disable a GUI element if the GUI element is not appropriate for the current process.
6. A window can be created but not shown. You have to explicitly tell the Java Virtual Machine to display the window by calling the `setVisible(true)` method.
7. You place a content pane in a container by calling the `setContentPane(ca)` method and passing it a reference to the content pane.
8. The purpose of a layout manager is to map areas of the container where you can position GUI elements.

9. You cannot explicitly specify the location of a GUI element in a window. Instead, you specify a relative position for each GUI element within the layout manager.
10. A major difference between creating a GUI in Java as opposed to creating a GUI in another programming language such as C++ is that you cannot explicitly position GUI elements in a window. This is because the Java Virtual Machine needs flexibility to adapt your GUI layout to various computers without you having to rewrite your program.

Chapter 13

1. A DBMS is software that enables you to organize and manage data by using SQL queries. Data stored in a file may or may not be organized and is managed directly by your program.
2. A resultset is a virtual table of data that is returned by a DBMS in response to an SQL query.
3. You retrieve data stored in a resultset by using the `getXXX()` method and passing the method reference to the column whose value you want to access.
4. You move the virtual cursor by calling the `next()`,`first()`, `last()`, `previous()`, `absolute()`, `relative()`, and `getRow()` methods.
5. You update a value in a resultset (if the resultset is an updatable resultset) by calling the `updateXXX()` method, where `XXX` is the data type of the column being updated. The `updateXXX()` method requires two parameters. The first identifies the column, and the second is the value that will be placed in the column.
6. You update a value in a table by creating and executing an SQL query that contains an update statement.
7. Metadata is data about data, such as a column's name, data type, and size.
8. You cannot update metadata. Metadata is set when you create a database and table. Metadata changes only when those components of a DBMS change.
9. You select a column in a resultset by referring to the position of the column in the resultset.
10. You retrieve metadata in order for your program to learn about the data stored in a table or about the table and database themselves.

Chapter 14

1. An applet is a type of Java program that is called by an HTML document.
2. Typically, an applet cannot access the clipboard, the local computer's event queue, the local computer's operating system properties, and the local computer's operating security properties.
3. An applet is executed by a browser when the browser encounters the `<applet>` tag in an HTML document.
4. The `main()` method is the entry point into a Java application. The entry point into an applet is where the browser encounters the `<applet>` tag in an HTML document. Therefore, an applet doesn't need to have a `main()` method.
5. You only have to overwrite methods of the `JApplet` class if you want to change the default behavior of those methods. Typically, you'll only need to change the default behavior of a few methods, not all the methods defined in the `JApplet` class.
6. An applet cannot be run from the command line because it does not have a `main()` method defined.
7. The `init()` method is called once when the applet first executes and usually has statements that initialize variables used by the other methods defined in the applet.
8. An HTML document does not have the capability to perform complex processing. Therefore, you would use an applet to enhance the capabilities of an HTML document.
9. The status line is used to display messages that keep the applet's user informed as to the status of the applet.
10. You pass a parameter to an applet by using the `<param>` tag in the HTML page that calls the applet. Parameters are then identified using the `name` and `value` attributes of the `<param>` tag.

Final Exam

1. An applet must be run using a browser or the appletviewer. A Java application can be run from the command line using the Java Virtual Machine.
2. Probably not. An applet is restricted in what it can do on the local machine. However, the local environment governs those restrictions. Many local environments protect the local file system from an applet.

3. No. An applet must be run from either a browser or the appletviewer.
4. The entry point into an applet is the browser. It is from there that the methods defined in the applet are called.
5. `init()`, `start()`, and `paint()`.
6. `init()`.
7. The `start()` method contains statements that are executed each time the applet is started.
8. Yes.
9. You run an applet by using the applet tag in an HTML document.
10. No, because an applet cannot be run from a command line. A parameter can be passed to an applet from an HTML document.
11. You call the `setVisible()` method and pass it a Boolean true.
12. Radio button, check boxes, combo boxes, and other GUI elements that use a list of items from which the user makes a selection.
13. Yes.
14. GUI elements are added to the content pane. The content pane is then placed in the container of the window.
15. False. A GUI element should be enabled only if it is used in the current process.
16. You call the `getContentPane()` method.
17. You call the `setBackground()` method and pass it a constant that corresponds to the color you want to use.
18. No. You cannot use pixel coordinates because they are machine specific, and their position may differ in various machines. Java is a machine-independent language; therefore, you must use relative coordinates rather than explicit coordinates to position GUI elements in a window.
19. The Gridbag Layout Manager enables you to specify the cell of the grid where a GUI element is to be positioned. The Grid Layout Manager places GUI elements in the next available cell in the grid.
20. In many programming languages, you can specify the exact location of each GUI element on the screen. In Java, you specify the relative position, and the Java Virtual Machine determines the exact placement of the GUI element.
21. An access specifier determines what parts of your program have access to members of a class.

22. An interface is a predefined set of methods that a class must define in order to implement the interface. The interface tells a programmer that he/she must define a specific set of methods in a class in order to use (implement) the interface.
23. True.
24. You can cause a class to inherit another class by using the keyword `extends` in the class header.
25. An abstract class is a class that cannot be instantiated.
26. Overloading is a technique of creating two or more versions of the same method, where the name of the method remains the same but the method signature is different in each version.
27. A method signature consists of the method name and an argument list.
28. Encapsulation refers to combining related data and methods into a class and protecting the data from other parts of the program.
29. The `main()` method is the entry point into every Java application.
30. The Java Virtual Machine is a machine-dependent executable program capable of translating Java bytecode into machine-readable instructions.
31. A Java application can run on any computer that has a Java Virtual Machine because the Java application's bytecode is machine independent and is interpreted by the Java Virtual Machine, which is machine specific.
32. A resultset is data returned to a Java application from a DBMS in response to an SQL query sent by the application.
33. An embedded query is an SQL query that is part of a program such as your Java program.
34. A DBMS is a database management system used to store, retrieve, and maintain large amounts of data, and it can follow instructions written in SQL.
35. Statements within a `while` loop may never be executed if the `while` loop condition expression is false. Statements within a `do...while` loop, however, always executes at least once, even if the `while` loop condition expression is false.
36. An int is a data type used for whole numbers. A float is a data type used for mixed numbers.
37. *System* is the name of the `System` class.
38. The `new` operator reserves memory for an object and returns a reference to that object and invokes a constructor method if one exists for the object.

39. This expression evaluates to false because the exclamation point reverses the logic of the expression. In other words, it says "x does not equal 10."
40. You use an endless loop whenever one or more statements within the loop determine when the loop should terminate.
41. The `Arrays` class provides methods that are used to manipulate elements of an array. An array does not have those methods.
42. The Java compiler generates bytecode, which can be executed on any computer that is running the Java Virtual Machine.
43. You cast the first data type to temporarily become the second data type.
44. A variable identifier represents the memory address where a value represented by the variable identifier is stored.
45. The precision of a value determines the accuracy of the value.
46. Yes.
47. A variable goes out of scope when the program leaves the code block within which the variable is declared.
48. A value of a character variable is an integer that corresponds to the Unicode value of that character; therefore, the character is represented as an integer in memory.
49. A single-precision value has seven significant digits to the right of the decimal.
50. The unary operator requires one operand.
51. Java follows the precedence rules, also known as the order of operation to evaluate an expression.
52. If the incremental operator precedes a value, such as `a = ++b`, then the value is incremented before being assigned. If the incremental operator succeeds a value, such as `a = b++`, then the value is incremented after the assignment.
53. Yes, if the `break` statement is not used within each `case` statement.
54. Use a default statement that executes if no `case` statement matches the `switch` value.
55. The second `if` statement is referred to as a *nested* `if` statement.
56. You insert a `continue` statement at the point where you want Java to return to the top of the loop.
57. You reference the name of the array followed by the array element's index value placed within square brackets.

58. You place your classes in a package that can be imported whenever you want to use them in other programs.
59. Polymorphism.
60. A static method.
61. A constructor is typically used to initialize member data when an instance of the class is declared.
62. A class.
63. A constructor is called automatically when an instance of its class is declared. A constructor can also be called directly. For example, you can use `super()` in a subclass to call the constructor of the superclass.
64. The `finalize()` method.
65. An argument list contains values required by a method to complete a process.
66. The subclass must comply with the "is a" rule, which states that the subclass "is a" superclass, such as "a graduate student 'is a' student."
67. You precede the name of the class with the keyword `final`.
68. The `Object` class.
69. You precede the method name with the keyword `super`.
70. You place the code that might generate the exception in a `try` block and then define one or more `catch` blocks to trap and react to exceptions.
71. You should trap any exceptions your program can recover from, including run-time exceptions.
72. Java's default exception handler will respond to the exception.
73. No. You can create your own exceptions that are thrown by statements in your program.
74. Yes. You can place those statements in a `finally` block. Java always executes the `finally` block regardless of whether exceptions occur in the program.
75. Multitasking.
76. Each thread is assigned an integer, 1 through 10, that indicates the thread's priority. The lowest priority is 1, and the highest is 10. A higher-priority thread should preempt a lower-priority thread.
77. Use the synchronization technique.
78. The `Runnable` interface.

79. Yes. Every program has a main thread that is created when the program executes.
80. You must override the `run()` method.
81. The easiest way to create a thread is to implement the `Runnable` interface and then overwrite the `run()` method. Statements within the `run()` method become the thread.
82. You serialize the class that contains the instance variables.
83. A stream.
84. The `File` class enables your program to interact with the file system.
85. First, you create a `BufferedReader` by declaring an instance of the `BufferedReader` class. Then, the methods defined in the `BufferedReader` class are used to read data from a file into a memory buffer and to read data from the memory buffer into your program.
86. The `getParent()` method returns the parent directory path of a subdirectory or file.
87. The `XXX` is replaced by the data type of the data being retrieved from the resultset.
88. No. Only updatable resultsets can be updated.
89. Metadata.
90. False. You can refer to the position of the column in the resultset.
91. The `last()` method positions the virtual cursor at the last row in the resultset.
92. The second argument is a Boolean value that determines whether data will be appended to the file. A Boolean true causes data to be written to the end of the file.
93. Double precision.
94. Machine language.
95. A memory address.
96. The modulus operator.
97. A Boolean value.
98. You use a bitwise operator.
99. Either `a == 10` or `b == 20`.
100. The normal flow of a Java application begins with the first statement in the `main()` method. Then statements are sequentially executed until the last statement in the `main()` method executes.

INDEX

B

C

F

G

H

I

M

N

T

U

V